Know all men that We
A.B. Forrest ... ...

... ... Emily _ a colored girl_ an
Orphan aged about ten years

to_ ... A. B. Forrest ... ... _until
of the age of_ Eighteen ... _years, during which time the
said_ Emily

shall obey the lawful commands, and faithfully serve the said A. B. Forrest
... ... and be in all things and respects subject to ... authority and con...
... ... Forrest ... on ... part covenants that ... will teach and instruct
the said_ Emily

the ... ...
in ... of ... ... and to read and write, or cause the same to be
done, if ... have sufficient capacity, and ... will also constantly find for the said
Emily

sufficient diet, lodging, washing and apparel, and other necessaries suitable for an apprentice
in sickness and in health, and also take care of ... morals and treat ... with humanity
... ... the end of the time for which ... ...
... suits of Clothes and the sum of
... in ... ...

This_ 26° _day of_ January _186 9_

... ...
for Shelby County ...

Judge of the County Court

A. B. Forrest

Bond of General Nathan B. Forrest, January 26, 1869
Courtesy of Shelby County Archives

WEST TENNESSEE'S FORGOTTEN CHILDREN
Apprentices from 1821 to 1889

by

Alan N. Miller

CLEARFIELD

Printed for
Clearfield Company by
Genealogical Publishing Co.
Baltimore, Maryland
2006

Reprinted, with revised index, for
Clearfield Company by
Genealogical Publishing Co.
Baltimore, Maryland
2007

ISBN-13: 978-0-8063-5309-8
ISBN-10: 0-8063-5309-0

Made in the United States of America

For Lucy and John

Texans with a
Tennessee Heritage

Table of Contents

List of Abbreviations

abt	about	mos	months
bnd	bound	prev	previous(ly)
canc	cancelled	prob	probably
d	days	req	request
dau	daughter	resc	rescinded
dcd	deceased	ret	returned
FB	Freedmen's Bureau	SCA	Shelby Co Archives
GF	grandfather	sib(s)	sibling(s)
GM	grandmother	sur	surety
illeg	illegtimate	yrs	years
ind	indenture		

Introduction

Apprenticeships have been known since ancient times, but the system which evolved in America had its roots in the England of the 16th century. The practice spread to the colonies along with other English customs but gradually became less of a method of training in the professions and crafts, evolving into a system whereby children who were or were likely to become indigent could be supported without cost to the local government.

When Tennessee became a state in 1796, she inherited the legal code of her mother state, North Carolina. Their laws of 1762 applicable to orphans specified the following:
1. Annually the names of all orphans who had no guardian or who were not previously bound were to be reported to the Orphan Court.
2. Where their estate was too small to support them, orphans or base-born children were to be bound as apprentices: the males until age 21, the females until age 18, and mulatto or mustee females until age 21.
3. The master was to provide "diet, clothes, lodging and accommodations, fit and necessary, and to teach or cause him or her to be taught to read and write."
4. At the expiration of the apprenticeship, the master was to pay the apprentice an amount specified by law [or in the indenture].
5. If the child were ill used or not taught as required, the court could cancel the indenture and rebind him or her.
6. The bond was to be by indenture, made between the presiding officer of the court (and his successor) and the master or mistress, recorded, and a copy kept in the clerk's office for the benefit of the apprentice.
7. Any ill-treated apprentice could prosecute in the name of the Justices of the Court and recover damages.

Originally, an orphan was considered to be any fatherless child. In 1825 Tennessee law was amended to include any child as bindable whose father had abandoned him or utterly failed and refused to support him, provided that the mother gave assent in open court. In the minutes these children also are sometimes referred to as orphans. In 1854 the courts were given the discretion to bind apprentices for shorter periods if desired. By 1858 the Code of Tennessee specified other changes, as follows:
1. No apprentice could be removed from the county without his consent and the consent of the court.
2. No householder could harbor or conceal any orphan child, or hire him, without first obtaining leave from some Justice of the Peace.
3. The apprentice was to be taught to read, write, and "cypher as far as the rule of three."
4. At the expiration of the indenture, in addition to the other stipulations, the master should pay to the apprentice $20 and furnish him with one good suit of clothes.
5. Illegitimate children could be bound out without their mother's consent if it were proved that she "disregarded their moral and mental culture and that she kept a house of ill repute, or lived in one."

Although these laws regarding the Master-Apprentice relationship remained in effect until the mid-20th century with few alterations, their application sometimes varied with court decisions and local practice. In different counties they seem to have been enforced with varying degrees of diligence. In no West Tennessee county was a record of an annual accounting found. Rather, they seemed to have been reported to the court at random by a JP or another interested individual, often the person to whom they were eventually bound. The mother's consent, when required and obtained, was not always recorded, leading at times to cancellation of the indenture.

Copies of the indenture were furnished to the Master, to the County Clerk and sometimes to the apprentice or his parent/guardian. Some indentures and bonds were recorded in full in the minutes, but most counties filed them in a Guardian Record Book or with Miscellaneous Bonds. Because copies of the indenture and accompanying bond seem to have vanished from most counties' archives, the Court Minutes are now the most complete record of these unfortunate children's fate. In some cases the complete indenture was recorded in the minutes along with the order binding the child; other clerks simply recorded that the child was bound, without further detail.

Of course not all bound children were indigent or orphans. A parent or guardian might bind a child in order to have a boy taught a useful trade or a girl the arts of homemaking. In a few cases financial arrangements were detailed in which the parent was to receive annual payments or a lump sum in return for for the child's services. It was occasionally stipulated in a will that an heir was to be bound out, and to whom. Also, not all indigent children were bound. Those not felt to have the physical or mental capacity to make a productive apprentice were relegated to care in the poor house or in a private home at county expense. Many ordered to be brought for consideration of binding could not be found by the sheriff so were not produced in court.

Orphanages began to appear before the Civil War and became a significant alternative for the care of indigent orphans in larger counties, especially Shelby County, following the War. Often children to be apprenticed or adopted were taken directly from these institutions.

Following the Civil War, many functions of the state courts which might affect the rights of the freed slaves were suspended. Apprenticeships made by the local courts were allowed only with the approval of the local Freedmen's Bureau Court or its representative. During this period the Bureau's own court system handled most of the apprenticeships. On May 26, 1866 the State Assembly passed an act defining the legal rights of "Persons of Color," and the Freedmen's Bureau responded by abolishing their courts in Tennessee. Some of the apprentice indentures which had been approved by the Freedmen's courts were re-recorded in the County Court Minutes, but most included here are taken from the Bureau's own records. They may be found in National Archives Record Group 105, Micropublication M999, Roll 20.

The following pages contain records of apprenticeships in the counties of West Tennessee from the earliest surviving records until the practice became uncommon, usually in the late 1870's or 1880's. During the latter years of the Civil War few meetings of the County Courts were held, and it was not until after the war that apprenticeships again began to be recorded. The usual problems in handwriting interpretation were encountered, and names were spelled many ways, sometimes within the same document. Original spellings have been retained, but entries have been abbreviated and the names of the court officials and bondsmen omitted in most cases. In entries where the date of the original bond or indenture is not given, the information is from a later reference, such as the cancellation of the indenture.

When a name is found, it is suggested that the researcher consult the microfilmed minutes for several years before and after the event for further clues as to the parentage and circumstances of the child. Often an insolvent estate, provisions for pauper care or burial, a bastardy case, or orders to bring to court other family members may be found. Also, it is worth looking for the original bond, as the names of the sureties may be significant. The Shelby County Archives is especially helpful in this regard. A date following a fact in the notes points to the source of that fact. An asterisk after an entry or date directs the reader to a source for further data. It is hoped that these records will help researchers locate ancestors who, because they were penniless and often without living parents, might be recorded nowhere else.

Records were copied from microfilm obtained from the Tennessee State Archives, the Shelby County Archives, the Library of the Church of Jesus Christ of Latter Day Saints, and the Dallas Public Library. My thanks to Larry Butler of the Tennessee State Archives, to Vincent L. Clark and John Dougan of the Shelby County Archives, and to Lloyd Bockstruck and Sammie Lee Townsend of the Dallas Public Library for their assistance in making microfilm available for this project.

Benton County

Name	Date	Age	Master	Notes
Cox, Shadrick	3July1843	Abt 13 yrs	Smith, William	Son of Hiram Cox, Dcd. Farming. Siblings Catherine & Nancy Feriby Cox 5June1843*
Cox, Harmon	3July1843	Abt 15 yrs	Cox, Johnathan B.	Orphan. Farming. 5June1843*
Nash, Zachariah	5Feb1844	1 yr	Colier, James	
Fullerton, David	6May1844	13 yrs	Merrick, James E.	Orphan. Farmer
Blanks, William	1July1844	10 yrs	Cate, Isaiah F.	Consent of father, Joseph Blank. Farmer
Blanks, John	1July1844	7 yrs	Cate, Isaiah F.	Consent of father, Joseph Blank. Farmer
Click, Jordan	2Mar1846	Abt 12 yrs	McElyea, Daniel F.	Mother unable to provide. Black smith
Dickerson, William	6Sept1846	Abt 14 yrs	Melton, Sion	Request of Zachariah Tomas, stepfather
Dickerson, Nancy Caroline	6Sept1846	Abt 8 yrs	Melton, Sion	Request of Zachariah Tomas, stepfather. To Sheriff's custody 4Sept1848. Ill-treatment
Dickerson, John L. F.	6Sept1846	Abt 11 yrs	Melton, Conrod	Request of Zachariah Tomas, stepfather
Dickerson, Lucinda	6Sept1846	Abt 10 yrs	Melton, Conrod	Request of Zachariah Tomas, stepfather. To Sheriff's custody 4Sept1848. Ill-treatment
Blanks, William L.	3May1847	13 yrs	Pfifer, John	Farmer. Cancelled 2July1849. William unable to work, so let out as pauper
Blanks, John M.	3May1847	11 yrs	Pfifer, John	Farmer
Townsend, Andrew Jackson	1May1848	Abt 16 yrs	Lowther, Hary	Orphan. Brick mason
Crutchfield, James M.	8Aug1848		Crutchfield, G. K.	Orphan of James Crutchfield, Dcd. Farmer. Taken from mother 7Aug1848*
Crutchfield, Sarah B.	8Aug1848		Crutchfield, G. K.	Orphan of James Crutchfield, Dcd. Taken from mother 7Aug1848*
Sanders, William R.	4Dec1848	Abt 3 yrs	Childers, James S.	Orphan
Jerman, Danil	3Sept1849		Simmonds, Bartley P.	Child of Nancy Jerman, who agrees
Jerman, Ellis Mary	3Sept1849		Cooper, John H.	Child of Nancy Jerman, who agrees

Name	Date	Age	Master	Notes
Jerman, Berry Ann	3Sept1849		Mulliniks, Pleasant	Child of Nancy Jerman, who agrees. Cancelled 2Feb1852 as Nancy B. Jarmon. Mulliniks dead
Jerman, Berry Ann	3Sept1849		Mulliniks, Pleasant	Child of Nancy Jerman, who agrees. Cancelled 2Feb1852 as Nancy B. Jarmon. Mulliniks dead
Council, W. C.	3June1850	Abt 2 yrs	Kelly, John	Orphan. Farmer
Haney, John	5Aug1850	Abt 2 yrs	Reddick, Kenneth	Orphan. Farmer
Robertson, William R.	7July1851	Abt 5 yrs	Tayloe, Haymon	Orphan. Farmer
Casteel, Martha	3Dec1851		Lashlee, John T.	Orphan
Casteel, James M.	3Dec1851	8 yrs	Presson, James F.	Orphan
Casteel, Pinkney	3Dec1851	7 yrs	Corbett, A. T.	Orphan
Jarmon, Nancy B.	2Feb1852		Tinker, J. B.	Orphan. See Berry Ann Jerman
Jones, Thomas	6Apr1852		Williams, John K.	Orphan
Spain, William Thomas	6Apr1852		Raybern, Henry	Orphan
Henderson, Pleasant	7Mar1853	14 yrs	Mulleniks, R. J.	Orphan
Bond, James Polk	4Apr1853		Harrison, James	Orphan. On 7Mar1853 three children of Elizabeth Bonds ordered brought to court
Ward, Josiah K.	4Apr1853		Davis, Henry W.	Orphan. Perhaps a son of Elizabeth Bonds. See above. Canc 2May1853. Josiah gone
Ward, William	4Apr1853		Presson, James	Orphan. Perhaps a son of Elizabeth Bonds. See above
Caststeel, Martha	4Apr1853		Lashle, J. C.	Orphan
King, William J.	3Apr1854	Abt 4 yrs	Barnes, Thomas	Orphan
Jordan, Berry	3July1854	Abt 15 yrs	Jordan, Jonathan	Until 18 yrs. Orphan
Ward, Joseph	4Sept1854		Bridges, James H. E.	For 6 yrs
Craig, Angeline	2Oct1854	11 yrs next spring	Presson, Needham	Until 16 yrs. Spincer [sic]
Lewis, Angeline	2Oct1854	6 yrs 5 mo	Bridges, Reuben	Until 16 yrs. Orphan. Spinster
Holomon, Thomas L.	4Dec1854	Abt 6 yrs	Arnold, James	Orphan
Tedder, John D.	4Dec1854	Abt 13 yrs	Smith, Andrew J.	Orphan
Tedder, James	1Jan1855	Abt 9 yrs	Johnson, William C.	Orphan. Farmer. Cancelled 6Aug1855. Uncontrollable. Heir of Elisha Teddler, Dcd 6Aug1855
Holaman, William H.	1Jan1855	Abt 14 yrs	Box, William	Orphan

Name	Date	Age	Master	Notes
McGill, John	6Aug1855	14 yrs	Mathews, Joseph R.	Orphan. Bound at McGill's request
Bryum, James	5Nov1855	14 yrs	Prudett, W. F.	Orphan
Leonard, William J.	3Mar1856	8 yrs	Bolen, G. M.	Orphan
Weaks, John	2June1856	11 yrs	Harrison, Benjamin	Orphan
Kilbreath, Lovey F.	3June1856	13 yrs	Utly, Burwell L.	Dau of William Kilbreath. Housekeeping. Canc 6April1857. Father now able to provide
Kilbreath, Moulton A.	3June1856	10 yrs	Allen, Isaac	Son of William Kilbreath. Farmer. Cancelled 1Dec1856, Allen having left county
Kilbreath, Sarah	3June1856	6 yrs	Kilbreath, James	Daughter of William Kilbreath, who consents. Sister of James. Mother living with James. Not formally bound
Kilbreath, William H.	7July1856	Abt 8 yrs	Pope, Leonard H.	Until 20 yrs. Son of William Kilbreath 3June1856* Cancelled 7Sept1857. Father now able to provide
Craig, Caroline	7July1856	7 yrs	Hudson, W. W.	Until 16 yrs. Orphan
Lewis, Angeline	1Dec1856		Malin, Martha	Formerly bound to Stephen Walker. Malin is Angeline's aunt
Kilbreath, A. M.	1Dec1856		Cardell, Charles	Formerly bound to Isaac Allen. Cancelled 7Sept1857. Father now able to provide
Craig, Louiza P.	2Feb1857	3 yrs	Greer, John	Until 16 yrs. Orphan. On 6Apr1857 Sarah Craig, pauper, let out for 6 mo
Taylor, James	2Nov1857	5 yrs	Williams, John K.	
Taylor, Hezekiah Forest	7June1858	8 yrs	Wheally, Ethelared	Orphan
Roswell, Mary L. B.	1Nov1858	4 yrs	Roswell, Lewis	Orphan
Craig, Matilda C.	1Nov1858	9 yrs	Craig, Charles	Orphan
Craig, Paralee	1Nov1858	6 yrs	Harper, Robert	Orphan
Hubbs, Henry	7Mar1859	Abt 9 yrs	Hubbs, William	
Phifer, Jonah	1Aug1859	10 or 11 yrs	Rushing, Richard B.	Orphan
Phifer, Elijah	1Aug1859	8 or 9 yrs	Markham, W. D.	Orphan
Sullins, Emaline	3Oct1859	11 yrs	Mitchel, James	Orphan
Baswell, Sarah E.	3Oct1859	8 yrs	Baswell, Elizabeth	Orphan. Elizabeth is Sarah E[lizabeth]'s stepmother 1Aug1859
Aden, Henry C.	5Nov1860		Bell, Alexander	Orphan
Akers, George L.	3Dec1860		Bomer, R. J.	Orphan of B. F. Akers, Dcd 6Nov1860*

Name	Date	Age	Master	Notes
Akers, William J.	3Dec1860		Cheatham, B. F.	Orphan of B. F. Akers, Dcd 6Nov1860*
Akers, Mary Bell	3Dec1860		Wynn, A. J.	Orphan of B. F. Akers, Dcd 6Nov1860* Cancelled 3Mar1862. Bell refuses to stay with Wynn
Aken (Allen?), Columbus	4Feb1861		Reeves, J. R.	Orphan
Price, Joseph	5May1862	13 yrs	Grissum, Willis	Orphan
Clinton, Henry			Starnes, Henry	Apprenticeship cancelled 6Feb1865
Arnold, Andrew M.	4Feb1867	Abt 6 yrs	Arnold, John	Orphan of Henry Arnold, Dcd. Cancelled 1Aug1867 as Martin Arnold. To his mother, Sarah Doyle
Smalley, James Monroe	1July1867	10 or 11 yrs	Smalley, Abner	Son of Elenor Smalley
Wheatley, William	2Dec1867	Abt 12 yrs	Farmer, Ichabod	
Dillian, Joseph	2Dec1867	Abt 11 yrs	Hatley, Luke	Cancelled June1872
White, Jerry	6Jan1868	12 yrs	White, James	Farming. Of color
White, Marcus	6Jan1868	11 yrs	White, James	Farming. Of color
Matlock, Andy	2Mar1868	Abt 11 yrs	Matlock, J. W.	Farming. Of color
Hubbs, John Wesly	2Mar1868	Abt 15 yrs	Matlock, William L.	Farming
Nowell, Jeptha G.	2Mar1868	Abt 6 yrs	Hale, Jesse	
Curtis, Cheatham	6July1868		Gibson, Sphen	
Swim, Nelson	6July1868		Gibson, Sphen	
Barker, Emer Jane	1Feb1869	Abt 10 yrs	Yarbrough, J. C.	
Bonds, Newton	5Apr1869	Abt 15 yrs	Bond, Granville	
Marchbanks, Marshal	3May1869	Abt 15 mo	Short, J. L.	
Erp, Elizabeth	4Jan1870	Abt 8 or 9 yrs	Swindle,	House keeping
Cupp, Thomas	7Mar1870	8 yrs	Hicks, J. D.	
Cupp, James Alfred	7Mar1870	Abt 5 yrs	Hargis, Judson	
Nowell, Caladonia	4July1870		Utley, M. V.	Had been let out to Utley 7Feb1870
Victrey, James	3Oct1870	Abt 6 yrs	Presson, J. N.	Cancelled 3Jan1871. James being cared for by friends
Lawson, Nevil	3Jan1871	Abt 13 yrs	Lashlee, Lewis	
Cooley, William	8Oct1872	Abt 8 yrs	Farmer, D. M.	Orphan
Allen, Moses D. H.	1June1874		Allen, J. A.	
Victor, James B.	3Aug1874	8 yrs	Spellings, G. C.	Cared for by Spellings past four years

Victor, William	3Aug1874	5 yrs	Spellings, G. C.	Cared for by Spellings past four years
Delain, Allice	7Dec1874	Abt 8 yrs (from adoption entry)	Barnes, Charlotte	Apparently is the Hannah Augustus adopted 2May1876* by William Simpson, of color, her reputed father. Mother dead
Alsup, Joseph	6Mar1876	14 yrs	Brewer, Nicholas	
Wilson, Robert Lee	4Dec1876	5 or 6 yrs	Cooley, James	Parents dead. Cared for by Cooley past 5 or 6 yrs
Aden, Vandella	7Oct1879	4 yrs	Aden, W. K.	Spinster. Abandoned by parents
Stigall, Hezekiah	7May1883		Hicks, Thomas	Farming
Watson, Burt	3Mar1884	12 yrs	Nowell, W. B.	Parents dead. Farming

Carroll County

Name	Date	Age	Master	Notes
Bennett, Francis Drake	15Sept1824	5 yrs	Bennett, Solomon	Farmer. Orphan
Lestin, William	6June1825		Bighim, Martin	Farmer. Orphan
Cooxey, Joseph	5Dec1825		Wood, David	Farming
Cooxey, Jemimah	5Dec1825		Wood, Samuel	Spinster. Canc 11Sept1832, as Jamima
Cooxey, Samuel	5Dec1825		Bigham, Joseph	Farmer
Wallis, Benjamine	12Mar1827	< 14 yrs	Allin, Samuel	Orphan. Farming. 14 & 15Dec1826*
Cox, Tillman	12Mar1827	6 yrs	Cox, Purity	Orphan 14Dec1826. Farmer. Ordered to court 12June1834
Eastes, Thomas	12Mar1827	4 yrs	Horn, John	Farmer. 13Nov1827* On 9June1828 Horn released as guardian & Drury Smith appt'd. Orphan of John Eastis, Dcd
Suliven, Patsey or Martha			Webb, Elijah	From entry 8Dec1828, when Webb ordered to answer charge of maltreatment. 15Dec1826*
Thrift, Mary Ann	4Sept1829		Neely, Andrew	Spinster
Thrift, Simpson	4Sept1829		Smoot, John N.	Tanner & currier
Lewis, James Washington	4Sept1829		Simons, John	Brick mason
Thrift, Eliza	4Sept1829		Johnson, Andrew	Spinster
Webb, Marvel	14June1830		Wilson, Plesant	Tanner
Seal, Thomas Jefferson	12Dec1831		Cathey, William	For 15 yrs. Blacksmith
Gillis, Murdock	12Mar1832		Nichol, David	Tanner

Name	Date	Age	Master	Notes
Empson, Susan	10Sept1832		Williams, John	For 7 yrs from November next. Spinster
Mary Ann	13Sept1832		Smithers, William H.	Until 18 yrs. Of color. Daughter of Penny
William Houston	13Sept1832		Smithers, William H.	Of color. Son of Penny
Russell, William	10June1833		Smith, Anderson H.	Taylor
Mitchell, Washington P.	11Mar1834		Briggance, John H.	For 7 yrs from 1Oct1833. Taylor
Williams, Marah Ann	9June1834		Williams, William	Spinster
Hicks, William C.	8Dec1834		Ward, Stephen	Farmer. On 3April & 1May1843 ordered brought to court
Hicks, Jackson	8Dec1834		Ward, Stephen	Farmer. On 3April & 1May1843 ordered brought to court
Carr, Frances Young	9Mar1835		Parks, William	Farmer
Wallis, Benjamin	9Mar1835		Gwin, Edward	Farmer
Harrison, William	11Mar1835		Jobes, William	Taylor
Woods, Lucinda	14Sept1835		Glover, George	Spinster
Calhoun, Martha Elizabeth	14Mar1836		Parks, William	
Calhoun, William M.	14Mar1836		Parks, William	
Wily, Jesse D.	3Jan1837		Peeples, D. D.	For 5 yrs. Sadler
Momord?, Israel	6Feb1837		Bigham, Mathis	Orphan. Wheel right
Seals, Thomas J.	7Aug1837		Gerr?, Edmond W.	
Good, Daniel	5Mar1838		Allen, Young W.	Of color
Good, Jefferson	5Mar1838		Allen, Young W.	Of color
Stewart, James	5Mar1838		Baxter, Samuel	Orphan of Hamilton Stewart
Scott, Thomas	6Mar1838		Williams, David	For 8 yrs
Momard, Isral C.	2July1838		Jobes, William	Taylor
Maren?, John P.	3Dec1838		Lindsey, John N.	For 5 yrs. Orphan. Possibly son of Levi Messer, Dcd, late of Humphreys Co. If so, has sib, Zoraan. 5Nov1838
Brandy, Martha	2Mar1840		Rust, Jeremiah T.	For 4 yrs
Ross, Daniell T.	2Mar1840		Williams, Nancy	For 10 yrs
Scoot, Keely T.	1Mar1841		Williams, Nancy	For 7 yrs 5 mos. Farmer
Gardner, Lary	7June1841		Hardin, Pation	For 9 yrs
Gardner, Melindy	7June1841		Horn, Wesley	For 4 yrs
Anderson, Nancy T.	4Oct1841		Duke, James D.	

Name	Name	Date	Notes
Anderson, Pateline	Duke, James D.	4Oct1841	
Anderson, Sally B.	Smith, Levi	4Oct1841	
Anderson, Mary O.	Park, James	1Nov1841	Cancelled 5Aug1844 at request of mother
Short, Pheby S.	Hull (or Null), Richward G.	6Dec1841	For 3 yrs
Williams, Levi D.	Nesbitt, Wilson	4Jan1842	For 10 yrs from last August. Farmer
Williams, Rowland A.	Rhodes, David	4Jan1842	For 13 yrs from last June. Canc 7Aug1843
Williams, Ephrem W.	Carter, John P.	4Jan1842	For 11 yrs
Williams, Willis G.	Corthen, Nathan	4Jan1842	For 8 yrs from last October
Williams, Ephrem M.	Pickler, John	6June1842	
Williams, Henry A.	Johnson, H. A.	4July1842	
Hicks, Jackson	Johnson, Stephen	5June1843	For 8 yrs
Hicks, William Carroll	Johnson, Williams	5June1843	Fpr 11 yrs
Williams, R. A.	Hamilton, Joseph	7Aug1843	
Rumley, Madison	Ruff, John L.	7Aug1843	For 10 yrs. Son of Henry Rumley, Dcd 3July1843*
Rumley, Sarah J.	Aven, C. W.	7Aug1843	For 5 yrs. Dau of Henry Rumley, Dcd 3July1843*
Rumley, Joseph	Ross, Samuel	7Aug1843	For 11 yrs. Son of Henry Rumley, Dcd 3July1843*
Seals, Thomas J.	Brigance, John H.	4Dec1843	For 3 yrs 2 mos
Anderson, Mary	Anderson, Rebecca B.	5Aug1844	Daughter of Rebecca
Martin, John D.	Johnson, Hiram A.	7Oct1844	
Phillips, Andrew Jackson	Brown, Wilson	2Dec1844	For 19 yrs 6 mo. Son of Nelly Phillips 4Nov1844
Green, Joseph	Bugance, John H.	2Dec1844	Son of Martha Green 4Nov1844
Burrow, Hezekiah	Moore, Thomas S.	6Jan1845	Son of Ephriam Burrow, Dcd. 2Dec1844
Burrow, Rebeca	Williams, Edward H.	7Jan1845	Dau of Ephriam Burrow, Dcd. 2Dec1844
Burrow, William	Palmer, John L.	7Apr1845	Son of Jincy Burrow 3Mar1845
Williams, James	Wood, James	5May1845	For 17 yrs. Destitute orphan.
Rumley, Madison	Hamilton, Calvin	6Oct1845	For 8 yrs 2 mos
Martin, John D.	Hameley, Joseph	7Apr1846	For 5 yrs
Vandiford, John	Barham, James H.	4May1846	For 7 yrs from 1Jan last
Phillips, John W.	Horton, Thomas	1Mar1847	

Name	Date	Age	Master	Notes
Williams, Alexander	5Apr1847		McMackins, William	
Ellis, Alsey	5Apr1847		Shelley, James T.	
Mainard, Israel	3May1847		Hardester, Elisha	
Burrow, Green	3May1847		Burrow, John S.	On 6July1847 support voted for widow and children of Martin Burrow, Dcd
Unnamed	2Aug1847		Ayres, George N.	
Ellis, John C.	5Oct1847		Rust, Jeremiah T.	
Park, Humphrey	1Nov1847		Ellis, Elijah H.	
Cutler (or Cutter), Edward	6Dec1847		Belam, Jacob	
Martin, John D.	8Feb1848		Wright, P. G.	Sadling
Webb, John	4Apr1848		Priest, Franklin	
Killough, John N.	1May1848		Pearce, Samuel M.	Cancelled 6Oct1851 on motion of Samuel D. Killough, Guardian
Booker, Frances M.	6June1848		Turbevill, A. H.	Male
Killough, Charles H.	4Dec1848		Manning, Micheal	For 4 yrs
Burrow,	1Jan1849		Burrow, Phillip	
Smith, Stephen	2Jan1849		Hern, Joseph T.	
Williams, Alexander	5Feb1849		Kile, E. S?.	
Wilson, Martha H.	5Feb1849		Taylor, P. P.	
Mainard, William J.	2July1849		Clement, Lewis T.	
Edward, Layfaett	7Jan1850		King, Chesley	
Swazne, Virinda C.	1July1850		Mitchell, William	Until 18 yrs, unless she shall sooner marry
Swazne, Newton	2July1850		Rogers, Nancy	
Harrell, Jr, Isaac	Nov1850		Harrell, Isaac	
Baker, Franklin	Nov1850		Moore, W. W.	
Crofford, Thomas N.	2Dec1850		Rolling, Alain	
Aspic, Robert	2Dec1850		Hardister, Elisha	
Wilson, Mary	2June1851		McKinney, E.	
House, Margarett	2June1851		Carter, Henry	
Phillips, Andrew J.	3Nov1851		Brown, Wilson	
House, Wilson	5Jan1852		Brooks, A. T.	

Name	Date	Term/Age	Master	Notes
Smith, G. W.	1Nov1852		Rowland, Aaron	
Smith, Thomas J.	6Dec1852		Rogers, William A.	
Kelough, John N.	7Mar1853		Basham, Thomas C.	
Ramsey, Maronda C.	5Sept1853		Woods, Sitizen S.	Orphan
Wilson, Mary	5Sept1853		Humphrey, James H.	Orphan of Charles Wilson, Dcd. Cancelled at Humphrey's request 1May1854
Ramsey, Maronda C.	5Sept1853		Woods, Citizen S.	?Corrected entry
Watson, Jessee	6Feb1854		Watson, Samuel S.	
Gibson, Wiley P.	4Apr1854		Parish, Claibourn	Orphan & heir of Jeremiah Gibson 7Feb1854
Mathis, William H. H.	4Apr1854		Woods, William W.	Orphan. Heir of John Mathis 1Jan1854
Mathis, Robert N.	4Apr1854		Conyers, John	Orphan. Heir of John Mathis 1Jan1854. Bond renewed 5Mar1860
Wilson, Mary	1May1854		Blackcome, Jacob	For 4 yrs
Black, Nancy Jane	7Aug1854		Haywood, H. B.	Heir of Samuel Black 3July1854. Cancelled 5Feb1855
Black, William	4Sept1854	12 yrs 6 mo	Kennon, William B.	Farmer. Heir of Samuel Black 3July1854
Hicks, John S.	2Oct1854	16 yrs 6 mo	Dwiggins, Robert	Orphan. Farmer
Black, Nancy J.	5Feb1855		Edwards, William	Spinster. Cancelled 3Mar1856
Wallace, John	5Feb1855			Orphan. Entry poorly legible
Wallace, James A.	2Apr1855		Blount, John B.	For 8 yrs
Pickles, Jessee	7May1855	12 yrs	Glowson, Jones?	Orphan. Farmer
Pickles, John	7May1855	10 yrs	Pickles, Jackson C.	Orphan. Farmer
Stafford, Robert S.	8May1855	11 yrs	Hames, S. G.	Orphan. Farmer
Busich, John	2July1855		Mitchall, Randolph	Orphan. Farmer
Jenkins, William	6Aug1855		Love, Robert B.	Farmer. Cancelled 7Apr1856
Litle, Jessee	5Nov1855		Phillips, John W.	For 11 yrs. Farmer
Bennet, John S.	8Jan1856		Wright, P. G.	For 3 yrs. Saddler
Driggers, William	3Mar1856		Moore, Thomas S.	Farmer. Driggers has option to cancel apprenticeship at age 18 yrs
Driggers, James	3Mar1856		Moore, W. W.	Farmer. Driggers has option to cancel apprenticeship at age 18 yrs

Name	Date	Age	Master	Notes
Black, Nancy Jane	3Mar1856		Hicks, Barton	House keeper
Jenkins, William	7Apr1856		Corelen, Joseph	Farmer
Jenkins, John A.	5Jan1858	Abt 7 yrs	Lawhon, Isaac	Taken from poor house. Farmer
Mitchell, William	9Jan1858	Abt 12 yrs	Parris, Clabron	Of color
May, James	5Apr1858	Abt 9 yrs	Roseberry, J. S.	Tobacconist
Smothers, William	5Apr1858	Abt 17 yrs	Pinkston, S. D.	Orphan. Farmer
Null, Louis? J.	3May1858	Abt 10 yrs	McAden?, Robert E.	
Barnett, John	3May1858		Curlee, Clabron	Farmer
Edwards, William H?.	5July1858		Simmins, John	Carpenter
Boston, Jacob	7July1858		Hickman, Stephen	Farmer. Cancelled 7Nov1860. Abandoned by Hickman
Boston, Jessee	7July1858		Carter, Thomas M.	Farmer
Boston, Samuel	7July1858		Wright, John H.	Farmer
May, Mary J.	2Aug1858	Abt 11 yrs	Gibson, John	Domestic
Niceler, Allert	2Aug1858	Abt 9 yrs	White, J. W.	Farmer
Nicely, Moses	2Aug1858	Abt 16 yrs	Duncan, Darrel	Farmer
Fiddler (or Feidler), Martha J	1Nov1858	Abt 5 yrs	Bowers, John	Domestick
Mitchell, Shim	7Feb1859		Butler, Johma	Of color. Farmer
May, Elizabeth	2May1859		Thompson, John W.	For thirteen years. Seamstress
Bevel, Henry J.	6Sep1859	b. 2Oct1857	Pinchly, Allen	Farmer
Jenkins, Mary Ann	3Oct1859		Neely, Samuel	Spinster
Alvis	7Nov1859	4 yrs	McAnly, James B.	Of color. Farmer
Jo	7Nov1859	6 yrs	McAnly, James B.	Of color. Farmer
Buyras, James	4Apr1860	Abt 14 yrs	Walker, Bazles	Bound at req of Martha L. Byrns. Farmer
Chandler, Elizabeth	May1860		Martin, Owen	Spinster
Niceler, Allert	4June1860		Allen, Samuel N.	Farmer
Jenkins, James	2July1860		Fisher, E. L.	Farmer
Rily, Robert	3Sept1860		Sole, Daniel	Farmer
Rily, Columbus	3Sept1860		Soles, J. B.	Farmer
Cantrell, Demarius	3Sept1860		Todd, Harley	Spinstress

Name	Date	Age	Master	Occupation/Notes
Walters Charles W.	1Oct1860		Palmer, William	Farmer
Hickey, Marshall	5Nov1860	7 yrs	McArthur, J. M.	Farmer
Bostin, Jacob	7Nov1860		Fuller, W. G.	Farmer
Nelson, William J.	1Apr1861		Smith, Hugh	Farmer
Nelson, George H.	1Apr1861		Ahsly, Joshua	Farmer
Henly, Martin	1July1861	Abt 8 yrs	Melune?, William E.	Farmer
May, Mary J.	2Mar1863		Moore, John	
Tosh, Samuel P.	4Dec1865		Sellers, J. W.	Farming
Tosh, Emerson C.	4Dec1865		Sellers, J. W.	Farming
Blair, Felix	4Dec1865		Blair, Andrew	Farmer
Louisa	1Jan1866		Alexander, J. H.	Orphan. Housewifery. Of color
Norman	1Jan1866		Alexander, J. H.	Orphan. Farmer. Of color
Benjamin	1Jan1866		Alexander, J. H.	Of color. Farmer. Info from entry 7Jan1867, when ordered brought to court at request of Ann Clabron Alexander, mother. Released to court 4Feb1867. Cancelled 5Feb1867
Robert	1Jan1866	11 yrs	Harrell, James H.	Orphan. Farmer. Of color
Martha or Mary	1Jan1866	12 yrs	Harrell, James H.	Orphan. Housewifery. Of color. Cancelled 5Oct1868
Herron, Columbus	1Jan1866	Abt 11 yrs	Herron, W. W.	Farmer. Of color
Herron, Celia	1Jan1866	Abt 9 yrs	Herron, W. W.	Housewifery. Of color
Unnamed female	1Jan1866	10 yrs	Kirk, William J.	Housewifery. Of color
Smith, Felix	1Jan1866	Abt 12 yrs	Smith, H. H.	Farmer. Of color
Hardister, Abram	1Jan1866	Abt 13 yrs	Smith, H. H.	Farmer. Of color
Pearce, Franklin	1Jan1866	Abt 10 yrs	McColl, Henry	Farmer. Of color
Wingo, Eliza	1Jan1866		Wingo, Dabney	Both of color. Information from entry 7Jan1867, when ordered brought to court*
Tush, Richard	6Feb1866	Abt 15 yrs	King, J. C.	Farmer
Smith, James H.	6Feb1866		Barnhart, Isabella	Farmer
Jordan, Emeline	6Aug1866		Morse, W. W.	Housewifery. Of color
Mcmachin, Jefferson	3Sept1866	Abt 8 yrs	Mcmachin, Lucinda	Farmer. Freedman
Hawley, Franklin	3Sept1866	Abt 10 yrs	Mcmachin, Lucinda	Farmer. Freedman

Name	Date	Age	Master	Notes
Hawly, Lewis	3Sept1866	Abt 14 yrs	Mcmachin, Lucinda	Farmer. Freedman
Williams, Sebron	3Sept1866		Kite, E. J.	Farmer. White
Williams, William	3Oct1866		Spelling, J. M.	Orphan. Farmer
Moore, Clay	3Oct1866	12 yrs	Moore, W. W.	Farmer. Of color
Baker, William	3Oct1866	9 yrs	Moore, W. W.	Orphan. Farmer. White
Baker, John	3Oct1866	7 yrs	Moore, W. W.	Orphan. Farmer. White
Adkison, Eliza	3Oct1866	13 yrs	Adkison, James	Spinstress. Of color
Adkison, Edward	3Oct1866		Adkison, James	Of color
Scriber, Lewis	6Nov1866	15 yrs	McCall, J. W.	Orphan. Farmer
Block, Alfred Jeremiah	3Dec1866		Not named	Farmer
Joshua	3Dec1866	Abt 14 yrs	Mom?, Jesse W.	Farmer
Jeremiah	3Dec1866	10 yrs	Black, Jeremiah	Farmer. Black of color
Boyd, Walter	1Apr1867	12 yrs	Townes, James M.	Orphan. Farmer
Boyd, George W.	1Apr1867	14 yrs	Townes, James M.	Orphan. Farmer
Alger, Alfred	3June1867	Abt 11 yrs	Alger, R. H.	Farmer. Of color
Alger, Jerry	3June1867	Abt 10 yrs	Moore, W. W.	Farmer. Of color
Grooms, Henry	1July1867	10 yrs	Grooms, Elizabeth	Orphan. Farmer
Grooms, Harriett	1July1867	6 yrs	Grooms, Elizabeth	Orphan
Carter, John C.	3Sept1867	Abt 10 yrs	Christenberry, William	Farmer. Christenberry to receive any effects in Henderson Co [TN] to which Carters are entitled & report to the court
Carter, Mahalla E. J.	3Sept1867	Abt 6 yrs	Christenberry, William	Spinstress. See above
Faulks, Jefferson	7Oct1867	11 5/12 yrs	Phillips, William	Farmer
Faulkes, John	7Oct1867	8 1/2 yrs	Phillips, William	Farmer
Foulks, Nancy	7Oct1867	Abt 14 yrs	Phillips, Benjamin	Spinstress
Montgomery, Jack	3Feb1868	11 1/4 yrs	Fry, G. W.	Farmer
Burrow, Matilda	3Feb1868		Hood, W. G.	General business. Cancelled 1June1868. To mother
Russell, John W.	3Mar1868	8 7/12 yrs	Springer, Jason	Farming
Rutlege, Thomas	6July1868	Abt 11 yrs	Whitsett, W. J.	Orphan
Johnson, Henry	3Aug1868		Gaskins, T. R.	Orphan. Son of Rebecca Johnson, Dcd. Of color
Johnson, Charity	3Aug1868		Gaskins, T. R.	Orphan. Daughter of Rebecca Johnson, Dcd. Of color

Name	Date	Term	Master/Employer	Description
Herron, John	7Sept1868		Fry, George W.	Farmer. Of color
McKenzie, Caty	1Feb1869	10 yrs	McKenzie, James M.	Orphan. Housewifery
Lansden, Dock	1Mar1869	14 yrs in Oct1869	Lansden, R. D.	Farming. Of color
Eason, Theodor	7Apr1869	9 yrs	Eason, W. H.	Farming. Of color
Unnamed female	7Apr1869	11 yrs	Eason, W. H.	Housekeeping. Of color
Johnson, Franklin	3May1869	7 yrs	Moore, James	Orphan. Farming
Adams, George	5July1869	10 yrs	Rowe, John M.	Orphan. Farming. Of color. Ordered returned to court 3Oct1869 at request of V. S. Allen, next friend. Cancelled 1Nov1869
Jones, John	1Nov1869		Manning, T. B.	Mother's consent. Of color
Adams, George	1Nov1869		Adams, D. E. (Mrs)	Mistress selected by George. Of color
Mebane, Ruth	1Nov1869	10 yrs	Woods, Virginia F.	Of color. Cancelled 8Feb1870*. Placed in custody of William Prince
Roper, David T.	7Feb1870	3 yrs	Brandon, John	Orphan. Farming
Burrow, Peter	7Feb1870	19 yrs	Burrow, John J.	Orphan. Farming
Scott, Nelson	7Mar1870	8 yrs	Scott, India V. (Miss)	Orphan. Farming
Pritchard, Willis	1Aug1870	12 yrs	Pritchard, Charles	Farming. Of color
Goodrum, G. W.	7Nov1870	14 yrs	Hawkins, S. D.	Farming. Of color
Cooper, Isaac	7Nov1870	9 yrs	Furgerson, Samuel H.	Farming. Of color
Cooper, Tilda	7Nov1870	12 yrs	Furgerson, Samuel H.	Household duties. Of color
Tompkins, John	5Dec1870	5 yrs	Henderson, F. H.	Farming. Of color
Timpkins, Lizzie	5Dec1870	3 yrs	Sneed, Garland	Household & kitchen work. Of color
Tompkins, Darcas	5Dec1870	7 yrs	Mebane, S. A.	Household & kitchen work. Of color
Tompkins, James	5Dec1870	11 yrs	Sneed, Garland	Farming. Of color
Collins, W. N.	6Feb1871	15 yrs	McKenney, J. C.	Farming
Clayton, Sarah	6Feb1871	4 yrs	Clayton, B. T.	Spinster. Of color
Clayton, James	6Feb1871	9 yrs	Clayton, B. T.	Farming. Of color
Pritchard, Allen	6Mar1871	8 yrs	Williams, William A.	Farming. Of color
Butler, Rese	14Apr1871	8 yrs	Butler, A. J.	Housewifery. Of color
Clayton, Nancy	1May1871	5 yrs	Sharp, William P.	Spinster
Travis, Sam	4Dec1871	14 yrs	McKenzie, J. D.	Farming. Of color

Name	Date	Age	Master	Notes
Travis, Susan	4Dec1871	7 yrs	McKenzie, J. D.	Spinster. Of color
Travis, Jinnie A.	4Dec1871	11 yrs	McKenzie, J. D.	Spinster. Of color
Lions, Martin	1Jan1872?	4 yrs	Kee, John	Farming. Of color
Morgan, Thomas	6May1872	9 yrs	Moore, Thomas S.	Farming
Pate, Joseph	8May1872	5 yrs	White, Richard	Farming. Both of color
Manley, W. H.	3June1872	9 yrs	Sneed, W. R.	Farming. Of color
Thompson, Robert Blake	3July1872	2 yrs	White, R. B.	Carpenter
Thompson, Mary M.	3July1872	4 yrs	White, R. B.	Orphan. Spinster
Milum, Charles	5Aug1872	6 yrs	Massey, William	Farming. Of color
Herald, John	4Nov1872	4 yrs	Greer, Joseph	Abandoned by parents. Farming. Of color
Rasberry, John J.	3Feb1873	14 1/2 yrs	McKenney, L. A.	Farming
Russell, Thomas P.	3Feb1873	5 yrs	Dildy, J. F.	Farming. Cancelled 1Sept1873
Clayton, John	6May1873	2 yrs	Bell, Eaton & Hariett	Farming. Of color
Allen, John J. J.	9July1873	14 yrs	Neace, Henry	White
Boyle, W. F.	4Aug1873	4 yrs	Humphrey, Enoch	Farming
Russel, Priestley	1Sept1873	5 yrs	Eskew, S. H.	Farming
Patton, Luvina	8Oct1873	10 yrs	Roberson, J. L.	Spinstress. Of color
Attkisson, Henry	3Nov1873	3 yrs	Attkisson, R. A.	Until 19 yrs. Farming. Of color
Attkisson, John	3Nov1873	4 yrs	Attkisson, R. A.	Until 19 yrs. Farming. Of color
Ray, Benjamin	8Jan1874	13 yrs	Crow, A. D.	Until 19 yrs. Common labor. Of color
Dozier, Billie	2Mar1874	12 yrs	Carnes, A. R.	Until 19 yrs. Farming. Of color
Douglass, Amanda	4May1874		Kee, Nelson	Housewifery. Of color
McMackin, William G.	8July1874	12 yrs	McMackin, David	Until 19 yrs. Farming
Shaw, Minnie	3Aug1874	12 or 13 yrs	Smith, J. W.	Spinstress
Hill, Lue E.	8Sept1874	9 yrs	Dilday, J. H.	Girl not to be moved out of the State
Hill, John E.	8Sept1874	12 yrs	McLeod, Daniel	Until 19 yrs. Not to be moved out of State. Terms of apprenticeship completed 7Sept1881
Allen, Samuel N.	9Sept1874	7 yrs	Palmer, T. M.	Until 18 yrs
Shofner, Sarah F.	7Oct1874	6 yrs	Sparks, M. F.	Orphan. Spinstress
Shofner, Willis	7Oct1874	13 yrs	Sparks, M. F.	Until 19 yrs. Orphan. Farming

Name	Date	Age	Guardian	Remarks
Dednum, Charles T.	2Nov1874	12 yrs	Dednum, M. E. (Mrs)	Until 19 yrs. Farming
Haywood, Curn L.	8Dec1874		Butler, Jr, P. T.	Until 19 yrs
Oliver, James	6Jan1875		Whitsett, W. J.	Until 19 yrs
Prince, Ephaine	6Jan1875		Bryant, R. A.	Until 19 yrs. Of color
Jones, Eddy N.	1Feb1875		Clark, J. J.	Orphan. Until 19 yrs
Dunn, Willis G.	1Feb1875	Abt 8 yrs	Brown, Isaac	Orphan. Until 19 yrs
Taylor, George F.	1Mar1875		Chambers, W. P.	Until 19 yrs. Of color
Oliver, Eudora	3May1875	8 yrs	Herrell, Lorenda	Orphan. Spinstress
Pearce, John	7June1875	13 yrs	Cooper, William	Until 19 yrs. Farming
Shanon, Pete	6Sept1875	8 yrs	Clay, W. E.	Until 19 yrs. Farming. Of color
Dyer, Charles	6Sept1875	8 yrs	Clay, W. E.	Until 19 yrs. Farming. Of color
Manley, Henryetta	5Jan1876		Collier, Z. T.	Until 19 yrs (sic). Spinstress. Of color
Killin, Sarah Ninie	9Nov1876	5 yrs	Bullington, D. A.	Spinstress. Of color. Adopted by Bullington on 5May1879. Petition states Sarah is illegitimate daughter of Elizabeth Killen & makes no mention of race
Young, Bettie	4June1877	Abt 9 yrs	McLain, E. N.	White
Russell, Henry A.	6Nov1877	3 yrs	Carter, J. L.	Until 19 yrs. Farming
Mann, Francis	11Jan1878	Abt 13 yrs	Sparks, Isaac	Keep house.
Jones, James	6May1878	3 yrs	Shad, Stephen	Until 19 yrs. Farming, Of color
Jones, Josephine	6May1878	9 yrs	Shad, Stephen	Farming. Of color
Jones, Callie	6May1878	12 yrs	Shad, Stephen	Farming. Of color
Jones, Nannie	6May1878	6 yrs	Shad, Stephen	Farming. Of color
Walker, Ricard	2Sept1878	10 yrs	Palmer, John	Farming
Boston, William H.	7Jan1879	7 yrs	Kyle, E. J.	Agriculturist
Quinn, Thomas	3Mar1879	12 yrs	Quinn, G. W.	Agriculturist
Allen, Thomas E.	3June1879	10 yrs	Smith, M. J. (Mrs)	2 1/2 y/o Thomas had been placed in her care & custody about 1July1872
Lions, Martin	1Dec1879	11 yrs	Cotton, J. M.	Until 19 yrs. Farming
Allen, Rufus	1Dec1879	4 yrs	Morrisett, L. D.	
Moore, Henry	2Aug1880	9 yrs	Strayhorn, H. S.	Orphan. Strayhorn of color

Name	Date	Age	Master	Notes
Moore, Willis	2Aug1880	13 yrs	Strayhorn, J. H.	Orphan. Strayhorn of color
Moore, Napoleon	2Aug1880	12 yrs	Strayhorn, J. H.	Orphan. Strayhorn of color
Bigham, Hayes	5Jan1881	5 yrs	Clay, J. T.	Orphan. Of color
Bigham, Harold	5Jan1881	9 yrs	Clay, J. H.	Orphan. Of color
Nesbitt, Sampson	6June1881	10 yrs	Nesbitt, Ed	Until 20 yrs. Orphan. Both of color
Snead, Wesley	6Mar1882	14 mos	Snead, Ned	Until 19 yrs. Of color
Marchbanks, Ernest	6Mar1882		Ridley, Rufus	Until 19 yrs. Of color
Marchbanks, King	6Mar1882		Howard, John	Until 19 yrs. Of color
Gilbert, Vina	6May1884	12 yrs	Crawford, Felix & Adline	Housekeeping. Crawford's given care of Vina by her father, Joe Gilbert, several years prior to his death. All of color
Grissom, C. W.	9June1885		Groom, W. C.	Until 20 yrs. Orphan. Farming

Crockett County

Name	Date	Age	Master	Notes
Willcox, Willie R.	2Apr1872	11 yrs on 31Oct next	Moore, James W.	Father dead. Consent of mother. Farmer
Jones, Samuel	6May1872		Perry, N. T.	Orphan. Of color
Hart, Jinnie	4June1872	11 yrs	Buck, Albert	Abandoned. Of color
Alton, George	2Sept1872	Abt 13 yrs	Woslin, J.	Orphan. Of color
Freeman, George W.	8Oct1872	Abt 11 yrs	Roberson, J. F.	Abandoned by parents. Of color. 1Dec1873*
McFarland, George	9Oct1872	Abt 17 yrs	McFarland, John W.	Orphan. Of color
McFarland, Elias Jackson	9Oct1872	Abt 13 yrs	McFarland, John W.	Orphan. Of color
McQuerter, Eller	4Nov1872	Abt 6 yrs	Boswell, C. A.	Mother unable to support. Female. Of color
Laman, John	3Feb1873	7 yrs in August 1873	Fouche, R. T. D.	Parents dead. Consent of relatives. Canc 5Jan1876. Also spelled John Layman
Todd, J. F.	4Feb1873	12yrs on 11June1873	Todd, J. C.	Parents dead. Consent of relatives. Farmer
Cox, John	3Mar1873	11 yrs	Roper, J. R.	Orphan. Of color
Hicks, Alice	9Apr1873	10 yrs	Hicks, A. G.	Orphan. Of color

Name	Date	Age	Apprenticed to	Remarks
White, Ella	7July1873		Rhoads, William	Orphan
Slayton, Joseph	3Nov1873		Browder, D. A.	Miss Slayton, mother, consents. Illegitimate
Robertson, Johnothan	3Nov1873		Ward, W. B.	Written consent of mother
Roseman, Samantha	1Dec1873		Lowry, James	Orphan of George Roseman. Brought to court by J. W. Roseman, Esq.
Dunnevan, Harvey	4Jan1875		Hay, R. J.	Farmer
Haynes, Jeff Davis	1Feb1875		Haynes, R. J.	Farming. On 3Feb1875 at request of Jeff's relatives rehearing ordered. Apprenticeship affirmed 2Mar1875. Appealed by next friend, Red McClellan
Shelton, Franklin C.	5Apr1875		Harmon, J. H.	Consent of mother, Sallie Shelton
Ward, Maggie	1Nov1875		Sinclair, J. F.	Req of mother, Tennessee Ward. Of color
Ward, Julie	1Nov1875		Sinclair, J. F.	Req of mother, Tennessee Ward. Of color
Ward, Gilbert	1Nov1875		Sinclair, J. F.	Req of mother, Tennessee Ward. Of color
Nichols, John	6Dec1875		Averry, T. H.	Consent of father, James W. Nichols
Laman, John	5Jan1876		Harmon, B. H.	
Perry, Micajah	2Oct1876		Nance, P. B.	Orphan
Dunnagan, Lucy	5Feb1877		Jones, W. S. A.	
Dunnagan, Rocksy	5Feb1877		Fallan, T. A.	
Works, Lucy	4June1877		Nunn, Jr, D. A.	
Corbitt, Willie	6Jan1879	6 yrs	Robertson, J. F.	Orphan. Farming
Johnson, Lee	5June1879		Sanders, Aaron	Orphan. Farming. Cancelled 5Aug1879, Johnson having mental & physical defects
Best, Turner	4Aug1879	4 1/2 yrs	Reddick, Noah	Orphan. Farming. Of color
Whitman, James	1Sept1879	5 yrs	McCuller, Abe	Orphan. Farming. Both of color
Lyas, John	1Sept1879	6 yrs	McCuller, Abe	Orphan. Farming. Both of color
Porter, Sarah	10Sept1879	8 yrs	Porter, Louisa	Orphan. House keeper. Of color
Johnson, Aslee	6Oct1879	4 yrs	Bell, Thomas	Orphan. House keeper
Dunagan, Lucy	4Oct1881	12 yrs	Williams, P. M.	Orphan. House keeper. Of color. Cancelled 5Dec1881. Mother's consent not obtained
Plunk, Hattie	7Nov1881	6 yrs	Humphreys, B. S.	Orphan. House keeper. Of color

Name	Date	Age	Master	Notes
Overton, Addie	7Nov1881	4 yrs	Robertson, J. F.	Orphan. House keeper. Of color
Overton, Rena	7Nov1881	7 yrs	Perry. John A.	Orphan. House keeper. Of color
Moore, William	7Nov1881	11 yrs	Robertson, J. F.	Orphan. Farmer. Of color
Pipkins, Miles W.	3Dec1883	3 yrs on 31Oct1883	Privett, Miles	Orphan. Farmer
Pounds, Francis	5May1884	5 yrs	Cormack, W. F.	Orphan. Housekeeper
Wade, Clarence	6Apr1886	9 yrs	Harper, Sam	Orphan. Farming. All of color
Wade, Jane	6Apr1886	7 yrs	Harper, Sam	Orphan. Housekeeper. All of color
Wade, Ines	6Apr1886	5 yrs	Harper, Sam	Orphan. Housekeeper. All of color

Decatur County

Name	Date	Age	Master	Notes
Alexander, James	2Aug1869	7 yrs	Davis, N. C.	Canc 7July1879, James having left Davis
Shanan, Joe	1Nov1869		Shanan, Thomas	Of color
Shanan, Mary	1Nov1869		Shanan, Thomas	Of color
Timberlake, George Turnley	6Dec1869		Pearcy, John H.	Canc 3Feb1873, George having run away
Timberlake, Lewis Scott	6Dec1869		West, M. B.	
Swims, Napoleon	6Dec1869		Petty, W. A. C.	
Kelly, Samuel	7Mar1870	7 yrs	Fisher, Jacob F.	Of color
Kelly, Hillman	7Mar1870	9 yrs	Fisher, Jacob F.	Of color
Smothers, Samuel	7Mar1870	8 yrs	Lacy, C. C.	
Simmons, Henry	7Mar1870	9 yrs	Lacy, C. C.	
Shanan, Rebecca	7Mar1870	9 yrs	Shanan, T. S.	Of color
Shanan, Eli	7Mar1870	10 yrs	Shanan, T. S.	Of color
Yarbro, Amice	3Oct1870		Yarbro, Joseph G.	On 4Oct1870 a copy of the will of Amon M. Yarbro recorded. Motion of Amanda J. Yarbro. Amice not mentioned
Thompson, Cattorin?	5Dec1870		Reynolds, W. H. H.	Female
Saint, George	7Feb1871		Brown, William A.	On 6March1871 Benjamin Saint appointed guardian of Mary M. Saint, minor heir of Thomas Saint, Dcd

Name	Date	Term/Age	Master	Notes
Thompson, Thomas	6Mar1871	6 yrs	Fisher, Jacob F.	Of color. Farming
Unnamed male			Lamm?, Theopilas	Of color. On 8Oct1872, indenture made "some years ago" cancelled, as Lamm had died and boy gone
Campbell, Miles	3Feb1873		Jamster?, J. W.	
Moore, Andrew	3May1875	9 yrs	Teague, Moses	Orphan. Farmer
Maness, George	6Sept1875	2 yrs on 15Sep1875	White, Abb?	Orphan. Farmer
Downey, Mary	2Jan1877	8 yrs	Currin, James W.	Orphan
Parrott, William	8Jan1878		Bray, John H.	Orphan. Farming. Of color
Parrott, James	8Jan1878		Coats, W. G.	Orphan. Farming. Of color. Canc 4Mar1878
Parrott, James	4Mar1878	Abt 12 yrs	Tate, James H.	Father dead. Mother unable to provide. Farming
Haney, Ruben Wesley	4Mar1878	13yrs on 21Jan1877	Harrell, George W.	Father dead. Stepmother cannot control him. Farming
Rease, Charly	4Mar1878	12 yrs in June1878	Smith, John	Orphan. Abandoned by father. Farming
Yarbro, Charly	4Mar1878	12 yrs	Fisher, J. F.	Of color
Yarbro, William	4Mar1878	9 yrs	Fisher, J. F. C.	Of color
Walker, Ruben	4Mar1878	9 yrs	Reynolds, W. H. H.	Of color
Walker, Carroll	4Mar1878	7 yrs	Reynolds, W. H. H.	Of color
Scott, Milton			Scott, David M.	Apprenticeship cancelled 8Oct1878, Milton, now abt 12 yrs old, having left. Of color.
Young, Ernett			Young, Robert	Apprenticeship cancelled 7Jan1879 with consent of Young heirs and Exec of Robert Young, Dcd, whose will proven same date
Young,			Young, Robert	Apprenticeship cancelled 7Jan1879 with consent of Young heirs and Exec of Robert Young, Dcd, whose will proven same date
Jones, Manuel	3Feb1879		Yarbro, Aaron	Abandoned by father. Farmer
Parrott, Jinna	4Aug1879	6 yrs	Fisher, W. H.	Father dead. Mother unable to provide
Parrott, John	4Aug1879	4 yrs	Fisher, W. H.	Father dead. Mother unable to provide
Dunn, James	6Jan1880	2 yrs abt 1Sept1879	Rushing, William F.	Orphan. Mother dead. Farming
Young, Jesse			Young, Penelope	Cancelled 7Feb1882, Jesse having left Young. Of color

Name	Date	Age	Master	Notes
Lemmons, Hester	5June1882	7yrs on 1June1882	Morgan, George	No father or mother. Keeping house
Moody, Robert Jefferson	6Nov1882	2 yrs	Teague, M. R.	Orphan. Farming
Lowe, Pitman	4Dec1882	2 yrs 3 mo 20 d	Pettigrew, Fred	Orphan. Farming
Lowe, Albert	4Dec1882	4 yrs 1 mo 20 d	Pettigrew, Fred	Orphan. Farming. Cancelled 2June1884. Father now able to support
Hensley, Emma Etta [or Etter]	6Aug1883	7yrs on 18May1883	Rushing, W. F.	Orphan. Mother, unable to provide, consents. Housewifery
Reed, Sammie	3Dec1883	14 yrs on 18May1883	Rushing, W. F.	Orphan. Farming. Cancelled 5July1886, Sam Reed (or Miller) having left Rushing
Butler, James J.	4Feb1884	12 yrs in Oct1882	Butler, W. F.	Parents dead. Cancelled 5July1886
Simmons, Viola Jane	7Jan1885		Prince, James	Orphan with neither father nor mother. Consent of stepfather, Lewis Morris. Housekeeping
Lemons, William	6July1885	8 yrs on 1July1885	Holland, John D.	No father or mother [sic] living. Lemons consents. Farming. Cancelled 3Aug1885 or 7Sept1885, as mother objected to binding
Lemons, William	7Sept1885	7 yrs in Nov1885	Morgan, George	Orphan. Farming
Maness, Angeline			Yarbro, Aaron	Both of color. Cancelled 4Jan1886
Stephens, Martha F.	6Apr1886	Abt 9 or 10 yrs	Holley, J. M.	Abandoned by parents. Housewifery
Blackburn, Joseph L.	6Feb1888	10 yrs 11 mo 15 d	Blackburn, R. H.	Orphan. Mother, unable to support, consents. Farming
Bird, Martha			Holley, J. M.	Cancelled 7Jan1889
Kemper, Jackson	7Apr1891	Abt 9 yrs	Harmon, C. M.	Neither father nor mother. Farming
French, Brown	6Feb1893	Abt 12 yrs	Fisher, W. H.	Orphan. Farming
French, Leslie	6Feb1893	Abt 14 yrs	Fisher, W. H.	Orphan. Farming
French, Reuben	6Feb1893	Abt 7 yrs	Fisher, W. H.	Orphan. Farming

Dyer County

Name	Date	Age	Master	Notes
Ferguson, Charlotte	2Sept1850		Burroughs, Henry W.	One of two daughters of Sally Ferguson 5Aug1850
Hathway, James	4July1853	10 yrs	Haynes, John B.	Tanner. Orphan. On 7Feb1853 Sarah Hathway's boys ordered brought to court
Lunsford, John	6Dec1853	8 yrs	Saunders, Ferdinand L.	Farmer. Orphan. On 7Nov1853 John & Harrison Lunsford ordered brought to court. Mrs Catherine Lunsford, widow, declared incompetent, Robert F. Crow, her Guardian. 7Feb1854*
Strayham, Andrew	6Feb1854	12 yrs	Davidson, Elizabeth G.	Orphan
Vaden, Fernando	6Feb1854	9 yrs	Chitwood, Edmund	Chitwood also appointed Guardian of Fernando, heir of Eliza Vaden
Williams, Thomas J.	6Nov1854	14 yrs	Harris, Allen	Farmer
Williams, Andrew J.	6Nov1854	14 yrs	Ledsinger, Charles H.	Orphan. Farming
Scott, Bailie Peyton	1Jan1855	11 yrs	Thurmond, Nancy	Orphan. Farmer
Lunsford, John	3Sept1855	10 yrs	Bogguss, R. D.	Orphan. Farmer
Hallum, William David	5Feb1856		Ledsinger, P. C.	
Hallum, Nancy Elizabeth	5Feb1856		Silsby, L. H.	
White, William	3Mar1856		Stephenson, J. H. D.	
Reddick, Lavinia	2Apr1866	13 yrs on 1Jan last	Reddick, Thomas J.	By FB. Orphan. Housework or farming. Of color
Reddick, John	2Apr1866	13 yrs on 4Mar last	Reddick, Thomas J.	By FB. Orphan. Farming. Of color
Wynne, Francis	7Apr1866	9 yrs on 9Feb last	Wynne, H. V. C.	By FB. Orphan. Housework or farming. Of color
Wynne, Susan	7Apr1866	6 yrs on 10Oct last	Wynne, H. V. C.	By FB. Orphan. Industry & spinning & sewing. Of color
Wynne, Sameller	7Apr1866	9 yrs on 5Mar last	Wynne, H. V. C.	By FB. Orphan. All kinds of work. Of color
Jones, Joseph	9Apr1866	Abt 11 yrs	Jones, Albert	By FB. Orphan. Farming. Of color

Name	Date	Age	Master	Notes
Jones, Monroe	9Apr1866	Abt 15 yrs	Jones, Albert	By FB. Farming. Of color
Woodson, Robert	16Apr1866	10 yrs on 25Dec last	Williams, Lewis M.	By FB. Orphan. Farming. Of color.
Woodson, Jane	26Apr1866	Abt 12 yrs	Westbrook, J. R.	By FB. Orphan. Of color
Howard, Margaret	1May1866	10 yrs on 1Apr last	Tipton, R. B. (Mrs)	By FB. Orphan. Cooking & sewing. Of color
Turpin, John	7May1866	9 yrs on 10Mar last	Turpin, Richmond (or Richard)	By FB. Orphan. Farming. Of color
Washington, Lewis	7May1866	Abt 13 yrs	Simmons, F. T.	Orphan
Ward, Susan	20May1866	8 yrs on 3Nov last	Hurt, William B.	By FB. Orphan. Housework & sewing. Of color
Warren, Henry	25May1866	12 yrs on 25Apr last	Tarkington, J. W.	By FB. Consent of mother, Raney Warren. Farming. Of color
Warren, Martha	25May1866	9 yrs on 6Dec last	Tarkington, J. W.	By FB. Consent of mother, Raney Warren. Sewing & cooking. Of color
Horton, Wyty	25May1866	5 yrs on 1June1866	Tipton, P. M.	By FB. Orphan. Farming. Of color
Horton, Josephine	25May1866	6 yrs on 4Jan last	Tipton, P. M.	By FB. Orphan. Sewing & cooking. Of color
Woodson, Mary	26May1866	7 yrs on 1Mar last	Westbrook, John R.	By FB. Orphan. Sewing & housekeeping. Of color
Woodson, Lewis	26May1866	13 yrs on 15Oct last	Westbrook, John R.	By FB. Farming. Of color
Watkins, Katy	26May1866	7 yrs on 10Mar last	Moss, Charles C.	By FB. Orphan. Sewing & housekeeping. Of color
Woodson, Jane	26May1866	12 yrs on 4Mar last	Westbrook, John R.	By FB. Orphan. Sewing & housekeeping. Of color
Watkins, Joseph	26May1866	11 yrs on 1May1866	Watkins, William M.	By FB. Orphan. Farming. Of color
Hathway, Maryann	4June1866	13 yrs on 15July next	Bledsoe, A. B.	By FB. Orphan. Sewing & housekeeping. Of color

Drane, Jo	2Oct1866	8 yrs	Drane, John M.	Male orphan
White, Bob	5June1866	18 yrs on 1May1866	Dolsen, Benjamin S.	By FB. Orphan. Farming. Of color
Drane, Sallie	2Oct1866	6 yrs	Drane, John M.	Orphan
Fuller, John	3Dec1866	14 yrs	Parks, Hamilton	Orphan
Fuller, Ann	3Dec1866	10 yrs	Parks, Hamilton	Orphan
Fuller, Amanda	3Dec1866	7 yrs	Parks, Hamilton	Orphan
Fuller, George	3Dec1866	5 yrs	Parks, Hamilton	Orphan
Lucas, Matt Franklin	3Dec1866	Abt 10 yrs	Lucas, J. M.	Orphan
Douglass, Matilda	9Jan1867	12 yrs	Douglass, Guy	Of color
Caruthers, Dandridge	9Jan1867	15 yrs	Caruthers, J. F.	Of color
Light, Assine	7Feb1867	7 yrs	Bunnell, W. A.	Of color
Allen, Sallie	7Feb1867		Allen, Thomas J.	Of color
Rhodes, James	6May1867	10 yrs	Bunnell, Isaac	White
Warren, John	1July1867	Abt 2 yrs	Rudder, James W.	Of color
Kent, Richard	1July1867		Spence, J. S.	Of color
Dowell, Wiley	5Aug1867	Abt 12 yrs	Davis, J. N.	White
Haskins, Milton	5Aug1867	Abt 9 yrs	Haskins, John C.	Of color
Haskins, Henry	5Aug1867	Abt 6 yrs	Haskins, John C.	
Fowlkes, Littleton	5Nov1867	Abt 10 yrs	McCoy, James	Of color
Chitwood, Reece	5Nov1867	Abt 10 yrs	McCoy, J. Henry	Of color
Jordan, Harriet	3Dec1867	Abt 8 yrs	Neal, Tom W.	Of color
Boon, Willard	3Dec1867	Abt 10 yrs	Boon, Henry	Of color. Entry struck out by court order
Jones, Ada	3Dec1867	Abt 14 yrs	Jones, Samuel J.	Of color
Smith, George	8Jan1868	11 yrs	Smith, Jo.	Of color
Smith, Henry	8Jan1868	9 yrs	Smith, Jo.	Of color
Smith, Armstead	8Jan1868	7 yrs	Smith, Jo.	Of color
Smith, Addison	8Jan1868	5 yrs	Smith, Jo.	Of color
Turner, Westley	2Mar1868	Abt 14 yrs	Fuller, William	Of color
Sugg, George Westly	2Mar1868	Abt 11 yrs	Hollowell, S. S.	White

Name	Date	Age	Master	Notes
Sharp, Luitene	1June1868	Abt 9 yrs	Bell, John E.	Of color
Pate, Dick	3June1868	Abt 15 yrs	Pate, E. C.	Of color
Boon, Billy	3June1868	Abt 6 yrs	Ferguson, H. F.	Of color
Sharp, Andrew	3Aug1868	Abt 7 yrs	Parker, John M.	Of color
Sharp, Scott	3Aug1868	Abt 5 yrs	Beasly, W. N.	Of color
Daniels, Wiley	7Sept1868	Abt 12 yrs	Parrish, Elias	White
Sharp, Erasmus	8Sept1868	Abt 10 mo	Beaumont, Joe	Of color
Steel, Hattie Ann	2Nov1868	Abt 13 yrs	Harris, William F.	Of color
Rushing, Richard	2Nov1868	Abt 7 yrs	Fryer, R. N.	Of color
Weakly, Henry	2Nov1868	Abt 10 yrs 8 mo	Weakly, D. C.	Of color
Robertson, Jeff D.	9Nov1868	8 yrs	Bigg, W. W.	Of color
Robertson, Albert	9Nov1868	6 yrs	Bigg, W. W.	Of color
Boon, Willard	7June1869	Abt 11 1/2 yrs	Wilbern, George	Of color
Tipton, Amanda	1Nov1869	Abt 5 yrs	Tipton, Pleas	Of color
Tipton, Sambo	1Nov1869	Abt 4 yrs	Tipton, Pleas	Of color
Neeley, Daniel	6Dec1869	Abt 10 yrs	Fumbanks, A. L.	Of color
Ray, Thomas	3Jan1870	Abt 9 yrs	Wesson, William	Of color
Lasley, Anderson	3Jan1870	Abt 12 yrs	Steel, R. S.	Of color
Echols, Margaret	6Jan1870		Leeroy, Mary A.	Of color
Palmer, Isabella	3May1870		Manley, J. A. C.	For nine years. Of color
Martha	7June1870	5 yrs	Griffin, Timothy	Of color
Neely, Amanda	1Aug1870	9 yrs	Enochs, W. S.	Of color
Smith, Martha	5Dec1870	15 yrs	Harris, Allen & Mary Ann	Of color
Smith, Jo	5Dec1870	13 yrs	Harris, Allen & Mary Ann	Of color
Smith, Spencer	5Dec1870	6 yrs	Harris, Allen & Mary Ann	Of color
Smith, Rowland	5Dec1870	4 yrs	Harris, Allen & Mary Ann	Of color

Name	Date	Age	Bound to	Notes
Smith, Hampton	5Dec1870	2/12 yrs	Harris, Allen & Mary Ann	Of color
Worrell, Daniel	5Dec1870	11 yrs	Perry, J. F.	White
Worrell, James H.	5Dec1870	9 yrs	Frost, Wilson	White
Parks, Blanch	3Jan1871	18 yrs	Parks, Sr, Hamilton	Of color
Parks, Margaret	3Jan1871	15 yrs	Parks, Sr, Hamilton	Of color
Parks, Anthony	3Jan1871	12 yrs	Parks, Sr, Hamilton	Of color
Parks, Fanin	3Jan1871	8 yrs	Parks, Sr, Hamilton	Of color
Parks, Sammie	3Jan1871	5 yrs	Parks, Sr, Hamilton	Of color
Talley, John	4Jan1871		Latta, S R.	Of color
Ferrill, Alice	7Feb1871	11 yrs	Ferrill, J. S.	Of color
Ferrill, Willie	7Feb1871	7 yrs	Ferrill, J. S.	Of color
Ferrill, Ella	7Feb1871	4 yrs	Ferrill, J. S.	Of color
Nora	5Apr1871	10 yrs	McCorkle, J. S.	Orphan. Of color
Biggs, Sam	5Apr1871	9 yrs	Biggs, W. W.	Orphan. Of color. On 5June1871 N. T. Perry, having possession of Sam (as Samuel Jones), asked apprenticeship to Biggs be cancelled. Denied 6Sept1871. Perry appealed to Circuit Court. Appeal denied
Enochs, Louisa	5June1871	11 yrs	Hale, Robert	Of color
Haskins, Peter	3July1871	6 yrs	Haskins, C.	Of color
Haskins, Sam	3July1871	8 yrs	Haskins, C.	Of color
Neely, Jo	7Aug1871	16 yrs	Neely, Robert H.	Male. Of color
Craig, Amanda	4Sept1871	5 yrs	Reamey, Sarah J.	Consent & application of mother. Of color
Parker, Richard	5Sept1871	12 yrs	Harris, J. P.	Consent of mother. Of color
Avery, Jonas	5Sept1871	12 yrs	Avery, H. B.	Consent of Jonas. Orphan. Of color
Moore, Dinkie	5Aug1872		Pierce, George W.	For 13 yrs. Orphan. Of color
Light, Nancy Adeline	3Mar1873	4 yrs 6 mo	Walker, W. H.	Request of mother. Of color
Donnel, George	6Oct1873	Abt 10 yrs	Parks, George	Farmer. Of color
Daniel, Callie	6Oct1873	6 yrs	Harrell, Rueben G.	Of color
Dunivant, Victoria	8Oct1873	12 yrs	Pendleton, E. B.	Housekeeping. Bound at request of mother. Father dead

Name	Date	Age	Master	Notes
Thompson, William	1Dec1873		Taylor, E. C.	White orphan
Mourae?	1Dec1873	11 yrs	Parker, J. W.	Farmer. Orphan. Of color
Brazier, Thomas	8Jan1874	13 yrs	Parrish, Elias	Farmer. Orphan. White
Gaulden, Fletcher	8Jan1874	6 yrs	Benton, Richard Johnson	Orphan. Both of color
Skipwith, John	2Nov1874	10 yrs	O'Dell, James A.	Farmer. Father dead. Mother unable to provide. 6Oct1874*
O'Neal, Charley	7Dec1874	Abt 5 yrs	Gardner, John	Farmer. Abandoned by father. Mother dead. White
Ketchum, Richard T.	7Apr1875	14 yrs in Feb1875	Wood, S. A.	Child of W. L. Ketchum & wife. Both present in Court & unable to provide.. White. Cancelled 2Oct1876. To father
Ketchum, John W. N.	7Apr1875	8 yrs in Sept1874	Wood, S. A.	Child of W. L. Ketchum & wife. Both present in Court & unable to provide.* White. Cancelled 2Oct1876 as John W. M. Ketchum. To father
Ferrell, Lucy	4Oct1875		Holland, S. K. P.	Orphan. Housekeeping. Of color
Perry, Jo	1Nov1875	Abt 10 yrs	Griffin, Thomas J.	Orphan. Of color. Appealed to Circuit Court by Robert Smith, of color, for boy, who does not wish to be bound to Griffin
Price, Agnes	6Dec1875	Abt 14 yrs	Stallings, E. G.	Agnes consents. Of color
Gentry, William	3Jan1876	11 yrs	Templeton, R. F.	Farming. Of color
Byrum, Callie	5Apr1876	Abt 10 yrs	Seat, James G.	Orphan. Housekeeping. On 5July1876 Willie Byrum sent to Poor House, as no one found to whom he can be bound. On 3June1878 Callie adopted by Nathan D. Fletcher
Douglas, Jane	2Jan1877	Abt 2 yrs	Walker, Ned	On 3Oct1876 mother, Ellen Douglas, said to be insane & ordered to Poor House. Now in jail. All of color
Douglas, Nick	2Jan1877	Abt 4 yrs	Walker, Ned	Farming. On 3Oct1876 mother, Ellen Douglas, said to be insane & ordered to Poor House. Now in jail. All of color
Butler, S. Mozello	2Jan1877	12 yrs in Aug1876	York, J. B. (Dr)	Duties pertaining to womanhood. Orphan.
Parker, Maggie	6May1878	Abt 7 yrs	Pace, A. R.	Mother in poor house. Father unknown. Of color
Canada, Maecenas	3July1878	Abt 7 yrs	Scharmahorn, James	Orphan. White
Walker, Joseph	5Sept1878	Abt 10 yrs	Walker, Phillip	Farming. Orphan. Both of color
Walker, Wash	5Sept1878	Abt 9 yrs	Walker, Phillip	Farming. Orphan. Both of color

Name	Date	Age	Master	Notes
Walker, Thomas	5Sept1878	Abt 8 yrs	Walker, Phillip	Farming. Orphan. Both of color
Pyles, Robert	4Dec1878	Abt 11 yrs	Bell, W. E.	Farming. Orphan. Of color
Sandford, Charley	5Mar1879	Abt 10 yrs	Love, John W.	Farming. White
Ivey, Sarah Francis	5May1879	Abt 10 yrs	Tate, W. G.	Father dead. Mother unable to provide. White
Given, Tenilla?	5Aug1879	Abt 11 yrs	Given, Stephen	Male orphan. Both of color
Parker, Thomas	4Oct1881	Abt 9 yrs	Atkins, James	Of color
McCoy, Samuel J.	6Nov1882	10 yrs in Spring 1882	Worrell, William F.	Farming. Orphan. White.
Douglass, Soran?	5Feb1883	Abt 6 yrs	Hudson, W. A.	Male orphan. Farming. Of color
Douglass, Shela	5Feb1883	Abt 4 yrs	Hudson, W. A.	Orphan. Of color

Fayette County

Name	Date	Age	Master	Notes
Isaacs, William R. G.	18Jan1828	12 yrs on 5Apr next	Moore, Alfred	Orphan. Cabinet work
Evans, Duncan	11Oct1829		Pair, Hamilton C.	For 7 yrs 6 mo
Evans, Chesly	11Oct1829		Pair, Hamilton C.	For 5 yrs 2 mo. Of color
Broomfield, John	14Apr1831	Abt 9 yrs	Cooper, John C.	Mulatto
Sophy	13Oct1831	18 yrs	Field, Drury S.	Dau of Betsey Finey, free woman of color
Washington	13Oct1831	15 yrs	Field, Drury S.	Son of Betsey Finey, free woman of color
Marthy	13Oct1831	12 yrs	Field, Drury S.	Dau of Betsey Finey, free woman of color
Betsy	13Oct1831	10 yrs	Field, Drury S.	Dau of Betsey Finey, free woman of color
William	13Oct1831	7. yrs	Field, Drury S.	Son of Betsey Finey, free woman of color
Sally	13Oct1831	4 yrs	Field, Drury S.	Dau of Betsey Finey, free woman of color
Elam, Henry	13Oct1831		Smith, David	Orphan
Elam, Wily	13Oct1831		Smith, David	Orphan
William	8Apr1833	6 yrs	Blackwell, John	Child of Nancy Perry, free mulatto. Of color. Indentures certified correct 2Jan1837

Name	Date	Age	Master	Notes
Sandy	8Apr1833	3 yrs	Blackwell, John	Child of Nancy Perry, free mulatto. Of color. Indentures certified correct 2Jan1837
Harriette	8Apr1833	1 yr	Blackwell, John	Child of Nancy Perry, free mulatto. Of color. Indentures certified correct 2Jan1837
Nesbitt, Henry	12Apr1833	Abt 13 yrs	Winset, Robert	Brick laying
Scott, Drury	8July1833	7 yrs	Harrass, Stephen	
Kesen, David	16Jan1834	12 yrs	Hill, David	
Kesen, Sarah Ann	16Jan1834	8 yrs	Hill, David	
Dunlap,	14Apr1834		Taylor, Cannon	For 6 yrs 6 mo. Orphan. Taylor
George, Isaac	17Apr1834	Abt 4 yrs	Myrick, J. W.	Orphan
Price, Sally	11Jan1836	10 yrs	Field, James	
Price, William	11Jan1836	7 yrs	Field, James	
Redding, Robert	11Apr1836	15 yrs	Malone, A. L.	Orphan
Blackwell, Jasper W.	5Dec1836		Blackwell, John	On 7Jan1837 cancelled at request of Polly Blackwell, mother. Appealed by John Blackwell to Circuit Court
Blackwell, Solomon G.	5Dec1836		Blackwell, John	On 7Jan1837 cancelled at request of Polly Blackwell, mother. Appealed by John Blackwell to Circuit Court
Blackwell, Hiram H.	5Dec1836		Blackwell, John	Mother Polly Blackwell 7Jan1837
Blackwell, Nathan B.	5Dec1836		Blackwell, John	Mother Polly Blackwell 7Jan1837
Blackwell, Polly A.	5Dec1836		Blackwell, John	Mother Polly Blackwell 7Jan1837
Blackwell, Newton G.	5Dec1836		Blackwell, John	Mother Polly Blackwell 7Jan1837
Blackwell, Bayles C.	5Dec1836		Blackwell, John	"Bayliss" in mother's petition 7Jan1837
Slaytor, Charles W.	2Jan1837		Wilson, William M.	Orphan. Taylor
Slaytor, Thadius W.	2Jan1837		Wilson, William M.	Orphan. Taylor
Edmondson, Thomas	6Feb1837	15 yrs	Burt, William S.	
Epps, Doney	6Feb1837		Harris, Jesse R.	
Houston, Carolin	6Mar1837	6 mo	Crawford, Joseph	Orphan
Duke, Stephen	3July1837	b. 4Mar1837	Langham, Thomas	Child of Caroline, of color.
Smith, Caroline	7Aug1837		Langham, Thomas	Of color. Rescinded next day
Baily, Lewis W.	2Oct1837	Abt 17 yrs	Floyd, Samuel	

Name	Date	Age/Term	Master	Notes
Cyles (or Llyles), William L.	5Mar1838	17 yrs on 1Apr1838	Booth, David C.	Of color
Walden, Barbery	4June1838		Floyd, Calvin S.	Orphan of John Walden. Has a sister, Lucy 6Feb1837* Lucy let out 2July1838
House, Emeline	4June1838		Birdsong, William	
Kirkpattrick, Plumer	2July1838	14 yrs	Giles, Thomas N.	Orphan
Futington, George Washington	1Oct1838	10 yrs	Johnson, Andrew	Orphan
Williams, James	5Nov1838	13 yrs at Xmas next	Phillips, Andrew	Orphan. Farmer
Bell, John Westly	3Dec1838	10 or 12 yrs	Wills, James S.	Orphan
Bell, William	3Dec1838	4 or 5 yrs	Wills, John B.	Orphan. Cancelled 6Jan1840
Walker, David G.	4Feb1839	10 yrs	Hooks, A. G.	
Rash, Jackson L.	4Mar1839	13 yrs on 13Sep1839	Wills, James S.	Orphan. Spring mashine making
Walden, Lucy	3June1839		Bayless, Thomas H.	Orphan of John Walden, Dcd. 6Feb1837*
Jones, Sarah	2July1839	Abt 16 yrs	Cooper, John C.	Of color
McCan, Fenan	2Sept1839	4 yrs	Douglass, Thomas	Consent of Mary McCan, mother. Of color
McCan, Washington	2Sept1839	3 yrs	Douglass, Thomas	Consent of Mary McCan, mother. Of color
McCan, Betsy	2Sept1839	7 yrs	Douglass, Thomas	Consent of Mary McCan, mother. Of color
Bell, William E.	6Jan1840	6 yrs	Morriss, John R.	Farmer
Tailor, John McKnight	3Feb1840		Thomas, Micajah	Farmer
Sanders, John A.	3Feb1840	7 yrs	Sullivan, William	Farmer
Sanders, James C.	3Feb1840	15 yrs	Gates, William A.	Farmer
Bell, Lutitia B.	4May1840	14 yrs	Mathews, John H.	Cancelled 7Sept1840
Johnson, Zachariah G.	7Sept1840	17 yrs 4 mo	Hardwick, L. C.	Consent of Sarah L. Johnson, mother
King, Mathew	7Dec1840	15 yrs on 5Aug1840	Butt, Samuel C.	Brick mason & plaster
King, William Henry?	7Dec1840	11 yrs	Webb, Jacob M.	Orphan. Tinner
Clinten?, Robert	4Oct1841	4 yrs next February	Williams, Isaac	Farmer

Name	Date	Age	Master	Notes
McLemore, Preston Perry	5Jan1842	12 yrs	Webb, David	On 4April1842 Mrs McLemore & family allowed $50 for their support until July term. Cancelled 6Aug1849, as Presly McLemore
Nesbit, Robert N.	2May1842	16 yrs in Sept next	Lynch, Moses & Branson, William	
McLemore, Sterling T.	3May1842	10 or 12 yrs	Winsett, Robert	On 4April1842 Mrs McLemore & family allowed $50 for their support until July term. 3July1843 Sarah McLemore awarded $25 for support of her and 3 small children
Daily, Permelia	6June1842	15 or 16 yrs	Jackson, Andrew	
McDaniel, David	5Dec1842	8 yrs next March	Farrish, A. J.	Farrish appt'd guardian in place of D. Chandler, Dcd. Orphan of David McDaniel, Dcd July1844 p.16. Cancelled 2Mar1846
Fulerton, Elijah	2Jan1843	11 yrs	Sisco, Z.	
McLemore, Ephram Columbus	3Jan1843	15 yrs next July	Hardwick, L. C.	Carpenter. Consent of McLemore. Cancelled 7Feb1848
Terrell, Solomon	6Mar1843	10 yrs	Hunter, Henry	Orphan. Cancelled 7Oct1844, as Solomon J?. High
Muncrief, Jasper	3Apr1843	13 yrs	Spear, Dennis	Farmer
Higdlburge, Samuel	1Jan1844	15 yrs on 29Mar next	Langham, James M.	Carpenter or mill wright. Consent of Higdlburge
Garrett, Henry	6May1844	Abt 8 yrs	Hopkins, Preston	Orphan. Farmer
Fulleton, Elijah	7Oct1844		Pickens, Andrew J.	
Koker, Ben F.	7Oct1844	Abt 6 yrs	Spear, John	Cancelled 2Dec1844 on demand of mother, Mary Koker
Koker, Nevil S.	7Oct1844	Abt 8 yrs	Spear, John	Cancelled 2Dec1844 on demand of mother, Mary Koker
Koker, Mary	7Oct1844	Abt 10 yrs	Spear, John	Cancelled 2Dec1844 on demand of mother, Mary Koker
Grant, Jackson	4Nov1844	Abt 10 yrs	Jordan, John	Farmer
Dickson, Thomas	2Dec1844	Abt 10 yrs last July	Siddle, Job	Farmer. Cancelled 2June1846. Is now with mother, Mildred J. Dickson
Bell, David E.	2Dec1844	10 yrs on 22July next	Cawood, John R.	Orphan. Farmer. Cancelled 3Nov1845 on application of Sarah Kennedy. Ill used
Wollam, Absalom C.	7July1845	Abt 12 yrs	Jones, Sr, Larkin	Farming. Cancelled 4Sept1848
Jones, Lovida	2Feb1846	Abt 5 yrs	Jones, Joel S.	Request of Sally Jones, mother. Of color
McDaniel, David	2Mar1846	11 yrs	Darden, Alfred H.	Farmer

Name	Date	Age	Master	Notes
Dickson, Thomas	4Jan1847		Hubbard, James D.	Farmer
Henderson, Edward	1Mar1847		Ward, P. W.	Farmer. Of color
Brinkley, Polly	6Sept1847	Abt 8 yrs	Martin, John W.	Orphan. Cancelled 3Nov1851
Smith, Edwin	4Oct1847	15 yrs	Allen, Amson	Mill wright
Swinney, Gerome P.	7Feb1848		Hamerick, Samuel	
Swinney, Louisa E.	7Feb1848		Hamerick, Samuel	Cancelled 3Feb1857, as Linny Janie Swiney. Ill treatment
Swanson, Willin? W.	7Feb1848	10 yrs	Hamerick Rheubin	Ink smudged
Swanson, Levi B.	7Feb1848	6 yrs	Hamerick Rheubin	
Swanson, Matilda Ann	7Feb1848	4 yrs	Hamerick Rheubin	
Woolam, Absalom Columbus	4Sept1848	Abt 15 yrs	Minter, William	Shoe maker
Cox, John W.	2Oct1848	Abt 9 yrs last August	Tucker, E. J.	
Dalton, John Calvin	5Dec1848	Abt 17 yrs	Webb, Jacob M.	Tiner
Perry, Martha	1Jan1849	11 yrs	Farish, L. B.	Of color. Farish also to support her mother
Perry, Joseph	1Jan1849	14 yrs	Farish, L. B.	Farmer. Of color. Farish also agrees to support his mother
East, John Henry	5Mar1849	10 yrs next April	Mason, John M.	Farmer
Morris, Mary Ann	7May1849	Abt 8 yrs	Elliott, A.	
McLemore, Presly	6Aug1849		Bowers, James	Carpenter
Fisher, David N.	4Mar1850	Abt 16 yrs	Fisher, William	
Ann	4Mar1851	Abt 16 yrs	Reeves, William C.	Orphan. Request of Eliza, mother. Card, spin, sew & weave. Of color
William	4Mar1851	Abt 14 yrs	Reeves, William C.	Orphan. Request of Eliza, mother. Planter & farmer. Make & burn brick. Of color
Mary	4Mar1851	Abt 12 yrs	Reeves, William C.	Orphan. Request of Eliza, mother. Card, spin, sew & weave. Of color
Sanders, Larkin P.	5May1851		Jones, Larkin	
Eliza Ann	6Oct1851	16 yrs (from 6Jan1858 entry)	Hodges, Margaret	Of color. On 6Jan1858 freedom confirmed & allowed to remain in Tennessee. Mulatto
Brinkley, Polly	3Nov1851	Abt 14 yrs	Snow, Stephen	White

Name	Date	Age	Master	Notes
Forbes, Alexander	1Dec1851	20 yrs on 4July1852	Walker, Simon H.	Cabinet maker
Newby, Wales	1Dec1851	Abt 18 yrs	Walker, S. H.	Cabinet maker
Gardner, Cornelius	6July1852	Abt 8 yrs	Carroll, W. B.	Mother, Mary Elizabeth Gardner, died at Carroll's house in April 1852. Of color. Blacksmith
Gardner, Elizabeth	6July1852	Abt 3 yrs	Carroll, W. B.	Mother, Mary Elizabeth Gardner, died at Carroll's house in April 1852. Of color. Spin, sew & weave
Gardner, Tom	6July1852	Abt 6 yrs	Carroll, W. B.	Mother, Mary Elizabeth Gardner, died at Carroll's house in April 1852. Now in Madison Co. TN. Of color. Blacksmith
Burrow, Robert	2Aug1852	Abt 13 yrs last April	Burrow, John W.	Farmer. Orphan of Freeman Burrow, Dcd 2May1859. 6Oct1859*
Burrow, Jarral	2Aug1852	11 yrs	Burrow, John W.	Farmer. Orphan of Freeman Burrow, Dcd 2May1859. 6Oct1859*
Cornelius	1Oct1855		Aston, C. S.	Servant. Of color
Morris, John	5Feb1856	Abt 16 yrs	Holloway, Q. T.	Farmer
Allen, James William	1Dec1856	6 yrs	Smith, John B.	Orphan. Farmer
White, Jabes H.	3June1857	Abt 17 yrs	Walker, Simon H.	Cabinet making
Baugh, Jenny	4Apr1859		Cawood, John R.	Abandoned by father
Skeggs, Charles B.	5Nov1860		Washer, Benjamin	Orphan
Jones, Joseph	14Nov1865	9 yrs	Jones, Martha A. (Mrs)	By FB at Memphis. Orphan. Of color
Jones, Samuel	14Nov1865	11 yrs	Jones, Martha A. (Mrs)	By FB at Memphis. Orphan. Of color
Jones, Richard	14Nov1865	11 yrs	Jones, Martha A. (Mrs)	By FB at Memphis. Orphan. Of color
Johnson, Charles	29Nov1865	12 yrs	Johnson, Dudley G.	By FB at Memphis. Orphan. Of color
Pullin, Judie	12Dec1865	12 yrs	Pullin, Fayette J.	By FB at Memphis. Orphan. Of color. Filed between Dickson & Dyer Co records
Smith, Scott	25Dec1865	11 yrs	Smith, G. F.	By FB. Orphan. Of color. Canc 9Jan1871, Scott having left Smith 27Dec1865.
[Smith], Jane	25Dec1865		Smith, G. F.	By FB. Orphan. Of color. Cancelled 7Dec1874 by consent of both. Data from cancellation entry. 6Mar1876*
House, Buck	17Jan1866	13 yrs	Williams, C.	By FB at Memphis. Orphan. Of color

Dora	25Jan1866	16 yrs at cancellation	Wells, James R.	By FB. Of color. Orphan. Cancelled 7Jan1871, Dora having married. Data from cancellation entry
Bryant, Davy	5Feb1866	10 yrs	Bryant, Andrew	By FB. Of color. Cancelled 6Oct1870. Data from cancellation entry
Rate, Emanuel	5Feb1866	10 yrs	Bryant, Andrew	By FB. Cancelled 4Dec1873 by petition of both. Data from cancellation entry
Crow, David O.	6Feb1866		Davis, Samuel M.	Request of Crow. Orphan. Farmer. Cancelled 5July1870
Champion, Sandy	10Feb1866		Champion, J. T.	By FB. Of color. Cancelled 10Aug1871, Sandy having left Champion about 20Dec1870. Data from cancellation entry
Champion, Frank	10Feb1866		Champion, J. T.	By FB. Of color. Cancelled 10Aug1871, Frank having left Champion about 13Feb1871. Data from cancellation entry
Rodgers, Louisa	11Aug1866	11 yrs	Walker, Edna B.	Orphan. Of color
Neblett, Emily	5Nov1866	10 yrs in Aug1866	Neblett, J. D.	Orphan. Of color. Canc 6Jan1870, as not an orphan. To parents, Alfred & Maria Payne
Hunter, Eve	5Nov1866	13 yrs	Hunter, J.	Orphan. Of color
Hunter, Eliza	5Nov1866.	13 yrs	Hunter, J.	Orphan. Of color
Paine, Ida	5Nov1866	6 yrs	Paine, B. M.	Orphan. Of color
Darden, Susan	5Nov1866	6 yrs	Darden, A, H.	Orphan. Of color
Darden, Polk	5Nov1866	8 yrs	Darden, A, H.	Orphan. Of color
Williams, Jennie	5Nov1866	9 yrs	Williams, Thomas R.	Orphan. Of color
Aston, Sam	5Nov1866	14 yrs	Hardin, M. L.	Orphan. Of color
Cannon, Jack	5Nov1866	13 yrs	Cannon, William J	Orphan. Of color
Jones, Allick	6Nov1866	4 yrs	Jones, Lovick	Orphan. Of color
Jones, Forrest	6Nov1866	2 yrs	Jones, Lovick	Orphan. Of color
Jones, Phoebe	6Nov1866	7 yrs	Jones, Lovick	Orphan. Of color
Roach, Sally	6Nov1866	12 yrs	Thomas, W. J.	Orphan. Of color
Cocke, Leana	6Nov1866	5 yrs	Cocke, Ann E. (Mrs)	Orphan. Of color
Cocke, Roberta	6Nov1866	3 yrs	Cocke, Ann E. (Mrs)	Orphan. Of color
Moore, Winny	7Nov1866	6 yrs	Moore, W. J.	Orphan. Of color
Moore, Cora	7Nov1866	5 yrs	Moore, W. J.	Orphan. Of color
Moore, Oliver	7Nov1866	10 yrs	Moore, W. J.	Orphan. Of color

Name	Date	Age	Master	Notes
Moore, Preston	7Nov1866	8 yrs	Moore, W. J.	Orphan. Of color
Jordan, Jesse	3Dec1866	10 yrs	Jordan, G. D.	Orphan. Of color
Wilson, Henry	4Dec1866	10 yrs	Gaither, J. G.	Orphan. Of color
Walker, Robert	4Dec1866	12 yrs	Thomas, James W.	Orphan. Of color
Walker, John	4Dec1866	9 yrs	Thomas, James W.	Orphan. Of color
Merriwether, Anderson	4Dec1866	12 yrs	Merriwether, F. A.	Orphan. Of color
Merriwether, Martha	4Dec1866	15 yrs	Merriwether, F. A.	Orphan. Of color
Harris, Marietta	12Dec1866	15 yrs	Hardin, M. L.	Orphan. Of color
Harris, Lucy Ann	12Dec1866	8 yrs	Hardin, M. L.	Orphan. Of color
Harris, Sarah Ann	12Dec1866	11 yrs	Harris, O.	Orphan. Of color
Harris, Alvin	12Dec1866	13 yrs	Harris, O.	Orphan. Of color
Miller, Pleasant	8Jan1867	11 yrs	Ragland, Milton E.	Orphan. Of color
Ivie, Lewis	9Jan1867	9 yrs	Ivie, Washington	Orphan. Of color
Lemon, George	14Jan1867	12 yrs	Maris, William	Orphan. Of color
Samuella	4Feb1867	12 yrs	Isbell, N. H.	Orphan. Of color
Fanny	4Feb1867	12 yrs	Isbell, N. H.	Orphan. Of color
Thomas	4Feb1867	11 yrs	Isbell, N. H.	Orphan. Of color
Elich	4Feb1867	8 yrs	Isbell, N. H.	Orphan. Of color
Alston, Lucinda	5Feb1867	8 yrs	Fraser, William L.	Orphan. Of color
Scott, Jainus	3June1867	8 yrs	Melcher, S. H.	Orphan. Of color
Scott, Wallace	3June1867	10 yrs	Melcher, S. H.	Orphan. Of color. Cancelled 2Sept1867
Hall, Kitty	5Aug1867	6 yrs	Hall, Zilla	Of color
Hall, Harriet	5Aug1867	4 yrs	Hall, Zilla	Of color
Ira	7Aug1867	12 yrs	Anderson, John V. & Elizabeth	Of color
Robert	7Aug1867	11 yrs	Anderson, John V. & Elizabeth	Of color
Solomon	7Aug1867	9 yrs	Anderson, John V. & Elizabeth	Of color
Crow, Martha E.	7Aug1867	10 yrs	Cocke, Thomas R.	Orphan

Name	Person	Age	Date	Notes
Scott, Wallace	Sutherland, Susan [J] [Mrs W. A.Sutherland]	8 yrs	2Sept1867	Orphan. Of color
Brown, Solomon	Mebane, William G.	10 yrs	2Dec1867	Orphan. Of color
Baird, Nancy	Baird, J. L.	10 yrs	5Dec1867	Orphan. Of color
Rivers, Fannie	Morgan, W. N.	14 yrs	9Jan1868	Of color. Cancelled 8Dec1870, Steven Rivers, her father, having taken her from Morgan a few weeks after binding
Granberry, Charles	Alexander, S. J.	6 yrs	3Feb1868	Orphan. Of color
Alexander, Phillis	Alexander, S. J.	8 yrs	3Feb1868	Orphan. Of color
Alexander, Joe	Alexander, S. J.	10 yrs	3Feb1868	Orphan. Of color
Tatom, Harriet A. E.	Small, W. A.	12 yrs	4Feb1868	Daughter of Susan H. Tatom, as Patsy Tatom declared a lunatic 6Aug1867* Dau of Richard E. Tatom Dcd & granddaughter of Martha E. Tatom 5Mar1867* Cancelled 3Nov1869, Small leaving Tennessee
Tatom, Mary Ellen	Bone, James P.	13 yrs	4Feb1868	Daughter of Susan H. Tatom, as Patsy Tatom declared a lunatic 6Aug1867* Dau of Richard E. Tatom Dcd & granddaughter of Martha E. Tatom 5Mar1867*
Tatom, Susan Ida	Thompson, Charles V.	7 yrs	4Feb1868	Daughter of Susan H. Tatom, as Patsy Tatom declared a lunatic 6Aug1867* Dau of Richard E. Tatom Dcd & granddaughter of Martha E. Tatom 5Mar1867*
Thompson, Jonah	Thompson, George	8 yrs	1June1868	Mother unable to provide. Of color
McRae, Lizzie	Lynn, Charles	5 yrs	6July1868	Of color. Cancelled 4Aug1873, Lizzie having left Lynn on 4Aug1872
Love, Henry	Love, W. R.	13 yrs	9Jan1869	Orphan. Of color
Jones, Matilda	Jones, Wiley B.	9 yrs	7Sept1869	Orphan. Of color
Boyd, William	Boyd, John		6Oct1869	Orphan. Mother dead. Of color
Tatum, H. A. E.	Scrugg, E. R.		3Nov1869	Until 17 yrs. See 4Feb1868 entry
Lincoln, Abraham	Pulliam, J. L.	6 yrs	3Nov1869	Orphan. Of color
Pirtle, Jesse	Crutchfield, J. S.	4 yrs	7Jan1870	Until 18 yrs. Parents dead. Of color
Pirtle, Lucinda	Crutchfield, J. S.	7 yrs	7Jan1870	Until 16 yrs. Parents dead. Of color
Pirtle, Ellen	Crutchfield, J.	12 yrs	10 Jan1870	Until 17 yrs. Orphan. Of color
Pirtle, Douglas	Crutchfield, J.	10 yrs	10 Jan1870	Until 18 yrs. Orphan. Of color

Name	Date	Age	Master	Notes
Pirtle, Susan	10 Jan1870	2 yrs	Crutchfield, J.	Until 17 yrs. Orphan. Of color
Murphy, Cyrene	6June1870		Griggs, Henry C.	Assent of mother, Jane Murphy. Sureties changed 8Nov1870
Murphy, Rose	6June1870		Griggs, Henry C.	Assent of mother, Jane Murphy. Sureties changed 8Nov1870
Wilson, Precilla	10Nov1870	13 yrs	Cooper, Henry J.	Orphan
Daly, Frank	6Dec1870	9 yrs	Tatum, J. G.	Illegitimate son of Emily Daly, who has 3 other children, is mentally unfit and fails to provide for their support. Of color. Cancelled 9Jan1873, Daly having left Tatum Aug1871
Daly, Lou	6Dec1870	6 yrs	Hodges, J. W.	Illegitimate daughter of Emily Daly, who has 3 other children, is mentally unfit & fails to provide for their support. Of color
Martin, Catherine	6Feb1871	5 yrs	Love, B. J.	Mother, Lucinda Martin, in Poor Farm
Parr, Felix	7Aug1871	10 yrs	Parr, William M.	Orphan. Of color
Ussery, Willis	8Oct1872	4 yrs	Ewell, Charles	Consent of mother, Sarrah Ussery, of color. No lawful father.
Williams, Robert	9Oct1872	13 yrs	Williams, Ed	No father or mother
Williams, Martha	9Oct1872	9 yrs	Williams, Ed	No father or mother
Anderson, Louisa	11Oct1872		Lawhorne, Jerry	Mother dead. Abandoned by father
Shivers, Mattie	7Nov1872	12 yrs	Blair, Lizzie	Without father or mother
Shivers, Louis	7Nov1872	8 yrs	Blair, Lizzie	Without father or mother
Wilson, Reuben	3Dec1872	8 yrs	Flippin, James A.	Orphan. Of color
White, Louis	9Jan1873	Abt 10 yrs	Tatum, J. G.	Orphan
Poston, Leonidas	8Oct1873	6 yrs	Poston, Louis	Orphan. Of color
Marlar, William	7Jan1874	4 yrs	Hooks, J. H.	Orphan
Williams, Martha	7June1875	Abt 6 yrs	Davis, L. L.	Bastard. Of color. Mother, Sally Jones, a "base and abandoned character"
Wells, Rufus	17Jan1877	14 yrs	McCully, J. M.	Request of Wells. No father or mother
Hammon, Nelson	6Apr1877	Under 14 yrs	Garnett, John H.	No father or mother living
Hammon, Saul	6Apr1877	Under 14 yrs	Garnett, John H.	No father or mother living
Tucker, Charlie	11Feb1878	3 yrs	Bailey, Albert	Consent of mother. Father a convict in State Prison. Of color
Leak, Mary	3July1878	Abt 10 yrs	Smith, John	No father or mother living. Of color
Grayton, William	6Aug1878	Abt 8 yrs	Carter, J. S.	Request of mother. No father. Of color

Name	Date	Age	Master	Notes
Lloyd, Lucy A. W.	7Mar1879		Scruggs, Fannie M. (Mrs)	Father dead. Mother in Poor House several years
Crawford, Rosa	2Mar1880		Boler, Ren	Father & mother dead
Ivy, Callie	1Sept1882	3 yrs	Jones, Henry	Mother dead. Deserted by father
Ivy, Sallie	1Sept1882	18 mo	Jones, Henry	Mother dead. Deserted by father

Gibson County

Name	Date	Age	Master	Notes
Ingram, Benjamin	Jan1825	13 yrs	Ferguson, William	Orphan
Dickson, Jackson	1Dec1828	12 yrs	Stanley, Thomas	Orphan
York, John	4Dec1828	10 yrs	Evans, John W.	Orphan
Shaw, Willis	4Mar1828		Shaw, Solomon	Orphan. Both parents dead. Canc 4Mar1830
Shaw, Zachariah	4Mar1830	b. 3May1813	Ferguson, William	
Shaw, Willis	4Mar1830	b. 7Apr1817	Ferguson, William	
Cantrell, Barry	7June1830	Abt 8 yrs	Lee, Abraham B.	Orphan. Cancelled 5Sept1831
Flowers, John	6Sept1830	12 yrs	Farmer, Nelson	Orphan
Cantrell, Berry	5Sept1831	Abt 9 yrs	Billingsly, Elijah	Orphan
Jones, John	Dec1831	Abt 13 yrs	Williams, Thomas	Orphan
Williams, Michael C.	7Sept1832	Abt 4 yrs	Underwood, Jeptha	Orphan
Williams, Susan	7Sept1832	Abt 6 yrs	Underwood, Jeptha	Orphan
Bartley	7Sept1832	16 yrs on 14Jan	Elam, Jonothan	Of color
York, John	16Sept1833		Evans, Catharine	Until 20 yrs. Orphan
Williams, Susan	16Dec1833	7 yrs	Morgan, John	Daughter of Susan Williams
Williams, Michael	16Dec1833	5 yrs	Morgan, John	Son of Susan Williams
Haily, Robert	19Sept1834		Hamilton, James	
Lewis, Joel	20Dec1834		Sellars, Robert	Child of William D. Lewis, Dcd
Lewis, Louisa	20Dec1834		Sellars, Robert	Child of William D. Lewis, Dcd
Davis, Jesse	16Mar1835		Williams, Beverly	Has option to leave Williams at age 17 yrs. Orphan son of John Davis, Dcd

Name	Date	Age	Master	Notes
Davis, Robert	15June1835	Abt 15 yrs	Williams, Johnston	For 5 yrs 6 mo. Orphan. Blacksmithing
Davis, Jesse	24Sept1835	13 yrs	Gee, John P.	
Webster, John	23Dec1835	16 yrs	Pybor, Nathanial	Orphan. Tailor
King, Nelson Franklin	Nov1836		Puckett, Peter P	Farming
Webb, Murrel	7Aug1837		Littlefield, William M.	Farming
Hall, Julius	4Dec1837	13 yrs	Eddings, Osborn	Orphan. Sadler
Hall, Calvin	4Dec1837	16 yrs	Gee, John P.	Orphan. Tanning
Hargrove, John A.	5Mar1838	15 yrs	Rogers, O[re]. U.	Cabbinet making. Cancelled 7Dec1840. Duties to Hargrove neglected by Roberts
Hall, Alfred D.	7May1838		Cox, Moses	For 2 yrs 4 mo. Brick mason. Heir of Warrin Hall, Dcd. Cancelled 3Sept1838*
Baker, Pinkney	6Aug1838		Baker, William G.	Brought to court by William Brent
Hall, Johnathan	3Sept1838		Tinkle, Robert	Heir of Warrin Hall, Dcd. Aaron Jackson, Adm. Jan1839 p. 71*
Ross, George W.	1Oct1838		Borren, Willis	For 15 yrs. Cancelled 5Apr1842. Ross to custody of Samuel Abbott, constable
Chamberlin, Thomas	1Oct1838		Hamilton, James M.	For 5 yrs. On 3Sept1838 Richard Dickins apptd adm of Thomas Chamberlain, Dcd
Man, Willis	6May1839	12 yrs	Gran, Jesse G.	Orphan. Farming
Chamberlin, Elizabeth			Parker, F. W.	Orphan. Cancelled 5Aug1839. Data from cancellation entry
Evans, Marian	2Dec1839	Abt 3 yrs	Parker, Amanda F.	Of color
Robins, William N.	6Apr1840	10 yrs	Ragsdale, Peter	Orphan. Blacksmith
Robins, George W.	6Apr1840	8 yrs	Bennett, Pernell	Orphan. Farming
Robins, John L.	6Apr1840	6 yrs	Bennett, Pernell	Orphan. Farming
Scott, William P.	3Aug1840	9 yrs	Fowler, Beaman	Orphan. Farming
Scott, Newton J.	3Aug1840	11 yrs	Fowler, James F.	Orphan. Farming
Cannon, William J.	2Nov1840	12 yrs	Hunt, James T.	Orphan. Farming
Hargrove, John	8Dec1840	17 yrs	Claiborn, Thomas B. & Davis, G.	Orphan. Book keeping
McGraw, David	5Jan1841	Abt 9 yrs	Giles, James C.	Orphan. Boot & shoe making
McGraw, John	1Feb1841	17 yrs	Boon, Benjamin	Orphan. Farming

Name	Date	Age	Master	Notes
Cannon, George W.	1Nov1841	4 yrs	McEwen, Hugh	Orphan. Farming
Cannon, Susan (or Susanah)	1Nov1841	8 yrs	McEwen, Hugh	Orphan. Housewifery
Cannon, John N.	3Jan1842	15 yrs	Bennett, Willis	Orphan. Farming
Nolin, Allen C.	8Mar1842	14 yrs	Blanton, Albert C.	Orphan. House carpenter. Canc 2Jan1844
Taylor, Joseph D.	2May1842	5 yrs	Basinger, John	Orphan. Farming
Taylor, Logan H.	2May1842	18 mo	Basinger, John	Orphan. Farming
Ross, George W.	2May1842	10 yrs	Dill, Jemmiah H.	Orphan. Farming
Spencer, Olaver H. P.	6Sept1842	7 yrs	Pole, John N.	Orphan. Taning & curing. Henry Franklin Spencer, orphan, sent to Poor House. Cancelled 9July1845
Sanders, Margaret E.	6Mar1843		Sanders, John	Orphan. Housewifery
Sanders, Aaron	6Mar1843		Hendricks, William	Orphan. Farming
Glisson, George W.	1May1843	14 yrs	O'Daniel, Stephen	Orphan
Glisson, William N.	1May1843	12 yrs	O'Daniel, Alexander	Orphan
Ross, George W.	6Nov1843	11 yrs	Ross, Charles H.	Orphan. Farming. Cancelled 7April1845
Mainard, John E.	6Nov1843	7 yrs	White, Joseph M.	Orphan. Farming
Knott, Henry	4Nov1844	15 yrs	Pritchett, Benjamin	Orphan. Taning & curing
Chamberlain, Leberry	6Jan1845	12 yrs	Chamberlain, Willam D.	Orphan. Farming. In Sept1843 term Jesse Bailey apptd guardian of Berry Chamberlain, heir of Thomas Chamberlain, Dcd
Ross, George W.	7Apr1845	Abt 13 yrs	McAlla, Richard	Orphan. Farming
Knott, William?	4Aug1845	Abt 13 yrs	Holt, William C[arroll].	Orphan. Farming. Securities released 6Nov1847, then called Green Knott
Knott, John	4Aug1845	Abt 11 yrs	Holt, Perry	Orphan. Farming. Securities released 6Nov1847
Dear, Wesley	2Feb1846	17 yrs	Billingsly, Elisha	Orphan. Farming
Shepherd, Thomas M.	5Oct1846		Blair, George D.	Cabbinet trade
Selph, Daniel	7Dec1846	12 yrs	Hunt, Wilson D.	Orphan
McLaurine, William	7Sept1847	Abt 12 yrs	Smith, Jacob T.	Orphan. Tayloring. Cancelled 4Mar1850, William having no aptness in learning trade
Furgerson, Harris J.	4Oct1847		Cole, S. H.	Orphan. Farming. Cancelled 6Dec1847
Crockett, David M.	May1848		Crockett, David	Orphan. Mother under jurisdiction of court. Farming. Cancelled 3Nov1851. Master dead

Name	Date	Age	Master	Notes
Cooper, Whitson C.	3Oct1848		Glasscock, Scarlett M.	Farmer
Evans, George Washington	4Dec1848	Abt 6 mo	Parker, Felix	Son of Dinah Evans. Of color
Amanda	3Feb1849	Abt 13 yrs	Taylor, Basil	Of color. Cancelled 4Nov1851
Spence, Elam C.	1Oct1849	16 yrs	Cashion, E. M.	Orphan. Cancelled 3Nov1851
Hunt, Caroline	1Dec1849	Abt 8 yrs	Ervin, William	Of color
Dickey, David	4Feb1850		Foster, John W.	For 12 mo. Saddling. Foster allowed $35 on 1April1850
Doud, William	6May1850	13 yrs	Dodson, William H.	Until 20 yrs. Orphan. Farming
Cook, John	3Mar1851	11 yrs	Hall, Hansford N.	Orphan
Hunt, Mary	3Mar1851	5 yrs	Irvin, William	Of color
Hunt Susan	3Mar1851	3 yrs	Irvin, William	Of color
Evans, Franklin	7July1851	Abt 1 mo	Parker, Felix	Servant. Son of Deanah Evans. Of color
Chamberlain, Berry			Shaw, Samuel	Rescinded 1Sept1851. Data from resc entry
Crockett, David M.	3Nov1851	13 yrs	McLain, John C.	Orphan. House carpenter
Amanda	4Nov1851		Davis, Joseph?	Of color
London, Thomas J.	6Jan1852	12 yrs	Ward, Isaac	Orphan
London, John C.	6Jan1852	8 yrs	Cossell, Henry F.	Orphan
Gordon, John W.	Feb1852?		Jones, Wesley F.	From cancellation entry 1Mar1852. Probable son of John Gordon, Dcd & Calista Gordon 5Jan1852, 3Feb1852. On 3Feb1852 Calista Gordon, a lunatic, & her 2 children sent to poor house
Speares, James D.	2Aug1852	12 yrs last January	Hudson, John S.	Orphan. On 7Nov1853 Hudson reported about to leave country. Ordered to bring Spear to Court
Gordon, Wilson	1Nov1852	Abt 15 yrs	Jones, John W.	Orphan. Heir of John Gordon, Dcd. Jones also apptd guardian
Manor, Riley	3Oct1853		Carroll, Charles	Of color
Branch, Elihu	6Mar1854	15 yrs	Conan, Isaac F.	
Hunt, Nancy Jane	3July1854		Cressup?, A. H.	Of color
Hunt, Susan Emily	3July1854		Cressup?, A. H.	Of color
Read, Peter	7Aug1854		Beard, James M. (Dr)	Orphan. Child of Jane Reed 3July1854
Read, Mary J.	7Aug1854		Waldrop, John	Orphan. Child of Jane Reed 3July1854. Cancelled 4Sept1854

Name	Date		Master	Notes
Read, James B.	7Aug1854		Beard, Wilson	Orphan. Child of Jane Reed 3July1854. Bond cancelled 1Oct1855, as Wilson Baird
Stephens, Margaret A.	8Aug1854		Baxter, John	Orphan
Reed, Mary J.	4Sept1854		Waldrop, Wiley A.	
Gordon, John W.	4Sept1854		Barksdale, N. T.	J. W. Jones, Security
Marsden, James E.	6Nov1854		Caldwell, Samuel M.	
Manen, John	4Feb1856		Belien, Govenor	
Webb, America	2Feb1857		Williams, L. L.	Female
Good, Patrick	4Jan1858		Wood, W. H.	Of color. Son of Manda Morton Nov1857. Cancelled 6Dec1859
Good, Nelson	1Feb1858		Goodloe, M. H.	Bound at January term. Of color. Son of Manda Morton Nov1857 p. 489
Good, Alex M.	7June1858		Farr, Poleman	Of color
Furgerson, William A.	1Nov1858		Cox, W. T.	Until 19 yrs
Arnold, Amanda	4Jan1859		Richardson, N. P.	
Arnold, Minerva	4Jan1859		Davis, Joseph	
Keathley, Alonzo J.	7Feb1859	Abt 12 yrs	Keathley, J. G.	Cancelled 7Oct1861. Apprentice ran away
Keathley, Jessee	7Feb1859		Cowan, Isaac F.	?Son of Archelous Keathly, Dcd 4June1860* On 4Sept1860* William M. Senter apptd Guardian ad litem. 5Sept1860* 8Jan1861*
Keathley, Elisha S.	7Feb1859		Halliberton, U. S.	On 4Sept1860* William M. Senter apptd Guardian ad litem. 5Sept1860* 8Jan1861*
, Stephen	8Feb1859		Hall, Herrod	
Ham, James W.	8Mar1859		Wood, Peyton	Until 20 yrs
Warren, John	4Mar1859		Wilson, B. F.	Until 20 yrs
Oliver, James H.	4Mar1859		Oliver, R. L. P.	Until 20 yrs
Mosely, Isaac A.	4Mar1859		Flowers, Thomas	Until 20 yrs
Lyons, John	2May1859		James, Isaac	Until 20 yrs*
Lyons, William S.	6June1859		Lowry, Stephen W.	Until 20 yrs. 2May1859* Cancelled 8June1859, as William T. Lyons
Lyons, Elizabeth B.	6June1859		Lowry, Stephen W.	2May1859* Cancelled 8June1859, as Catharine Lyons

Name	Date	Age	Master	Notes
Lyons, William S.	7June1859		Pybas, James S.	Until 20 yrs. Cancelled 7May1860
Lyons, Elizabeth	1?July1859		Morris, Charles	
Mosley, A. C.	3Oct1859		Whitehurst, A. B.	Until 20 yrs
Ferrell, William	4Oct1859		Ferrell, Thomas	Until 20 yrs
Shelby, Charles A.	1?Feb1860	Abt 5 yrs	Ferrell, Charles	Until 20 yrs. Orphan
Lyons, William	7May1860		Hatchett, Thomas	Cancelled 4Mar1861
Cannon, W. H.	4June1860		Melton, Robert	Until 20 yrs
Coples, William T.	6Aug1860		Tatum, A. H.	Until 20 yrs. Father & mother assented. Cancelled 3Dec1867 as W. T. Capps, Capps having left Tatum
Wallace, Lee	3Sept1860		Connell, James	Until 20 yrs
Davis, James	1July1861	9 yrs	Cooper, Whitson	Until 20 yrs
Roberson, Meriah	2Sept1861		Levy, Lewis	Until 20 yrs. Consent of mother, Sarah A. Roberson. Of color. Cancelled 7July1868
Roberson, Betty Jane	2Sept1861		Levy, Lewis	Until 20 yrs. Consent of mother, Sarah A. Roberson. Of color
Roberson, Mary F.	7Oct1861	6 yrs	Fite, John R.	Until 20 yrs. Mother consents. Of color
Roberson, Nancy P.	7Oct1861	4 yrs	Fite, John R.	Until 20 yrs. Mother consents. Of color
Harper, Stephen T.	7Oct1861	Abt 12 yrs	Nevel, R. J.	Until 20 yrs
Patrick, W. H.	3Oct1865		Patrick, J. J.	Until 20 yrs. No father or mother
Patrick, John W.	3Oct1865		Patrick, N. S.	Until 20 yrs. No father or mother
Camden, Thomas	1865-66		Camden, M. J.	Of color. Cancelled 6May1873, Thomas not controllable. Data from cancellation entry
Camden, Mary	1865-66		Camden, M. J.	Of color. Cancelled 6May1873. Mary now married. Data from cancellation entry
Camden, Watson	1865-66		Camden, M. J.	Of color. Cancelled 6May1873, Watson having left. Data from cancellation entry
Camden, Zilpha	1865-66		Camden, M. J.	Of color. Cancelled 6May1873. Zilpha now married. Data from cancellation entry
Camden, Ellen	1865-66		Camden, M. J.	Of color. Data from cancellation entry
Camden, Lewis	1865-66		Camden, M. J.	Of color. Data from cancellation entry
Keathley, Elisha S.	5Feb1866		Bottoms, P. L.	Son of Archelous Keathley, Dcd 4June1860*

	6Aug1866	11 yrs [from canc]	McMurray, L. P.	Of color. Canc 6May1873. Oscar absconded
Caldwell, Oscar				
McMurray, Mary	6Aug1866		McMurray, L. P.	Of color
McMurray, Minerva	6Aug1866		McMurray, L. P.	Of color
Arnold, Lou	6Aug1866		Balentin, Samuel D.	Of color
Nance, Wilson	5Nov1866		Nance, W. W.	
Nance, Jacob	5Nov1866		Nance, W. W.	
Seward, Jennie	7Jan1866		Seward, Benjamin	Of color
Roe, Green	8Jan1867		Roe, John A.	
Roe, Charity	8Jan1867		Roe, John A.	
Williams, Aley	8Jan1867		Williams, A. J.	
Williams, Ellen	8Jan1867		Williams, A. J.	
Lasiter, Collin	8Jan1867		Lasiter, A. J.	Cancelled 2Jan1871, at age 17 yrs. To mother & relatives. Of color
Thompson, Ben	4Feb1867		Thompson, John A.	
Thompson, Eliza	4Feb1867		Thompson, John A.	
Thompson, Martha	4Feb1867		Thompson, John A.	
Thompson, Zoe	4Feb1867		Thompson, John A.	
Seat, James?	4Feb1867		Seat, S. G. B.	
Roe, Jessee	4Feb1867		Roe, John A.	
Watson, Andrew	4Feb1867		Watson, E. F.	
Patton, Mariah?	4Feb1867		Patton, N. C.	
Newhouse, Emma	4Feb1867		Newhouse, F. M.	
Newhouse, Allen	4Feb1867		Newhouse, F. M.	
Jackson, Margaret	5Feb1867	8 yrs	Jackson, P. H.	
Jackson, Alice	5Feb1867	7 yrs	Jackson, P. H.	
Fly, Paris	5Feb1867	10 yrs	Fly, F. L.	
McClelland, John	6Mar1867	12 yrs	Hicks, A. R. A.	Of color
Edwards, John	1Apr1867	14 yrs	Moore, Needham	
Jail?, Mary	3Apr1867		Oppenheimer, M.	

Name	Date	Age	Master	Notes
Williams, Benjamin	5May1867		Wheeler, W. T.	
Hunter, Hannah	5May1867	10 yrs	Williams, Z. N.	Of color
(Hazlewood), Kate	5Aug1867		Hazlewood, Elizabeth	
(Hazlewood), Alice	5Aug1867		Hazlewood, Elizabeth	
(Hazlewood), Greer	5Aug1867		Hazlewood, Elizabeth	
Ollendem, Polly	5Aug1867	7 yrs	Nichold, Lazarus	Of color
Dodson, Buck	2Sept1867		Dodson, W. H.	Of color
Dodson, Belle	2Sept1867		Dodson, W. H.	Of color
Bradford, Tennessee	2Sept1867		Bradford, Harris	Until 21 yrs. Female. Of color
Patterson, William	2Sept1867		Patterson, Carson	Of color
Patterson, George	2Sept1867		Patterson, Carson	Of color
Patterson, Hannah	2Sept1867		Patterson, Carson	Until 21 yrs. Of color
Patterson, Samuel	2Sept1867		Patterson, Carson	Of color
Green, Erasmus	3Sept1867		McGee, R. B.	Of color
Avery?, Mary	7Oct1867	11 yrs	Epperson, J. L.	Until 21 yrs. Of color
Claudius Caesar	4Nov1867	Abt 6 yrs	Dunlap, Ebenezer	Of color
Cora Edna	4Nov1867	Abt 4 yrs	Dunlap, Ebenezer	Of color
Minnie	4Nov1867	Abt 3 yrs	Dunlap, Ebenezer	Of color
Donaldson, Lucinda	5Nov1867	14 yrs	Donaldson, Ebenezer	Until 21 yrs
Donaldson, William	5Nov1867	12 yrs	Donaldson, Ebenezer	
Donaldson, Charles	5Nov1867	11 yrs	Donaldson, Ebenezer	
Donaldson, Harriet	5Nov1867	11 yrs	Robinson, James W.	Until 21 yrs
Hays, Jeff	5Nov1867	9 yrs	Lee, W. A.	Of color
Stott, Jim	5Nov1867		Holder, J. S.	Of color
Stott, Frank	5Nov1867		Holder, J. S.	Of color
Stott, William	5Nov1867		Holder, J. S.	Of color
Sinclair, Dick	2Dec1867	Abt 6 yrs	Fields, Mary M.	Of color
Cox, Daniel? Della	2Dec1867		Cox, J. F. M.	Of color
Cox, Charles Henry	2Dec1867		Cox, J. F. M.	Of color
Cox, Jack Moss	2Dec1867		Cox, J. F. M.	Of color

Name	Age	Date	Master	Notes
Pigece, Ella		2Dec1867	Arnold, E. J.	Of color
Pigece, George		2Dec1867	Arnold, E. J.	Of color
Pigece, William		2Dec1867	Arnold, E. J.	Of color
Pigece, John		2Dec1867	Arnold, E. J.	Of color
Tyree, Bob		3Dec1867	Tyree, E. G.	Of color
Tyree, Green		3Dec1867	Tyree, E. G.	Of color. Cancelled 3July1871, as Mrs C. Tyree dead
Tyree, Patsy		3Dec1867	Tyree, E. G.	Of color. Cancelled 3July1871, as Mrs C. Tyree dead
McAulay, Amanda	Abt 13 1/2 yrs	4Dec1867	McGee, R. B.	Until 21 yrs. Of color
Green, Mary	Abt 13 yrs	6Jan1868	Scrape, W. H.	
Johnson, Robert	10 yrs	6Jan1868	Elder, B. F.	
Unnamed female	Abt 12 yrs	8July1868	James, Joseph	White orphan
Rutledge, Beverly	Abt 12 yrs	3Aug1868	Taylor, David A.	White orphan. Cancelled 5May1873
Childress, Rebecca Jane	10 yrs	7Sept1868	Cox, W. T.	Orphan. With her mother, an inmate of the Poor House 6Apr1868
Caldwell, Willis	8 yrs	8Sept1868	Caldwell, J. M.	Orphan. Of color
Corley, Bet	6 yrs	2Nov1868	Corley, N. H.	Orphan. Of color
Corley, Sam	8 yrs	2Nov1868	Corley, N. H.	Orphan. Of color
Reed, Victoria A.		2Nov1868	Martin, C. W.	Orphan
Johnson, Chloe	12 yrs	1Feb1869	Gleason, Timothy	Orphan. Of color. Caroline Johnson, mother, protests and appeals to Circuit Court
Johnson, Henry	5 yrs	1Feb1869	Gleason, Timothy	Orphan. Of color. Caroline Johnson, mother, protests and appeals to Circuit Court
Tucker, Aphmerson?	8 yrs	1Feb1869	Parker, O. P.	Orphan. Of color
Johnson, Cherry	Abt 6 yrs [sic]	2Feb1869	James, G. W.	Orphan. Canc. Had been previously bound
Johnson, Henry	Abt 12 yrs [sic]	2Feb1869	James, G. W.	Orphan. Canc. Had been previously bound
Harvey, Rachel	Abt 2 yrs	1Mar1869	Harvey, W. H.	Of color
McAlilly, James	Abt 7 yrs	5Apr1869	Riley, William	Orphan. White
Mitchell, Joanna	Abt 12 yrs	5Apr1869	Harper, J. B.	Mulatto
Runnells, Jefferson	Abt 12 yrs	3May1869	Bledsoe, W. E.	Orphan
Warren, Jesse	11 yrs	2Aug1869	Warren, J. T.	Orphan. Of color

Name	Date	Age	Master	Notes
Nance, Eliza	1Nov1869	10 yrs	Nance, James A.	Of color
Burns, Anthony	1Nov1869	Abt 11 yrs	Burns, Robert H.	Orphan. Of color
Claxton, Isaac	6Dec1869	10 yrs	Tucker, J. T.	Of color
Claxton, Newman	6Dec1869	5 yrs	Tucker, J. T.	Of color
Wade, Clara	6Dec1869	10 yrs	Wade, Lewis	Orphan. Of color
Flippin, William	6Dec1869	Abt 8 yrs	Smith, James H.	Orphan
Ivie, Agnes	6Dec1869	8 yrs	House, Ambrose	Orphan
Flippin, Thomas L.	6Dec1869	15 yrs	Smith, W. R.	Orphan
Hamlett, Bill	6Dec1869	Abt 12 yrs	Elam, W. A.	Orphan. Of color
Adams, George	4Jan1870		Coleman, J. F.	Of color
Fly, Fillmore	7Feb1870	11 yrs	Fly, G. W.	Orphan. Of color
Greer, Thomas A. Guillom	8Feb1870	Abt 3 yrs	Williams, William	Orphan
Craig, Belle	7Mar1870	7 yrs	McKnight, W. H.	Consent of mother, Rebecca Wood. Of color. Cancelled 14Sept1874. Belle tried to set fire to McKnight's house
Crider, W. L.	4Apr1870	9 yrs	Crider, D. B.	Orphan
Jones, John A.	4Apr1870	8 yrs	Mays, A. P.	Orphan
Barnes, John	5Apr1870	8 yrs	Butler, E. T.	Petition of mother, Adaline Barnes. Cancelled 4July1871 at request of mother, now able to support & educate him
Walker, Luanna	2May1870		Simmons, S. F.	Orphan. Of color
Stevens, Harvey	2May1870		Senter, Sr, J. W.	Orphan. Of color. Cancelled 2Jan1870. To father, Eli Stevens
January, John	2May1870	Abt 7 yrs	January, W. H.	Orphan. Of color
Swain, Susan	5July1870	8 yrs	Hicks, R. A. (Dr)	Orphan
Vance, Sam	5July1870	15 yrs	Lyon, J. W.	Orphan. Of color
Vance, Bill	5July1870	9 yrs	Lyon, J. W.	Orphan. Of color
Vance, Moris	5July1870	7 yrs	Lyon, J. W.	Orphan. Of color
Vance, Suart	5July1870	3 yrs	Lyon, J. W.	Orphan. Of color
McAlilly, Mary Rozena	1Aug1870	11 yrs	Hassell, John	Orphan. White
Reeves, Balaam P.	3Oct1870	7 yrs	Reeves, W. L.	Orphan
Reeves, Josie M.	3Oct1870	5 yrs	Reeves, W. L.	Orphan
King, Anna Lennetta	7Nov1870	4 yrs	Sharp, Malinda	Of color

Name	Date	Age	Bound to	Notes
Blackwell, Bettie	9Nov1870	8 yrs	McGee, W. C.	Of color. Cancelled 11Dec1871
Fuqua, John	5Dec1870	Abt 12 yrs	Stewart, James	Orphan. Of color
Thomas, Everline	2Jan1871	8 yrs	Organ, James	Assent of mother, Melvina Thomas. Of color
Mosley, Sir Isaac N.			Rank, S. G.	Cancelled 2Jan1871, Sir Isaac having absconded. Data from cancellation entry
Shoultce, Rutha	6Feb1871	Abt 12 yrs	Mayfield, J. N.	Orphan. Cancelled 6Mar1871. Rutha, true age 14 years, allowed to choose her master
Shoultce, Anoline?	6Feb1871		Higgerson, R. P.	Orphan
Vandeford, George	13Feb1871	12 yrs	Wade, Lewis	Orphan. Of color
Vandeford, John	13Feb1871	12 yrs	House, W. B.	Orphan. Of color
Shoultse, Rutha	6Mar1871	14 yrs	Ridgeway, Sarah (Mrs)	Orphan
Sharp, William	3Apr1871	5 yrs	Webb, Gardner	Orphan. Both of color
Hill, Rolander	3Apr1871	13 yrs	Hale, J. P.	Orphan
McCutchon, Stephen	1May1871	9 yrs	Hood, C. H.	Abandoned by parents. Of color
McCutchon, Yancey	1May1871	11 yrs	Hood, C. H.	Abandoned by parents. Of color
Nesbitt, Peter	1May1871	Abt 5 yrs	Nesbitt, Robert	Orphan. Of color
Tyree, Green	3July1871	13 yrs	Smith, J. R.	Orphan. Of color
Tyree, Patsey	3July1871	11 yrs	Smith, J. R.	Orphan. Of color
Tyree, Robert	7Aug1871	Abt 16 yrs	Tyree, C. H.	Orphan. Of color
Sims, James Washington	4Sept1871	13 yrs	Sims, G. W.	Orphan. Of color. Same date G. W. Sims & S. S. Caldwell apptd to lay off years support for Martha Sims, infant daughter of Elmos & Amanda Sims, Dcd
Sims, Mary Elizabeth	4Sept1871	11 yrs	Sims, G. W.	Orphan. Of color. See above
Sims, Sarah	4Sept1871	4 yrs	Sims, G. W.	Orphan. Of color. See above
Sims, John Millis	4Sept1871	9 yrs	Caldwell, S. S. (Dr)	Orphan. Of color. See above
Sims, Susan Leonora	4Sept1871	6 yrs	Caldwell, S. S. (Dr)	Orphan. Of color. See above
Basham (Barham?), Buck	4Sept1871	Abt 6 yrs	Barksdale, G. T.	Orphan. Of color
Army, Lee	4Sept1871	14 yrs	Sims, G. W.	Orphan. Of color
Army, Jane	4Sept1871	13 yrs	Sims, G. W.	Orphan. Of color
Army, Toney	4Sept1871	9 yrs	Sims, G. W.	Orphan. Of color

Name	Date	Age	Master	Notes
Army, Dilla	4Sept1871	8 yrs	Epperson, J. L.	Orphan. Of color
Chaffin, Hewit	4Sept1871	11 yrs	McGee, J. P. (Dr)	Orphan. Of color. Cancelled 6May1873. Hewit absconded
Dunevant, James	6Nov1871	Abt 7 yrs	Hill, John	Parents unable to provide support
Dunevant, Oscar	6Nov1871	Abt 6 yrs	Coop, G. B. H.	Parents unable to provide support
Brown, Simon	6Nov1871	Abt 11 yrs	McCulloch, Woodson	Orphan. Both of color
Wesley, John	6Nov1871	Abt 3 yrs	Moore, Aaron	Orphan. Both of color
Givens, Lucy	13Nov1871	Abt 10 yrs	Penny, Haywood	Orphan. Both of color
Arnold, Peyton	4Dec1871	12 yrs	Coop, G. B. H.	Orphan. Of color
Arnold, Joan	4Dec1871	10 yrs	Coop, G. B. H.	Orphan. Of color
Idleburg, Louann	5Dec1871	Abt 7 yrs	Elrod, J. W.	Orphan. Of color
Idleburg, Amos	5Dec1871	Abt 4 yrs	Elrod, W. P.	Orphan. Of color
Blackwell, Betty	11Dec1871	9 yrs	Kelly, W. O.	Orphan. Of color
Barham, Harriet	1Jan1872	Abt 11 yrs	Pearce, Arthur C.	Orphan. Of color
Witherington, John R.	2Jan1872		Gardner, William	Orphan. Consent of Nancy Witherington, grandmother
Thomas, Francis Marion James	5Feb1872	Abt 11 yrs	Brooks, Thomas	White
Lassiter, Anna	5Feb1872	Abt 12 yrs	Harbert, Thomas C.	Orphan. Of color
Ivie, Fanny	5Feb1872	5 yrs	Bright, R. S.	Orphan. Of color
Ivie, Austin	5Feb1872	7 yrs	Bright, R. S.	Orphan. Of color
Johnson, William Henry	4Mar1872	Abt 13 yrs	Sanders, M. M.	White
Thomas, Charles B.	4Mar1872	Abt 3 yrs	Campbell, I. B.	Orphan
Witherington, James	4Mar1872	Abt 13 yrs	O'Daniel, J.	Abandoned by mother. White
Dunnegan, Mariah	4Mar1872	Abt 10 yrs	Dunnegan, J. C.	Abandoned by parents. Of color
Dunnegan, Esther	4Mar1872	Abt 8 yrs	Dunnegan, J. C.	Abandoned by parents. Of color
Dunnegan, George	4Mar1872	Abt 6 yrs	Dunnegan, J. C.	Abandoned by parents. Of color
Hazlewood, Ann	1Apr1872	9 yrs	Hazlewood, B. F.	Orphan
Hazlewood, Eliza	1Apr1872	12 yrs	Hazlewood, B. F.	Orphan
Alvis, Elijah	6May1872	Abt 8 yrs	Davis, F. M. (Dr)	Orphan. Of color. On 3June1872 Jim Sharp, his stepfather, asks for custody of Elijah. Judged not a proper person to have custody. Mother dead. Sharp appeals to Circuit Court

Name	Date	Age	Master	Notes
Dunnegan, Victoria	3June1872	10 yrs	Howell, J. W.	Orphan
Hoover (Alvis), Fanny [sic]	3June1872	Abt 16 yrs	Goodloe, P. R.	Orphan. Of color
Mitchell, Riley	7Oct1872	Abt 7 yrs	Sanders, M. M.	Orphan
Foreman, Henry	4Nov1872	6 yrs	Fitzgerald, O. G.	Nancy Foreman, mother, unable to maintain. Of color
Foreman, Unnamed female	4Nov1872	2 yrs	Fitzgerald, O. G.	Nancy Foreman, mother, unable to maintain. Of color
Hunt, Sally	4Nov1872	10 yrs	Crim, P. D.	Fanny Hunt, mother, unable to maintain
Mitchem, Eliza	4Nov1872	12 yrs	Durley, W. H. (Dr)	Orphan. Of color. Appealed to Circuit court by Lewis Hart, grandfather. Has sibs Aggy & Lewis 21Oct1872*
Unnamed male	6Nov1872	9 yrs	Hart, Louis	Both of color
Unnamed male	6Nov1872	11 yrs	Hart, Louis	Both of color
Dickson, William Jefferson Davis	4Feb1873	12 yrs	Harbert, Thomas C.	Of color
Dickson, Emma	4Feb1873	8 yrs	Harbert, Thomas C.	Of color
Rutledge, Beverly	5May1873	17 yrs	Taylor, Simeon	Orphan. Male. Cancelled 6July1874, Beverly having left Taylor
Hundley, Sarah	2June1873	Abt 14 yrs	Mangum, Mary Ann	Orphan. White
Page, Emma	14July1873	11 yrs	Page, Joseph	Daughter of Martha Page, Dcd, a pauper. Of color. Ed Williams appeals to Circuit Court. Cancelled 10Nov1877
Page, Mary	14July1873	7 yrs	Page, Joseph	Daughter of Martha Page, Dcd, a pauper. Of color. Ed Williams appeals to Circuit Court. Cancelled 10Nov1877
Vick, Robert	14July1873	6 yrs	Vick, J. N.	Orphan. Of color
Hunt, Aaron	13Oct1873		Nelson, G. F.	Orphan. Of color
Mallett, Maclin	1Dec1873		Bowers, Abe	Of color
Arnold, Lee	1Dec1873		Arnold, W. S.	Orphan. Of color
Haley, Michael	2Feb1874	12 yrs	Gary, Martin O.	Orphan
Needham, John W.	2Feb1874	12 yrs	Tilghman, R. C.	Orphan. Same day Tilghman apptd guardian of child of Thomas Needham, Dcd, unnamed
Skinner, Minerva S.	9Mar1874		Caldwell , S. W.	Taken from Calvin Smith. Illegitimate. Of color. Cancelled 14Dec1874. To mother
Shannon, Kate	6Apr1874	8 yrs	Edmonds, C. W.	Orphan. Cancelled 1Mar1875, Edmonds having left the state without Kate
Shannon, Andy	6Apr1874	10 yrs	McKinzie, N. J. H.	Orphan

Name	Date	Age	Master	Notes
Shannon, Boss	6Apr1874	12 yrs	McKinzie, N. J. H.	Orphan
Price, James	6Apr1874		Perkins, Joseph	Orphan. "See Will Book G" beneath entry
Price, John	6Apr1874		Perkins, Joseph	Orphan. "See Will Book G" beneath entry
Scott, Fannie	1June1874	8 yrs	Scott, W. D.	Orphan. Of color
Scott, Ann	1June1874	6 yrs	Scott, W. D.	Orphan. Of color
Thomas	14Sept1874		Johns, W. R.	Orphan
Dodd, Nancy	7Dec1874	11 yrs	Banks, W. T.	Orphan
Brown, James William	7Dec1874	11 yrs	Brown, M. H.	Orphan
Harrison, Nuity?	14Dec1874		Harrison, W. H.	Female orphan. Of color
Harrison, Rufus	21Dec1874	4 yrs	Christman, A. M.	Orphan
Shannon, Kate	1Mar1875		Thorn, W. W.	Orphan
Unnamed female	1Mar1875	14 yrs	Smith, C. F.	Orphan. Of color
Givens, R. S.	7June1875	7 yrs	Arnold, W. F.	Orphan. Of color
Dodd, Willie	14June1875	13 yrs	Givins, S. D.	Orphan. Of color
Dodd, Sammie	14June1875	11 yrs	Givins, S. D.	Orphan. Of color
Bell, Mary Joratha	2Aug1875	12 yrs	Sappington, J. B. (Dr)	Orphan. Consent of mother, Narcisa Bell
Ballentine, Corra	6Sept1875		Forsythe, S. F.	Orphan. Of color
Rachel, Sue	13Sept1875	8 yrs	Rachel, Henry	Bastard. Barney & Henry Rachel apply to be guardians or masters of Lawyer & Judge Rachel, their 3 or 4 y/o bastard twin nephews, and of Newton Rachel. Mother is dead. Denied 2Nov1875. * Appealed to Circuit Court
Hesse, Sam T.	12Dec1875	7 yrs	King, Henry A.	Orphan
Harper, Gardner	3Jan1876	5 yrs	Gleason, Timothy	Of color. Amanda Harper, mother, consents
Elliott, Giles	4Jan1876	Nearly 10 yrs	Hooker, D. R.	Orphan. Of color
Hessie, E	5June1876	5 yrs	Bass, John J.	Male orphan at County Poor House
Hessie, James	7Aug1876		Bass, H.	Orphan
Walker, Ellen	7Aug1876		Hole, J. P.	Orphan
Lee, Robert	4Feb1877	3 yrs	Foster, J. W.	Orphan
Williams, Edney	3Apr1877	7 yrs	Matthews, E. D.	Orphan. Of color
Cooper, Gracie	3Apr1877	10 yrs	Brown, C. P.	Orphan. Of color . On 4June1877 petition to reverse denied

Name	Date	Age	Bond	Remarks
Page, Emma	10Nov1877		Page, H. N.	Of color
Page, Mary	10Nov1877		Page, H. N.	Of color
Blackwell, Diisy	22Jan1878		Raines, A. W.	Orphan
Blackwell, Lewis	4Feb1878	5 yrs	Jetton, J. W.	Until 18 yrs. Orphan. Of color
Dewberry, Amarintha	4Mar1878	8 yrs	Sanders, William T.	On petition of John Dewberry, father
Donaldson, Milly	12Aug1878		Crim, P. D.	Until 18 yrs. Orphan. Of color
Donaldson, Calvin	12Aug1878		Crim, P. D.	Until 18 yrs. Orphan. Of color
Donaldson, Mattie	12Aug1878		Crim, P. D.	Until 18 yrs. Orphan. Of color
Donaldson, Benjamin	12Aug1878		Crim, P. D.	Until 18 yrs. Orphan. Of color
Donaldson, Leonidas	12Aug1878	9 yrs	Crim, A. T.	Until 18 yrs. Orphan. Of color
Pike, Annstead	3Feb1879	8 yrs	Williams, G. C.	Orphan girl
Pike, Isaah	3Feb1879	12 yrs	Williams, E. H.	Until 18 yrs. Orphan
Pike, Eliza	3Feb1879	10 yrs	Williams, E. H.	Orphan
Ing, Isaac	3Feb1879	12 yrs	Ing, J. M.	Until 18 yrs. Orphan
Ing, Mittie	3Feb1879	8 yrs	Ing, J. M.	Orphan
Martin, Samuel	13Oct1879	8 yrs	Harvey, W. H.	Until 18 yrs. Orphan. Of color
Penn, Ernest	4Jan1880	13 yrs	Martin, Willis	Until 18 yrs. Mother consents. Of color
Penn, Lou	4Jan1880	7 yrs	Penn, Amy	Mother consents. Of color
Weaver, Margaret	9May1881	8 yrs	McLouren, John M.	Orphan
Spivey, Navett	7Nov1881	9 yrs	Dungan, James A.	Until 18 yrs. Orphan. Of color
Spivey, William	7Nov1881	11 yrs	Morgan, C. J.	Until 18 yrs. Orphan. Of color
Ray, Richmond	2Jan1882	13 yrs	Banks, W. T.	Until 18 yrs. Orphan. Of color. Cancelled 16Jan1882*
Ray, Mary	2Jan1882	10 yrs	Seat, W. B.	Orphan. Of color. Cancelled 16Jan1882*
Ray, John	2Jan1882	7 yrs	Seat, W. B.	Until 18 yrs. Orphan. Of color. Cancelled 16Jan1882*
Ray, John	16Jan1882	7 yrs	Seat, W. B.	Until 18 yrs. Father & mother dead. Of color
Ray, Mary	13Feb1882	Abt 10 yrs	Seat, W. B.	Father & mother dead. Has been with Seat for 18 mo, placed there by mother. Of color
Weaver, Maggie	25May1883		Hall, W. L.	Cancelled 14July1884, Hall having moved to Texas. Margaret now at Mrs. Morgan's in District #6

Hardeman County

Name	Date	Age	Master	Notes
Satterwhite, Drucilla	7Apr1828	7 yrs	Williams, Jeremiah	Orphan. On 6April1829 an account sales of the estate of Drucilla Satterwhite, Dcd was returned by R. Moore, Administrator
Miller, John	7July1828		Kirkpatrick, Alexander	Hatting business
Birdsong, Miles	9Jan1829		May, Abram	
Read, Samuel A.	10Apr1829	15 yrs	Kirkland, Henry	For 4 years. Bricklaying & plastering
Miller, Joseph	5Apr1830		Mott, Randolph	Orphan. Consent of Joseph. Tailor
Barnett, Benjamin	5Apr1830		Kirkpatrick, Alexander	Orphan. Hatter.
Pritchett, Judy	5Apr1830		Hodges, John	Of color. Consent of Ludy Pritchett, mother. Certificate from Dinwiddie Co, VA dated 12Dec1822 attests to Ludy's freedom
Pritchett, Hannah	5Apr1830		Hodges, John	Of color. Consent of Ludy Pritchett, mother. Certificate from Dinwiddie Co, VA dated 12Dec1822 attests to Ludy's freedom
Satterwhite, Drucilla	5July1830		Taylor, Joseph	
Satterwhite, Martha	5July1830		Bradford, John M.	
Willis, John	4July1831	Abt 17 yrs	Bright, Greenberry	Tanner
Bellen, William C.	8Jan1833		Hitchcock, Moses	Consent of Bellen
Minton, Valentin	1Apr1833	12 yrs	Mott, John	Request of mother. Tailor. Canc 7Apr1834
Walden, Hugh	1July1833	Abt 12 or 13 yrs	Looney, Lunsford L.	
Wren, James	6Jan1834	15 yrs	Chace, William	Consent of James & his mother. Tailor
Edwards, Betsey Ann	7Jan1835	Abt 11 yrs	Steele, William G.	Request of father, Sampson Edwards. Cancelled 4Apr1836. Child still with parents
Edwards, David	7Jan1835		Burnett, Thomas M.	Request of father, Sampson Edwards. Tanner. Canc 4Apr1835. Still with parents
Sykes, Agnes	6Apr1835		Baker, Jonas	Of color. Consent of Judy Pritchett, mother. Certificate from Dinwiddie Co, VA dated 12Dec1822 attests to Judy's freedom. On 3Dec1838 ordered returned to court, as Baker likely to leave Tennessee
Sykes, Hannah	6Apr1835		Baker, Jonas	Of color. Daughter of Judy Pritchett. On 3Dec1838 ordered returned to court, as Baker likely to leave Tennessee

Child	Bound to	Date	Age	Notes
Ratcliff, Jean	Basden, Kinch	6July1835	3 yrs	Orphan
Milton, John	Hatly, Josiah	5Oct1835		For 4 yrs. Of color. Probably the John M. Davis, formerly bound to J. Hatly, who on 6Nov1848* at age 24 applied for permission to remain in county
Barnett, Benjamin?	Ramsey, William	6Oct1835		Orphan
Fletcher, Caroline	Breeding, Shahan			Orphan. Previously bound. On 8Oct1835 Breeding released of arithmetic obligation
Fletcher, Lucinda	Breeding, Shahan			Orphan. Bound before 8Oct1835
Fletcher, Lucinda	Rogers, John	4Jan1836		Orphan
Ray, Samuel G.	Oliver, Eliza	4July1836	Abt 7 yrs	Prob one of two children of Betsy Ray, "in a helpless condition" 3May & 6June1836. Cancelled 4Dec1837
Lambert, Elizabeth	Carley, William	4Sept1837		
Lambert, Julia Ann	Carley, William	4Sept1837		
Ray, Samuel G.	Oliver, George	4Dec1837		Cancelled 1Oct1838
Houston, Jefferson	Parks, Barbary	5Feb1838	8 yrs	
Raines, James W.	Gough, Jesse	3Apr1838		Child of Stephen & Clara Raines. Mother consents. Abandoned by father. Cancelled 3Dec1838
Raines, Amanda M.	Gough, Jesse	3Apr1838		Child of Stephen & Clara Raines. Mother consents. Abandoned by father. Cancelled 3Dec1838
Reynolds, John Q.	Stovall, George	3Sept1838	12 yrs	
Reynolds, Thomas P.	Stovall, George	3Sept1838	10 yrs	
Reynolds, Hugh A.	Stovall, George	3Sept1838	8 yrs	
Ray, Samuel G.	Warren, John	1Oct1838		
Rogers, David	McComan, Isaac N.	5Nov1838		Without parents. David consents. On 1Oct1860 inquest on body of David Rogers ascribes death to accidental gunshot*
Whitaker, Lewis	Bright, Granberry	5Nov1838		Without parents in this state. Lewis consents
Sykes, Agness	Sykes, Judah	7Jan1839	13 yrs	On 7Apr1840 Judy, mother, posted bond to keep child from becoming a county charge
Sykes, Hannah	Sykes, Judah	7Jan1839	10 yrs	On 7Apr1840 Judy, mother, posted bond to keep child from becoming a county charge
Dunn, William H.	Mohunded, William H.	4Feb1839		

Name	Date	Age	Master	Notes
Tilmon, Calvin	7Oct1839		Briant, James B.	Orphan
Bland, Morris	1Mar1841	Abt 10 yrs	Marsh, R. A.	Tanner
Baugh, Ann	6Sept1841		Lee, Henry	Orphan. Of color. Cancelled 5Feb1851, as Anna Baugh. Appealed by Lee
Baugh, William	6Sept1841		Lee, Henry	Orphan. Of color. Cancelled 5Feb1851. Appealed by Lee
Baugh, Mary	6Sept1841		Lee, Henry	Orphan. Of color. Cancelled 5Feb1851. Appealed by Lee
Bray, Henry Lewis	6Nov1841		Brooks, Matthew	
Vaughn, Lucretia	2Jan1843		Nuckolly, John	Bound by mother, Dolly Vaughn
Vaughn, Thomas Benton	2Jan1843		Nuckolly, John	Bound by mother, Dolly Vaughn
Nichols, George	1May1843		Hervey, Abner	
Nichols, Noah	1May1843		Hervey, A. Mull?	
Washington, Mathew	4Dec1843		Brooks, Mathew	
High, Solomon E.	2Dec1844	Abt 13 yrs	Wills, H. S.	
Oakes, John	7Apr1845		Mayfield, W. E. C.	
Thrailkill, James	7Apr1845		Clarley, John W.	
Wiggi[n]s, Harriss	7July1845		Bright, Grunby	Taner. Cancelled 1Apr1850
Vaughn, George	7July1845		Mills, Elvis	
Vaughn, Martha J.	7July1845		Erwin, William C.	
Wiggins, Francis M.	7July1845		Lambert, Abner	
Wiggins, William	4Aug1845		Gardner, Thomas J.	Cancelled 6Jan1851
Wiggins, James	1Sept1845		Bright, Grunby	Cancelled 4Oct1852
Stinson, Isaac N.	6Oct1845		Oliver, Thomas A.	Cancelled 7Feb1848, as Newton Stinson
Vaughn, Martha Jane	6Apr1846		Mills, Elvis	
Smith, John	7Dec1846		Campbell, C.	
Tate, Jason (James?) B.	1Mar1847		Toon, Jans (James?)	
Flowers, Henry V.	7June1847		Strickland, David	
Flowers, Nancy	7June1847		Strickland, David	
Flowers, John H.	7June1847		Strickland, David	
Williams, John	4Oct1847		Smith, William	Cancelled 3Jan1848
Williams, Newton	4Oct1847		Farriss, Moses B.	Cancelled 7Oct1850, as Isaac Newton Williams

Name	Date	Term/Age	Master	Remarks
Spurlin, Eli	4Oct1847		Taylor, John	Cancelled 4Feb1850. Back to mother
King, William	1Nov1847		Fewell, William H.	Cancelled 4Mar1851
Crisp, Moses P.	6Dec1847		Gardner, Thomas J.	Cancelled 4Dec1849
Eaton, D. W.	6Dec1847		Plunkett, James R.	Cancelled 7Feb1848, as David W. Eaton
Crisp, Gilbert Longstreet	7Dec1847		Reynolds, William	Cancelled 3Jan1848
Stinson, Newton	6Mar1848		Thompson, J. N.	
Carnard, Thomas	1May1848		Johnson, John P.	
Duke, John P.	4Sept1848		Edwards, Jacob T?.	
Guthrie, Felix	6Aug1849	6 yrs next November	Jackson, Mark	Orphan. Farming. Canc 2Dec1850. To care of Louis D. Wells, a relation "by affinity"
Crisp, Moses P.	4Dec1849		Teague, Josiah	Saddler. Cancelled 10Jan1851 with consent of Elihu C. Crisp, Guardian. Son of Moses Crisp, Sr, Dcd 3Mar1851
Carnard, James	1July1850		Kelly, James	Cancelled 7Aug1856, as James Kinnard, for ill usage & cruelty
Wiggins, William W.	6Jan1851		Biggs, R. W.	Cancelled 10Apr1852, Biggs having moved to Shelby Co. Another cancellation 8Nov1858, Wiggins having absconded. Had been rebound to Biggs?
Rhodes, Thomas	3Feb1851	10 or 11 yrs	Janey, W. H.	Orphan
King, William	4Mar1851		Myrick, Alfred A.	Until 20 yrs. Son of Enoch King, Dcd. Same date Myrick appt'd administrator of estate of Enoch King, Dcd
Carley, Jesse I?.	5May1851	4 yrs	Rook, A[mon]. Y.	Until 20 yrs. Cancelled 7July1851
Carley, Jesse I?.	7July1851		Waller, George	
Wisdom, Amanda	4Aug1851	4 yrs	Moore, Miles P.	
Wisdom, Blakely	4Aug1851	12 yrs	Harris, West	
Kinnard, Thomas	1Sept1851	9 yrs	Kelly, James	
Wisdom,	1Sept1851	10 yrs	Usery, Welcome	Farming
Steward, James	7Oct1851	15 yrs	Homes, John J.	Farmer
Chuning, James	4Nov1851	11 yrs	Wells, D. J.	Son of ___ Chuning, Dcd
Chuning, Thomas	4Nov1851	9 yrs	Ellington, L. B.	Son of ___ Chuning, Dcd. Waggon & carriage making
Chuning, Andrew	4Nov1851	7 yrs	Ellington, L. B.	Son of ___ Chuning, Dcd. Waggon & carriage making
White, Mary Ann	1Dec1851	9 yrs	Thomas, Jesse M.	

Name	Date	Age	Master	Notes
White, William	1Dec1851	17 yrs	Watson, Thomas	
White, Marion	1Dec1851	14 yrs	Mullins, Edward A.	Farmer
White, Catherine	1Dec1851	12 yrs	Glidewell, James	Spinster
White, Louisa	1Dec1851	5 yrs	Glidewell, James	Spinster
Terrie, Eli	2Feb1852	11 yrs	Cox, Joseph	Farmer. Canc 7Mar1855 for mistreatment on petition of Susan Terry, mother
Rogers, W. O.	2Feb1852	6 yrs	Huddleston, P. M.	House & sign painter
Wiggins, William	3May1852	11 yrs	Casey, H. D.	Orphan 10Apr1852
Baugh, Lewis	7June1852	10 yrs	Boyle, Thomas	Consent of mother, Eliza Baugh. Farming. Of color
Baugh, Robert	7June1852	8 yrs	Boyle, Thomas	Consent of mother, Eliza Baugh. Farming. Of color
Baugh, Parthena	7June1852	6 yrs	Boyle, Thomas	Consent of mother, Eliza Baugh. Farming. Of color
Baugh, Anderson	7June1852	4 yrs	Boyle, Thomas	Consent of mother, Eliza Baugh. Farming. Of color
Baugh, Isabella	7June1852	2 yrs	Boyle, Thomas	Consent of mother, Eliza Baugh. Farming. Of color
Henson, Joseph Martin A.	6Sept1852	4 yrs	Henson, John	Illegit child of Eliza King. Farmer. Same date child's surname changed from King to Henson. On 5Oct1857 Samuel Henson appt'd admin of John Henson, Jr Dcd. Martha Henson his widow. On 3Apr1860, as Joseph M. A. King, reputed son of John Henson , adopted by Martin Jackson
Wiggins, James	4Oct1852		Kearley, John	
Gibson, James Henry	1Nov1852		Gibson, E. P.	Illegitimate son of Gibson & of Mary, Davis, Dcd. Same date surname changed from Davis to Gibson. Farming
Robertson, Narcissa Elizabeth	8Mar1853		Robertson, Patrick F.	Illegitimate daughter of Frances Dyson. Robertson reputed father. Surname changed from Dyson to Robertson same date.
Shofer, Rufus	8Nov1853	13 yrs in Oct last	Hamilton, Alexander B.	Orphan son of Frederick Shofer, Dcd. Consent of Rufus. Farming
Grantham, James Henry	7Aug1854	Abt 14 yrs	Grantham, Lewis	Until 19 yrs. Request of James. Son of Sion Grantham, Dcd. Mother dead. Lewis is James' uncle
Kinnard, James	8Aug1855	9 yrs	Sinclair, Daniel	Orphan. Cabinet making. Canc 2Feb1857
Wilkinson, Henry C.	5Nov1855	4 yrs	Burges, Madison	Until 20 yrs
Hill, James R.	7July1856	7 yrs	Jones, Samuel	Farming. Cancelled 4Feb1857

Name	Date	Age	Master	Notes
Dandridge	6Jan1857	5 yrs	Farris, L. B.	Farming. Of color
Kinnard, James	2Feb1857		Smith, James	
Henson, Joseph A.	2Nov1857	10 yrs	Jackson, Martin	
Johnson, John Henry	7Dec1857	8 yrs	Norton, Jacob A.	
Perry, William Arthur	5Jan1859		Johnson, Nathan	Until 20 yrs. Orphan. Of color
Perry, Fayette	5Jan1859		Johnson, Nathan	Until 20 yrs. Orphan. Of color
John	5Dec1859	6 yrs	Boyle, Thomas	Orphan. Of color
Laura	5Dec1859	4 yrs	Boyle, Thomas	Orphan. Of color
Eveline	5Dec1859	2 yrs	Boyle, Thomas	Orphan. Of color
Joseph	5Dec1859	1 mo	Boyle, Thomas	Orphan. Of color
Thompson, James C.	5Dec1859	Abt 4 yrs	Wilson, Jessee	Orphan
Thompson, William	6Feb1860	8 yrs	Wilson, William	
Perry, Fayette	2Apr1860	4 yrs	Farris, L. B.	Farming. Of color. On 2Apr1867 Farris avers that Fayette taken to Fayette Co by Rhoden Bowers abt 26Feb1867. Asks his return.
Perry, William A.	2Apr1860	2 yrs	Farris, L. B.	Farming. Of color
Hill, James	8May1860	11 yrs	Laney, Julius	Orphan. Farmer
Hull, Petsor?	9Nov1865	6 yrs	Hull, Daniel C.	Father dead. Abandoned by mother. Of color. Sureties changed 5July1869
Hull, Paul	9Nov1865	4 yrs	Hull, Daniel C.	Father dead. Abandoned by mother. Of color. Sureties changed 5July1869
Hull, Sophia	9Nov1865	2 yrs	Hull, Daniel C.	Father dead. Abandoned by mother. Of color. Cancelled 1Mar1868
Hull, Sophia	9Nov1865	2 yrs	Hull, Daniel C.	Orphan. House keeping & farming. Of color. Entry from FB records
Polk, Isibell	4Dec1865	9 yrs	Polk, J. J.	FB consent. Orphan. House keeping & farming. Of color
Davis, Ellen	4Dec1865		Davis, W. J.	FB consent. Orphan. House keeping & farming. Of color
Davis, Francis	4Dec1865		Davis, W. J.	FB consent. Orphan. House keeping & farming. Of color
Davis, Jery	4Dec1865		Davis, W. J.	FB consent. Orphan. House keeping & farming. Of color
Davis, Hariett	4Dec1865		Davis, W. J.	FB consent. Orphan. House keeping & farming. Of color

Name	Date	Age	Master	Notes
McCarley, Joseph	8Dec1865	8 yrs	McCarley, W. W.	By FB. Orphan. Farming
Ferguson, Isebeller	8Dec1865	12 yrs	Ferguson, D. A.	By FB. Orphan. House keeping
Woods, Solomon	8Dec1865	13 yrs	Wood, George (Dr)	By FB. Orphan. Farming
Woods, Fountain	8Dec1865	7 yrs	Wood, George (Dr)	By FB. Orphan. Farming
Wood, Eugenia	8Dec1865	11 yrs	Wood, John R.	By FB. Orphan. House keeping & farming
Cradic, Gamer	11Dec1865	7 yrs	Carter, R. S.	By FB. Orphan. Farming
Cradic, Wesley	11Dec1865	2 yrs	Carter, R. S.	By FB. Orphan. Farming
Cradic, Sura	11Dec1865	13 yrs	Carter, R. S.	By FB. Orphan. House keeping & farming
Bray, Benjamin	11Dec1865	7 yrs	Bray, J. H.	By FB. Orphan. Farming
Bowers, Fred	11Dec1865	10 yrs	Bowers, John W.	By FB. Orphan. Farming
Bowers, Albert	11Dec1865	11 yrs	Bowers, John W.	By FB. Orphan. Farming
Jarratt, Harbut	12Dec1865	11 yrs	Jarratt, Gregory	By FB. Orphan. Farming
Jarratt, Lucy	12Dec1865	9 yrs	Jarratt, Gregory	By FB. Orphan. House keeping & farming
Jones, Ellen	12Dec1865	9 yrs	Jones, Paul T.	By FB. Orphan. House keeping & farming
Jones, Lydia	12Dec1865	11 yrs	Jones, Paul T.	By FB. Orphan. House keeping & farming
Patrick, Hugh	13Dec1865	7 yrs	Patrick, George	By FB. Orphan. Farming
Patrick, Ham	13Dec1865	12 yrs	Patrick, George	By FB. Orphan. Farming
Scott, Zerus	14Dec1865	8 yrs	Scott, John D.	By FB. Orphan. Farming
McClelen, William H.	14Dec1865	12 yrs	McClelen, J. H.	By FB. Orphan. Farming
Rodgers, Jeff	15Dec1865	10 yrs	Webb, J. M.	By FB. Orphan. Farming. Mother consents
Rodgers, Chance	15Dec1865	8 yrs	Webb, J. M.	By FB. Orphan. Farming. Mother consents
Grove, Agga	16Dec1865	10 yrs	Grove, Margaret C. (Mrs)	By FB. Orphan. House keeping & farming
Grove, Laura A.	16Dec1865	7 yrs	Grove, Margaret C. (Mrs)	By FB. Orphan. House keeping & farming
Grove, Osker	16Dec1865	5 yrs	Grove, Margaret C. (Mrs)	By FB. Orphan. Farming
Grove, Allen Osker	16Dec1865	11 yrs	Grove, Margaret C. (Mrs)	By FB. Orphan. Farming
Miller, Mattie	18Dec1865	15 1/2 yrs	Miller, Austin	By FB. Orphan. House keeping. Of color

Name	Date	Age	Bound to	Remarks
Miller, Bube (?Beebe)	18Dec1865	11 yrs	Miller, Austin	By FB. Orphan. Farming. Of color
Miller, Billy	18Dec1865	15 yrs	Miller, Austin	By FB. Orphan. Farming & planter. Of color
Miller, Frank	18Dec1865	13 yrs	Miller, Austin	By FB. Orphan. Farming & planter. Of color
Miller, Lilla	18Dec1865	8 yrs	Miller, Austin	By FB. Orphan. House keeper. Of color
Cheshier, Richard	18Dec1865	11 yrs	Cheshier, W. D.	By FB. Orphan. On 9Nov1867 Malinda Cheshier, of color, alledges maltreatment of Dick & Layton. Complaint dismissed 2Dec1867 and boys rebound to Cheshier
Cheshier, Leyton	18Dec1865	8 yrs	Cheshier, W. D.	By FB. Orphan. Farming. See above
Brogdon, Charles	18Dec1865	10 yrs	Brogdon, George M.	By FB. Orphan. Farming
Brogdon, Lavenia Lucy	18Dec1865	4 yrs	Brogdon, George M.	By FB. Orphan. House keeping & farming
Brogdon, Prudence	18Dec1865	8 yrs	Brogdon, George M.	By FB. Orphan. House keeping & farming
Anderson	19Dec1865	11 yrs	Coleman, A. A.	By FB. Abandoned. Farming
McNeal, Nanna	20Dec1865	10 yrs	McNeal, Ezekiel P.	By FB. Orphan. House keeping & farming
McNeal, Lucy	20Dec1865	12 yrs	McNeal, Ezekiel P.	By FB. Orphan. House keeping & farming
McNeal, Leonidas	20Dec1865	4 yrs	McNeal, E. P.	By FB. Orphan. Farming
McNeal, Ellen	20Dec1865	6 yrs	McNeal, Ezekiel P.	By FB. Orphan. House keeping & farming
McNeal, Napoleon	20Dec1865	8 yrs	McNeal, E. P.	By FB. Orphan. Farming
McNeal, Horace	20Dec1865	10 yrs	McNeal, Ezekiel P.	By FB. Orphan. Farming
McNeal, Emma	20Dec1865	14 yrs	McNeal, Ezekiel P.	By FB. Orphan. House keeping & farming
Fort, Noah	20Dec1865	12 yrs	Fort, Willie	By FB. Abandoned by father. Farming
Fort, West	20Dec1865	7 yrs	Fort, Willie	By FB. Abandoned by mother. Farming
Fort, Eva	20Dec1865	2 yrs	Fort, Willie	By FB. Abandoned by mother. House keeping & farming
Harlan, Ellen	21Dec1865	7 yrs	Black, S. A.	By FB. Orphan. House keeping
Crisp, Amelia	22Dec1865	14 yrs	Crisp, E. C.	By FB. Orphan. House keeping & farming
Crisp, Edmond	22Dec1865	11 yrs	Crisp, E. C.	By FB. Orphan. Farming
Dodson, Archer	23Dec1865	17 yrs	Ingram, R. M.	By FB. Orphan. Farming
Ingram, Virginia	23Dec1865	12 yrs	Ingram, R. M.	By FB. Orphan. House keeping & farming
Black, Walker	25Dec1865	12 1/2 yrs	Black, Amos	By FB. Orphan. Farming
Newbern, Henry	25Dec1865	11 yrs	Newbern, David J.	By FB. Orphan. Farming
Newbern, Thomas	25Dec1865	10 yrs	Newbern, David J.	By FB. Orphan. Farming

Name	Date	Age	Master	Notes
Harris, William	25Dec1865	12 yrs	Harriss, James B.	By FB. Orphan. Farming
Harris, Green	25Dec1865	11 yrs	Harriss, James B.	By FB. Orphan. Farming
McKinney, Fanny	25Dec1865	10 yrs	Miller, James M.	By FB. Orphan. Farming
Black, Charles	25Dec1865	6 yrs	Black, H.	By FB. Orphan. Farming
Thermond, Moses	27Dec1865	13 yrs	Robinson, James H.	By FB. Orphan. Farming
Harriss, Daniel	28Dec1865	13 yrs	Harriss, Thomas H.	By FB. Orphan. Farming
White, Harriet	28Dec1865	13 yrs	White, Alexander	By FB. Orphan. Housekeeping & farming
Oates, Eliza Jane	28Dec1865	11 yrs	Oates, Fannie G. (Mrs)	By FB. Orphan. House keeping
Newbern, Anna	28Dec1865	15 yrs	Black, H.	By FB. Orphan. House keeping & farming
Boyle, Frank	29Dec1865	13 yrs	Boyle, Thomas	By FB. Orphan. Farming
Boyle, Fanny	29Dec1865	13 yrs	Boyle, Thomas	By FB. Orphan. Housekeeping & farming
Boyle, James	29Dec1865	7 yrs	Boyle, Thomas	By FB. Orphan. Farming
Grove, Ellen	29Dec1865	13 yrs	Grove, J. H.	By FB. Orphan. Housekeeping & farming
McKinney, Nervy	29Dec1865	8 yrs	McKinney, Parthenia	By FB. Orphan. Housekeeping & farming
Smith, William	30Dec1865	9 yrs	Collier, Louisa (Mrs)	By FB. Orphan. Farming
Bowling, George	1Jan1866	9 yrs	Bowling, J. M.	By FB. Orphan. Farming
Craddock, Vicy	1Jan1866	12 yrs	Craddock, J. T.	By FB. Orphan. House keeping
Lax, Elisha	1Jan1866	11 yrs	Lax, William	By FB. Orphan. Farming
Lax, Dawson	1Jan1866	9 yrs	Lax, William	By FB. Orphan. Farming
Lax, George	1Jan1866	7 yrs	Lax, William	By FB. Orphan. Farming
Miller, Thomas	1Jan1866	12 yrs	Miller, John	By FB. Orphan. Farming. Of color
Fort, Carra	1Jan1866	10 yrs	Ruffin, T. J.	By FB. Female orphan. Mother willing. Farming
Fort, William	1Jan1866	8 yrs	Ruffin, T. J.	By FB. Orphan. Mother willing. Farming
Sain, Henry	1Jan1866	4 yrs	Sain, Enoch	By FB. Orphan. Farming
Shivers, Elin	1Jan1866	13 yrs	Scott, Robert	By FB. Orphan. Farming
Shaw, Martha S.	2Jan1866	8 yrs	Shaw, Susan	By FB. Mother willing. House keeping
Moorman, Polly	3Jan1866	14 yrs	Moorman, R. A.	By FB. Orphan. Housekeeping & farming
Smith, Delia	4Jan1866	5 yrs	Smith, Cannon	By FB. Orphan. Housekeeping
Hicks, Caroline	4Jan1866	10? yrs	Whitlow, N.C.	By FB. Orphan. Housekeeping
Hicks, Moriah	4Jan1866	6 yrs	Whitlow, N.C.	By FB. Orphan. Housekeeping

Name	Date	Age		Remarks
Boyd, Panthea	5Jan1866	9 yrs	Boyd, Robert A.	By FB. Orphan. Housekeeping & farming
Cross, Louis	6Jan1866	10 yrs	Coleman, E. G.	By FB. Orphan. Farming
Cross, Fillis	6Jan1866	8 yrs	Coleman, E. G.	By FB. Orphan. Housekeeping & farming
Cross, Aaron	6Jan1866	6 yrs on 20Aug last	Coleman, E. G.	By FB. Orphan. Farming
Cross, Isham	6Jan1866	4 yrs on 24Sept last	Coleman, E. G.	By FB. Orphan. Farming
Cross, Margaret	6Jan1866	5 yrs on 28Oct last	Coleman, E. G.	By FB. Abandoned by mother in 1862. Farming & housekeeping. On 2Jan1872 Coleman allowed to remove Margaret from county. Margaret assents
Cross, Jane	6Jan1866	8 yrs on 6April last	Coleman, E. G.	By FB. Abandoned by mother in 1862. Farming & housekeeping
Cross, Alice	6Jan1866	10 yrs on 15Feb next	Coleman, E. G.	By FB. Abandoned by mother in 1862. Farming & housekeeping
Clinton, Ellen	6Jan1866	13 yrs	Clinton, M. L.	By FB. Orphan. Housekeeping & farming
Macon, Hester	8Jan1866	9 yrs	Patrick, Thomas G.	By FB. Orphan. Housekeeping & farming
McKinie, Milton	8Jan1866	3 yrs	Bailey, Thomas	By FB. Orphan
Allin, George	10Jan1866	13 yrs	Dodson, George	By FB. Orphan. Farming. Both of color
McCommans, Juda	11Jan1866	11 yrs	McCommon, J. M.	By FB. Orphan. Housekeeping
Pugh, Rose	11Jan1866	12 yrs	Pugh, Eliza B.	By FB. Orphan. Housekeeping
Pugh, Ann	11Jan1866	10 yrs	Pugh, Eliza B.	By FB. Orphan. Housekeeping
Smith, Louis	11Jan1866	11 yrs	Smith, Guy	By FB. Orphan. Farming
Elliotte, Luenda	11Jan1866	6 yrs	Elliotte, W. W. R.	By FB. Orphan. Housekeeping
Pucket, Susan	12Jan1866	10 yrs	Pucket, Winnefred (Mrs)	By FB. Orphan. Housekeeping & farming
Pucket, Columbus	12Jan1866	8 yrs	Pucket, Winnefred (Mrs)	By FB. Orphan. Farming
Rodgers, Jake	16Jan1866	11 yrs	Rogers, Richard	By FB. Orphan. Farming
Powell, Hannah	22Jan1866	6 yrs	Powell, N. J.	By FB. Orphan. Farming
Powell, Davy	22Jan1866	8 yrs	Powell, N. J.	By FB. Orphan. Farming
Powell, Easter (or Ester)	22Jan1866	10 yrs	Powell, N. J.	By FB. Orphan. Farming
Smith, Nelus	5Feb1866	13 yrs	Smith, N. M.	By FB. Orphan. Farming

61

Name	Date	Age	Master	Notes
Smith, Tom	5Feb1866	9 yrs	Smith, N. M.	By FB. Orphan. Farming
Smith, Jack	5Feb1866	10 yrs	Smith, N. M.	By FB. Orphan. Farming
Smith, Fanny	5Feb1866	10 yrs	Smith, N. M.	By FB. Orphan. Housekeeping & farming
Swinebroad, Ben	6Feb1866	2 yrs	Swinebroad, G. W.	By FB. Orphan. Farming
Swinebroad, Viney	6Feb1866	5 yrs	Swinebroad, G. W.	By FB. Orphan. Housekeeping & farming
Lincoln, Abe	6Feb1866	6 yrs	Swinebroad, G. W.	By FB. With mother's consent. Farming
Swinebroad, Calvin	6Feb1866	6 yrs	Swinebroad, G. W.	By FB. Orphan. Farming
Smith, Sallie	8Feb1866	10 yrs	Smith, J. L.	By FB. Orphan. Housekeeping & farming
Coburn, Ginny	10Feb1866	10 yrs	Coburn, James L.	By FB. Deserted by father. Farming & housekeeping
Smith, Fanny	12Feb1866	10 yrs	Hamilton, Mary K.	By FB. Orphan. Housekeeping & farming
Smith, Jack	12Feb1866	10 yrs	Hamilton, Mary K.	By FB. Orphan. Housekeeping & farming
Dickerson, Cora	19Feb1866	7 yrs	Patrick, Thomas G.	By FB. Orphan. Housekeeping & farming
Gwyn, Pattie	2Mar1866	10 yrs	Gwyn, Sallie D.	By FB. Orphan. Housekeeping
Mask, Jim	5Mar1866	12 yrs	Mask, W. A.	By FB. Orphan. Farming
Jones, Charles	30Mar1866	12 yrs	Jones, Bruce	By FB. Orphan. Farming
Dickerson, Jesse	30Mar1866	11 yrs	Dickerson, Jack	By FB. Orphan. Farming
Mask, Enoc	15May1866	6 yrs	Pybass, James	By FB. Farming. Mother not able to support
Mask, Nancy Jane	15May1866	4 yrs	Pybass, James	By FB. Farming & housekeeping. Mother not able to support
Jones, Ephram	28May1866	13 1/2 yrs	Jones, W. B.	By FB. Orphan. Farming
Wood, Jessee	16July1866	11 yrs	Polk, Marshall T.	By FB. Orphan. Farming
Higgs, Sophia	1Oct1866	6 yrs	Orfford, Andrew	By FB. Farming & housekeeping
Welch, George W. W.	2Oct1866	6 yrs	Reynolds, Jerry	Father & mother dead
Welch, Rebecca M.	2Oct1866	10 yrs	Reynolds, Jerry	Father & mother dead
Gibbon, Clara	16Oct1866	5 yrs	Davis, L. J.	By FB. Farming & housekeeping
Gibbon, Henry	16Oct1866	3 yrs	Davis, L. J.	By FB. Orphan. Farming
Hardin, Jack	4Dec1866	11 yrs	Hardin, G. W.	By FB. Orphan. Farming
Jim	8Jan1867	9 yrs	McCarley, W. W.	Of color
Conner	8Jan1867	10 yrs	Robinson, D. A.	Of color

Name	Date	Age	Bound to	Notes
Coates, George	9Jan1867		Coates, Amanda L. M. (Mrs)	Until 18 yrs. Illegitimate. Freed boy. On 10Jan1867 James McNeal, of color, petitions to adopt 13 y/o George, his son by Catherine, who died in George's infancy. Granted. Surname changed to McNeal
New, John	11Jan1867	14 yrs	Wilkerson, A.	Orphan. All of color
New, Jordan	11Jan1867	13 yrs	Wilkerson, A.	Orphan. All of color
New, Adaline	11Jan1867	12 yrs	Wilkerson, A.	Orphan. All of color
New, Early	11Jan1867	5 yrs	Wilkerson, A.	Orphan. All of color
New, Martha	11Jan1867	3 yrs	Wilkerson, A.	Orphan. All of color
Wood, Jessee	12Jan1867	13 yrs	Wood, R. H.	Of color
McNeal, Evelina	12Jan1867	13 yrs	Wood, R. H.	Of color
Webb, William Henry	4Feb1867	5 yrs	Neely, J. S.	Orphan
Sills, J. M. M.	5Feb1867	8 yrs	Rush, William	Until 18 yrs. Mother consents. Of color.
Sills, Reuben I.	5Feb1867	6 yrs	Rush, William	Until 18 yrs. Mother consents. Of color
Taylor, Paul	5Feb1867	9 yrs	Taylor, John	Mother consents. Of color
Taylor, Silas	5Feb1867	6 yrs	Taylor, John	Mother consents. Of color
Taylor, Manuel	5Feb1867	3 yrs	Taylor, John	Mother consents. Of color
Yopp, Jim	4Mar1867	15 yrs	Yopp, W. T.	Of color. Cancelled 6July1869. Ran away
Yopp, Bob	4Mar1867	13 yrs	Yopp, W. T.	Of color. Cancelled 6July1869. Ran away
Yopp, Maria	4Mar1867	10 yrs	Yopp, W. T.	Of color. Cancelled 6July1869. Ran away
Yopp, Burrell	4Mar1867	8 yrs	Yopp, W. T.	Of color. Cancelled 6July1869. Ran away
Hall, Henry	4Mar1867	8 yrs	Hall, M. W.	No father or mother. Of color
Sills, John	4Mar1867	10 yrs	Nailor, George	Until 18 yrs. Mother consents. White
Forbes, Susan	5Mar1867	14 yrs	Forbes, Robert L.	Neither mother nor father. Of color
Forbes, Wallace	5Mar1867	9 yrs	Forbes, Robert L.	Neither mother nor father. Of color
Forbes, Wilson	5Mar1867	12 yrs	Forbes, Robert L.	Neither mother nor father. Of color
Forbes, Henry	5Mar1867	7 yrs	Forbes, Robert L.	Neither mother nor father. Of color
Holmes, Lucy	6May1867	11 yrs	Holmes, John H.	No parents. Of color
Potts, Chaney	4June1867	8 yrs	Blaylock, Jesse	Female. Mother consents. Of color. Cancelled 5Feb1868 at mother's request

Name	Date	Age	Master	Notes
Potts, Winiford	4June1867	11 yrs	Blaylock, Jesse	Female. Mother consents. Of color. Cancelled 5Feb1868, as Winny Potts
Potts, Dawson	4June1867	4 yrs	Blaylock, Jesse	Mother consents. Of color. Cancelled 5Feb1868 at mother's request
Potts, Samuel	4June1867	6 yrs	Blaylock, Jesse	Mother consents. Of color. Cancelled 5Feb1868 at mother's request
Cugo, Fanny	4June1867	6 yrs	Blaylock, Jesse	No living parents. Of color
Cugo, Betha Ann	4June1867	10 yrs	Blaylock, Jesse	No living parents. Of color
Bradford, Minerva	1July1867	8 yrs	Bradford, George	Neither mother nor father. Of color
Bradford, Jordan	1July1867	3 yrs	Rook, A. T.	No parents. Of color
Bradford, Moses	1July1867	3 yrs	Rook, A. T.	No parents. Of color
McGowan, Mariah	2July1867	8 yrs	Eubanks, J. T.	No parents. Of color
McGowan, Thomas	2July1867	10 yrs	Eubanks, J. T.	No parents. Of color
McGowan, Jordan	2July1867	6 yrs	Eubanks, J. T.	No parents. Of color
McGowan, Stephen	2July1867	4 yrs	Eubanks, J. T.	No parents. Of color. On 3Feb1868 surrendered to Leroy McNeal, father
McGowan, Spencer	2July1867	2 yrs	Eubanks, J. T.	No parents. Of color. On 3Feb1868 surrendered to Leroy McNeal, father
Graham, Dock	7Oct1867	7 yrs	Graham, G. W.	Orphan. Of color
Graham, John Henry	7Oct1867	10 yrs	Graham, G. W.	Orphan. Of color
Graham, Robert	4Nov1867	5 yrs	Graham, G. W.	No parents. Of color
Cheshur, Dick	2Dec1867		Cheshur, Washington D.	Orphan. Of color
Cheshur, Layton	2Dec1867		Cheshur, Washington D.	Orphan. Of color
Cheshur, Malinda	2Dec1867	17 yrs	Garratt, Ted	Orphan. Of color
Turner, Thomas	5Dec1867	6 yrs	Gray, W. C.	No parents. Of color
Turner, Harriet	5Dec1867	5 yrs	Gray, W. C.	No parents. Of color
Cheshur, Hezekiah	9Jan1868	13 yrs	Webb, Pryor	No parents living. Of color. Cancelled 6Sept1870, "Zach" having left Webb

Name	Date	Age	Bound to	Notes
Eagin, Ellen	9Jan1868		Brooks, Matthew	Bastard. Abandoned by mother. Of color
Thompson, John Calhoun	3Feb1868	15 yrs on 2Mar1868	Toone, Sr, James	Mother dead. Father unable or unwilling to support, consents to binding. White
Thompson, Leroy	3Feb1868	11 yrs	Toone, Jr, James	Mother dead. Father unable or unwilling to support, consents to binding. White
Potts, Chaney	5Feb1868		McGuire, James	Request of mother, Phillis Potts. Father dead. Of color
Potts, Winney	5Feb1868		McGuire, James	Request of mother, Phillis Potts. Father dead. Of color
Potts, Dawson	5Feb1868		McGuire, James	Request of mother, Phillis Potts. Father dead. Of color
Potts, Samuel	5Feb1868		McGuire, James	Request of mother, Phillis Potts. Father dead. Of color
Reed, Alfred	7Apr1868	10 yrs	Wood, Frances	Orphan. Of color
Wilks, Dock	6July1868	14 yrs	Wilks, Benjamin	No living parents. Of color
Wilks, Isaac	6July1868	11 yrs	Wilks, Benjamin	No living parents. Of color
Turner, Jonah	8Sept1868	10 yrs	Pybass, James	No parents. Of color
Tatum, Adeline	7Dec1868		Lineberger, William C.	Baseborn orphan. Mother deranged. Of color
Hannah	10Dec1868		Hornerly, W. S.	Mother deranged. Of color
Warren, Fanny	2Feb1869	8 yrs	Warren, Abner	Father supposed to be dead. Mother a prostitute & "non compos mentis." Of color
Polk, Rose	1Mar1869	4 1/2 yrs	Polk, M. T.	No parents. Of color
Newsom, Hannah	1Mar1869	4 1/2 yrs	Wilkes, Perry C.	No parents. Of color
Hull, Sophia	1Mar1869	4 yrs	Wood, Abram	Both of color
Smith, A. G.	2Mar1869	14 yrs	Yopp, W. T.	No parents. White
Adams, Charles	2Mar1869	6 yrs	Adams, J. G.	Baseborn. Mother dead. Of color
Smith, Delia	4Mar1869	8 yrs 3 mo	Smith, Cannon	Without living parents. Bound previously to Smith by FB at deathbed wish of mother. Of color
Pirth, Jesse	7Apr1869	9 yrs	Fawcett, J. B.	No living parents. White
Pepkin, John	3May1869	11 yrs	Joyner, Jonathan	Request of father, William Pepkin
Pepkin, Jesse	3May1869	12 yrs	Joyner, Jonathan	Request of father, William Pepkin
Hanet?, Clinton	7June1869	8 yrs	Polk, H. M.	Illegitimate. No mother. Of color
Collier, William	5Oct1869	10 yrs	Neely, J. J.	No parents. Of color

Name	Date	Age	Master	Notes
Miller, Ann	5Oct1869	14 yrs	Miller, Simon	No parents. Both of color
Robertson, Willis	1Nov1869	7 1/2 yrs	Robertson, P. F.	No mother. Bastard. Of color
Waller, George Franklin	4Jan1870	11 yrs	Nuckells, Richard	Father dead. Mother in poor house. White
Turner, Patton	7Mar1870	8 yrs	Turner, L. D.	Parents consent. Of color
Turner, Bryant	7Mar1870	13 yrs	Turner, Andrew	Parents consent. Of color
Turner, Milly	7Mar1870	4 yrs	Turner, L. D.	Parents consent. Of color
Turner, Joseph	7Mar1870	11 yrs	Turner, John C.	Parents consent. Of color
Turner, Fanny	6Apr1870	9 yrs	Parker, Henry M.	Until 21 yrs. Mother consents. Of color
Marsh, Mary	3May1870	9 yrs	Keller, A. J.	Mother consents. Father dead. Of color
Marsh, Margaret	3May1870	5 yrs	Smith, James M.	Mother consents. Father dead. Of color
Marsh, Jerry	3May1870	7 yrs	Marsh, John T.	Mother consents. Father dead. Of color
Armstead, Ann	6June1870	7 yrs	Parran, Thomas A.	Parents dead. Of color
Armstead, Sherman	6June1870	5 yrs	Parran, Thomas A.	Parents dead. Of color
Turner, William	5Sept1870	9 yrs	Robinson, James L.	Of color. On 6Dec1870 Dan & Ann Turner, parents, protest binding. On 3Jan1871 apprenticeship confirmed
Bradford, Martha	4Oct1870	9 yrs	Joyner, J. T.	Orphan. Of color
Bradford, Nancy	7Oct1870	13 yrs	Bradford, William G.	Orphan. Of color
Harriss, Salte	7Oct1870	9 yrs	Armistead, W. T.	Thomas Harriss, father, consents. Mother dead. Male. Of color
Bradford, Austin	5Dec1870	8 yrs	Letner, Nannie C.	Orphan. Of color
Buford, Alex	6Feb1871	16 yrs	Neely, James C.	Orphan. Alex consents. Of color
Bradford, Susannah	8Feb1871	5 yrs	Homesby, W. M.	Neither father nor mother living. Of color
Smith, Rachel	6Mar1871	9 yrs	Moore, L. C.	Orphan. Of color
Smith, Henry	6Mar1871	13 yrs	Guthrie, W. W.	Orphan. Of color
Smith, Richard	6Mar1871	11 yrs	Brown, H. B.	Orphan. Of color
Lanier, Thomas	6Mar1871	14 yrs	Shearin, G. W.	Orphan. Of color
Ramsey, Julia	8Mar1871	10 yrs	Ramsey, Alex	Orphan. Of color
Shaw, Miller	3Oct1871	12 yrs	Joyner, Alex	Orphan. Both of color
Pitman, Simon	1Jan1872	13 yrs	Mills, William R.	Orphan. Cancelled 4Mar1872, as Mary Stitt, mother, of color, proves her ability to care for Simon. 7Feb1872*

Name	Date	Age	Bound to	Notes
Ferguson, Turner	5Aug1872	6 yrs	Shinault, Alfred	Orphan. Both of color. On 6Nov1872 Isaac Hadley avers he is Turner's father & legal custodian, asks cancellation of indenture for fraud. On 8Jan1873 cause dismissed
Daniel, Robert L.	6Nov1872	8 yrs	Harris, Cynthia	Father & mother dead
Warr, Charles	3Nov1873	14 yrs	Warr, Henderson	Orphan. Consent of Mary Robertson, formerly Mary Warr, mother. Of color. 7Oct1873*
Warr, Tandy	3Nov1873	11 yrs	Warr, Henderson	Orphan. Consent of Mary Robertson, formerly Mary Warr, mother. Of color. 7Oct1873*
Allen, Joseph C.	2Mar1874	17 yrs	Patrick, T. G.	Orphan. Allen consents
Harriss, Calvin	7Apr1874	16 yrs	Harriss, Albert	Orphan. Both of color. Cancelled 7Sep1875. Albert unfit & incompetent
Harriss, Jesse	7Apr1874	10 yrs	Harriss, Albert	Orphan. Both of color. Cancelled 7Sep1875. Albert unfit & incompetent
Harriss, Moses	7Apr1874	7 yrs	Harriss, Albert	Orphan. Both of color
Harriss, John	7Apr1874	6 yrs	Harriss, Albert	Orphan. Both of color
Harriss, Isaac	7Apr1874	13 yrs	Harriss, Ambrose	Orphan. Both of color
Thomas, Andrew C.	7Jan1875	16 yrs	Hammons, A. B.	Orphan
Thomas, Martha E.	7Jan1875	13 yrs	Hammons, A. B.	Orphan
Thomas, John A.	7Jan1875	7 yrs	Hammons, A. B.	Orphan
Harriss, Calvin	7Sept1875		Harriss, Burrus	Orphan. All of color
Harriss, Jesse	7Sept1875		Harriss, Burrus	Orphan. All of color
Partridge, James	3Nov1875	7 yrs	Hornesby, James H.	Father dead. Mother has left state
Wood, Wesley	7Aug1876	12 yrs	Wood, Flem	Flem is father of Wesley. Both of color
McGowan, Ann	8Aug1876	14 yrs	Wood, David	Both of color. No legal parents living
Dickenson, Mollie	2July1878	Abt 12 yrs 3June1878	Dickenson, William	Without father or mother living. On 3June1878 apprenticeship objected to by Isaac Dickenson. Objection denied. Of color
Partridge, Harmon Verton	9Apr1879	Abt 9 yrs	Hornesby, K. E.	Without father or mother
Brooks, Rinda	8June1880	12 yrs	Wood, Charles	Female. Of color

Hardin County

Name	Date	Age	Master	Notes
Stanfield, Female	5Apr1821		Huddleston, Benjamin	Illegitimate daughter of Polly Stanfield. Termed guardianship in entry
Eddridge, Elijah	5Apr1821	10 yrs	Eads, Gabriel	Blacksmith. Orphan. Cancelled Thursday, April 1823 term, as Elijah Edwards
Fuller, Jefferson	1Oct1821		Harbour, Samuel	Until 20 yrs. Released 19Sept1825. Agreement altered 23Sept1825*
Edwards, Elijah	July 1823		Boyd, James	Orphan. Cancelled Oct 1823 term
Crotts, Joseph	Oct 1823		Hitchcock, Isaac	Blacksmith. Orphan. Same date Isham Cherry appointed administrator of David Crotts, Dcd & guardian of Elizabeth Crotts
Crotts, Elizabeth	Oct 1823		Pauley, Elijah	See above
Crotts, Lewis	Oct 1823		Pickens, Jonathan R.	Blacksmith. See above
Lewis, William	Jan 1824	Near 10 yrs	Gammill, Ebenezer	Orphan
Crotts, Valentine	Jan 1824	Abt 16 yrs	Cherry, Isham	Orphan. See Joseph Crotts
Boyd, John	21Mar1825	12 yrs	Tybus, John	Orphan. Hatter. On 21Dec1824 will of James Boyd, Sr, Dcd proven. James Boyd granted Letters of Administration
Burks, Patsey	20June1825	6 yrs on 26Dec next	Murkinson, Keneth	
Cherry, Joseph	20June1825	6 yrs on 17Dec1824	Wood, Walter	
Cherry, Franklin	20June1825	10 yrs	Gibbs, Coonrod	
Haire, Martha	15Sept1834	11 yrs	McClain, James	Pauper
Haire, Cason	15Sept1834	8 yrs	Farrar, John	
Haire, William	15Sept1834	5 yrs	Graham, James	
Robbins, John	16Mar1835		Stout, Robert	

Name	Date	Age	Bound to	Notes
Williams,			Church, Johnathan M.	Previously bound. On 21Sept1835 ordered brought to court by Sheriff, then returned to Church. Elizabeth Williams' appeal denied 23Dec1835
Williams,			Church, Johnathan M.	Previously bound. On 21Sept1835 ordered brought to court by Sheriff, then returned to Church. Elizabeth Williams' appeal denied 23Dec1835
Williams,			Church, Johnathan M.	Previously bound. On 21Sept1835 ordered brought to court by Sheriff, then returned to Church. Elizabeth Williams' appeal denied 23Dec1835
McBride, Mary Jane	21Dec1835	Abt 11 yrs	Baine, Daniel	
McBride, Robert	21Dec1835	Abt 9 yrs	Baine, George	
Hare, Richard	4July1836		Nevill, Alexander	Orphan
Dennum, Wilson	1Aug1836	6 yrs	Kerr, Thomas A.	Orphan
Tankerley, James	3Dec1836	17 yrs in May1837	Wood, Charles	
Leaky, Rachel	1May1837	13 yrs in Oct 1837	Sweeney, James	Orphan. On 1Jan1838 William C. Hughes apptd guardian & given custody. See below
Leaky, Phebee	1May1837	10 yrs	Hunter, Daniel H.	Orphan. See below. Cancelled 3Sept1838
Leaky, Rhody	1May1837	9 yrs	Gray, Thomas	Orphan. On 5June1837 William F. Blanton paid $20 for caring for Mary Leaky & bringing her to court. Mary, a pauper, bid off for 4 wks to James Sweeney
Roberts, Margaret	5Feb1838		Barnes, John L.	Mulatto. Taken from Washington B. Turner for maltreatment
Lakey, Phebe	3Sept1838	11 yrs on 13Mar1838	Brumley, Willis	
Freeman, Benjamin Rush	1Oct1838		Thornton, Isaac	Same date James Robinson appointed administrator of William P. Freeman, Dcd
Freeman, William Andrews	1Oct1838		Blakely, Thomas	See above. Cancelled 5July1841, as William P. Freeman
Freeman, John Lewis	1Oct1838		Robinson, Dawson H.	See above. Cancelled 1June1840
Freeman, James Jasper	1Oct1838		Campbell, W. G.	See above. Cancelled 7July1845
Freeman, Adeline Catherine	1Oct1838		Edwards, Willie B.	See above
Freeman, Sarah Jane	1Oct1838		Lucus, Willis	See above

Name	Date	Age	Master	Notes
Frely, Solomon	5Nov1838	Abt 10 yrs	Frely, Andrew J.	Same date Sarah Frely & Andrew J. Frely granted administration of estate of Martin Frely, Dcd. 7Jan1839*
Aikin, William	3Dec1838	Abt 15 yrs	Randolph, Rix A.	
Waters, Robert	7Jan1839	11 yrs	Owen, Daniel	Daniel Owen's noncupative will probated 4Nov1839. Mary Owen, Executrix. Mary Owen's will probated 7Sept1840. Joel C. Hancock, Executor
Clingan, David	2Sept1839		Baker, Solomon H.	Tanner. Cancelled 7 Nov1842, Clingan refusing to remain with Baker
Nancy	2Sept1839		Campbell, A. B.	Spinster. Of color. Cancelled 5Oct1842, as Nancy Mitchel
Thompson, Jackson	4Nov1839		Campbell, A. B.	Tanner. Of color. Cancelled 5June1843, as Jackson Mitchell. John Hannah appointed guardian.* See Jack Mitchell
Grinage, James M.	2Mar1840	11 yrs	Head, William	Orphan
Redding, James M.	6Apr1840	Abt 9 yrs	Wyatt, William	
Freeman, John L.	1June1840		Hurst, Thompson	House carpenter
Freeman, John L.	5Oct1840	Abt 10 yrs	Whitlow, Paschal	Cancelled 3July 1843. Runaway
Freeman, Sarah	5Oct1840	Abt 11 yrs	Whitlow, Paschal	Until 21 yrs
Freeman, Elizabeth Ann	2Nov1840	Abt 4 or 5 yrs	Woodward, Fielder	Spinster. Until 21 yrs
Copeland, Solomon	4Jan1841		Yount, Larkin	Blacksmith
Lilly			Russell, William	Of color. On 1Feb1841 term of service expired. Russell to comply with indenture
Copeland, Solomon	5Apr1841	12 yrs	Polk, Thomas	Orphan
McBride, Robert	3May1841	Abt 15 yrs	Kerr, Andrew	Orphan. Farmer
Cagle, John J.	7June1841	Abt 14 yrs	Dinkins, Edward G.	Orphan. Farmer
Cagle, Charles	5July1841		Gray, Thomas	Orphan
Crissman, Jane	3Jan1842	Abt 13 yrs	Brumley, Jefferson C.	Orphan
Robins, Sarah Alexander	1Aug1842	Abt 3 yrs	Robinson, David	Until 21 yrs
Mitchel, Nancy	5Oct1842	Abt 8 yrs	Campbell, Thomas P.	Until 21 yrs
Jackson, Calvin	4Sept1843	Abt 11 yrs	Dowdey, William	Orphan
Oneal, Mary	4Dec1843	Abt 16 yrs	Bell, Larkin F.	Orphan. On 4Sept1843 ordered brought from house of Richard Orton

Name	Date	Age	Person	Notes
Gorforth, Alfred	1July1844		Polk, Michael L.	Farming
Mitchel, Manuel	5Aug1844	14 yrs	Davis, Henry W.	Farming, Mulatto. Cancelled 6Oct1845
Lacy, Elinor	4Nov1844	Abt 7 yrs	Blake, James G.	Consent of Rachel Lacy. Mulatto. Child of Jacob Lacy 4Nov1845* 6July1846*
Lacy, Mary	4Nov1844	Abt 4 yrs	Blake, James G.	Consent of Rachel Lacy. Mulatto. Child of Jacob Lacy 4Nov1845* 6July1846*
Holland, Thomas F.	2Dec1844	Abt 16 yrs	McCorkle, John	Farming. White
Holland, James M.	2Dec1844	Abt 11 yrs	Holland, William M.	Farming. White
Scott, Margaret	7July1845	Abt 11 yrs	Duncan, William C.	Cancelled 6Oct1845. To father, G. B. Scott
Garner, Joshua	6Oct1845		Hudeburgh, Solomon S.	Request of Garner. Blacksmithing. Cancelled 3Nov1845. Runaway
Mitchell, Manuel	6Oct1845		Hardin, Alexander S.	Request of Abby Mitchell, mother
Mitchell, William Henry	6Oct1845		Hardin, Alexander S.	Request of Abby Mitchell, mother
Mitchell, Jim	6Oct1845		Hardin, William K.	Request of Abby Mitchell, mother. See 2Jan1860 petition for free papers by James & Linda Mitchell & children, George Washington Mitchell & James Jackson Mitchell
Mitchell, Elijah	3Nov1845	17 yrs	Russell, Alexander	Request of Mitchell. Bond signed 1Dec1845. Of color. Cancelled 7Sept1846
Mitchell, Elijah	7Sept1846		Clifton, Eldridge	Cancelled 4Oct1847
McQueen, Thomas	1Feb1847		Carroll, Isaiah	
McQueen, John	1Feb1847		Carroll, Isaiah	Request of Carroll & "the widow McQueen"
Sellers, Riley	5July1847	5 yrs	Russell, William	Mother's consent. Saddler. Of color. Cancelled 2Apr1860
Brumly, William A.	6Sept1847		Perkins, E. M.	Bond cancelled 5Jan1852, terms of indenture having been completed
Mitchel, Elijah	4Oct1847		Baily, Robert P.	Of color
Ramsey, Henry C.	4Sept1848		Staly, J. C.	Cancelled 4Sept1854
McQueen, Hiram	4Sept1848		Wilkerson, R. J.	Until 20 yrs
Nix, Franklin	6Aug1849		Keeton, Reason	
Ray, Elizabeth	3Sept1849		Davidson, J. J.	
Smith, Susan	3Sept1849		Shull, Joseph	
Byrd, Robert	3Sept1849		Davis, H. W.	

Name	Date	Age	Master	Notes
Ray, Emanul F.	3Sept1849		Davis, H. W.	
Sellers, John	5Nov1849		Donahoo, John D.	Consent of mother. Of color
Morriss, Thomas J.	1July1850		Morriss, C. M.	Consent of mother, Sarah Morriss. Pauper. Cancelled 4Dec1854, as C. W. Morris
Damerell, Zachariah	3Feb1851		Rushing, Mark	No father or mother
Hanna, J. W.	5Nov1851	12 yrs	Hanna, Thomas	Orphan
Laxton [Laxson], Jessee	5Apr1852		Shull, Joseph	Orphan. Spelled "Laxon" in 1850 census
Laxan [Laxson], Mary E.	5Apr1852		Shull, Joseph B.	Orphan. Spelled "Laxon" in 1850 census
Laxcan [Laxson], Lucy C.	5Apr1852		Milam, Thomas F	Orphan. Spelled "Laxon" in 1850 census
Wolverton, Laura Jane	4Nov1852	12 yrs	Wolverton, John	Orphan
Wolverton, Wiley Green	4Nov1852	14 yrs	Wolverton, John	Orphan
Austin, G. A.	7Feb1853		Austin, S. A.	Until 21 yrs. Cancelled 7Nov1853. Heir of David M. Austed (sic) 7Nov1853
Austin, A. J.	7Feb1853		Austin, S. A.	Until 21 yrs. Cancelled 7Nov1853. Heir of David M. Austed (sic) 7Nov1853
Austin, D. J.	7Feb1853		Austin, S. A.	Until 21 yrs. Cancelled 7Nov1853. Heir of David M. Austed (sic) 7Nov1853
Austin, J. W.	7Feb1853		Austin, S. A.	Until 21 yrs. Cancelled 7Nov1853. Heir of David M. Austed (sic) 7Nov1853
Robinson, J. W.	7Feb1853		Weatherspoon, M[oses]. C.	Cancelled 2Oct1854. Weatherspoon leaving county 4Sept1854
Robinson, Wiley G.	7Feb1853		Weatherspoon, M[oses]. C.	Cancelled 2Oct1854. Weatherspoon leaving county 4Sept1854
Tinsley, James F.	6June1853	8 yrs	Polk, Green H.	Orphan
Tinsley, Emily F.	6June1853	16 mo	Parrish, Lewis B.	Orphan
May, Frances	6June1853	7 yrs	Loyd, William	Orphan
Outlaw?, Martha A.	7Nov1853		Blankenship, D. W.	
Austin, Andrew J.	7Nov1853		Franks, W. H.	
Austin, George A.	7Nov1853		Franks, W. H.	
Austin, J. W.	7Nov1853		Yount, Larkin	Cancelled 7May1855, as James Austin

Name	Date	Age	Master/Guardian	Notes
Taylor, Sarah L.	3July1854		Huling, William	
Williams, John	4Sept1854	16 yrs	Hames, Robert	
Morris, Thomas J.	4Dec1854		Tucker, R. B.	
Edwards, Susan	2Apr1855		Jones, Jessee	Orphan. Cancelled 7Jan1856, Susan having left Jones
Bradford, George W.	7May1855	Under 13 yrs	Counts, William	No father, mother, or legal guardian
Jones, Sarah?	6Aug1855	Abt 14 yrs	Capoot, James	Female orphan
Newman, Wesley	6July1857	10 yrs	Newman, Henry	Orphan
Mitchell, Sarah J.	6Oct1857	6 yrs	Campbell, T. J.	Orphan
Mitchell, Henry T.	6Oct1857	5 yrs	Campbell, T. J.	Orphan
Mitchell, Martha E.	6Oct1857	4 yrs	Campbell, T. J.	Orphan
Bourland, Robert	1Feb1858	15 yrs	Cunningham, J. M.	Orphan. Son of John Bourland, Dcd. James Counce, Guardian 1Aug1859. 3Jan1859*
Hardin, William	1Feb1858	16 yrs	Wells, Washington	
South, John	1Feb1858	13 yrs	South, Levi	
Kincannon, Nancy E.	4Oct1858	b. 17June1843	Mosier, William	
Kincannon, Thomas W. P.	4Oct1858	b. 15June1845	Mosier, William	
Kincannon, Rebecca J.	4Oct1858	b. 20July1847	Mosier, William	
Kincannon, James F.	4Oct1858	b. 11June1849	Mosier, William	
Davidson, John	1Nov1858	16 yrs	Davidson, S. S.	Orphan
Miller, James	1Nov1858		Luther, Jacob	Orphan
Mitchell, Jack		b. 1834	Campbell, A. B.	Apprenticeship completed 5Dec1859* Of color. See Jackson Thompson
Baker, Newton			Reed, Amzi	Cancelled 5Aug1861
Stinnet, Robert	5Feb1866	8 yrs	Lindsey, W. P.	White
Harbour, Joseph	6Aug1866	14 yrs on 15Sep1866	Maxwell, Thomas	Consent of Mary Harbour, mother. Of color
Harbour, Alexander	6Aug1866	13 yrs on 13Oct1866	Maxwell, Thomas	Consent of Mary Harbour, mother. Of color. Cancelled 6Sept1869, with mother's consent
Harbour, Wesley	6Aug1866	11 yrs on 15Nov1866	Maxwell, Henry	Consent of Mary Harbour, mother. Of color. Cancelled 1Feb1870. To mother

Name	Date	Age	Master	Notes
Marshal or Marsh	6Aug1866	9 yrs	Irwin, Nancy S.	Without father or mother. Of color. Cancelled 7Sept1874, Marshall having run away
Harbour, Calvin	6Aug1866	12 yrs	Howard, James	Without father or mother. Of color
Harbour, Wiley	6Aug1866	10 yrs	Howard, James	Without father or mother. Of color. Cancelled 5Oct1874
Smith, Amanda Jane	7Jan1867	Abt 10 yrs	Blevins, Wilson	White. Cancelled 1May1871
Smith, Hiram E.	4Feb1867	7 yrs in Sept1866	East, John H.	Without parents
Parker, James M.	4Mar1867	9 yrs	Ross, William A.	Without father or mother
Parker, John Walker	4Mar1867	11 yrs	Ross, James T.	Without father or mother
Loyd, Dick Fanny	3June1867	9 yrs	Bentley, A. W.	Without parents in Hardin Co. Of color
Harvill, Robert	1July1867	10 yrs	Ingram, W[illiam] C.	Orphan. Same date inquest on body of Warren Harvill reports death on 10May1867 caused by a limb falling on him while at his plow. D. S. Harvill, JP
Harvill, Samuel	1July1867	8 yrs	Ingram, W[illiam] C.	Orphan. See above
Jenkins, Martha E.	4Nov1867		Roberts, Martha H.	Until 21 yrs. Of color
Low, Jr, Thomas	2Nov1868	9 yrs	Irwin, L. B.	Consent of mother. Orphan. Cancelled 5July1869, Low having an ungovernable temper.* To mother
Davey, Bartlett	2Aug1869	9 yrs	Davey, Thomas	Of color. Cancelled 1May1876
Davey, Bradford	2Aug1869	7 yrs	Davey, Thomas	Of color. Cancelled 1May1876
Lincoln, G. B.	2Aug1869	9 yrs	Moon, F. G.	Male. Of color
Choat, Edmond	6Sept1869	12 yrs	Davey, T[homas]	Of color. Cancelled 6May1872, as Ed Shoat
John	6Sept1869	14 yrs	Watson, Margarett	Of color
Marshall	6Sept1869	11 yrs	Watson, Margarett	Of color
Mathews, William	6Sept1869	12 yrs	White, F. M.	
Pickens, Dick	1Nov1869	13 yrs	Franks, James L.	Of color
Spears, Robert	6Dec1869	12 yrs	Davis, Joseph	Cancelled 5Feb1872. Taken by mother, Nancy Clifton
Nichols, George	7Feb1870	Abt 11 yrs	Franks, Jr, W. H.	Of color
Jones, Thomas	6June1870	11 yrs	Churchwell, John C.	Orphan. Cancelled 6Sept1875
Hendrix, Sylvester	1Aug1870	9 yrs	Journey, John F.	Orphan
Davis, Monroe	1Aug1870	12 yrs	Hardin, Charles	Both of color. Cancelled 5Jan1874
Gardner, John	5Sept1870	11 yrs	Howard, J. M.	Of color. Cancelled 6Oct1873, Gardner having run away

Name	Date	Age	Master	Notes
Jackson, Green	3Oct1870	Abt 7 yrs	Yant, W. D.	Of color
Smith, Margarett E.	7Aug1871	Abt 10 yrs	Gammill, Arch	Orphan. Cancelled 4Nov1872
Franks, John T.	2Oct1871	5 yrs	Vanhoose, John A.	Orphan. Twin. Cancelled 3Sept1883, "Frank" having left Vanhoose
Franks, Samuel A.	2Oct1871	5 yrs	Vanhoose, John A.	Orphan. Twin. Cancelled 3Sept1883, Sam refusing to be controlled
Mathews, William P.	6Nov1871	14 yrs	Dillon, Joseph	Orphan. Cancelled 3Aug1874
Branch, Alfred	1Jan1872		Thomas, J. R.	Orphan. "Boy"
Bunch, Albert	3Feb1873	Abt 13 yrs	Davey, J. L.	Of color
Boyd, Robert	4Aug1873	14 yrs	Howell, D. W.	
Pickens, Thomas	1Sept1873	12 yrs	Franks, James L.	Of color. Cancelled 6Sept1875
Harvill, William H.	3Nov1873	4 yrs	Barnett, J. W.	Cancelled 6Apr1874
Yancey, Beckey	1Dec1873	Abt 9 yrs	Dodds, John A.	Of color
Barns, Felix	2Mar1874	11 yrs	Doran, W. P.	Farming. Illegitimate mulatto child of Lou Barns, now wife of Samuel Holt
Brown, Thomas B.	1June1874	13 yrs	Dillon, Joseph	Of color. Cancelled 3Aug1874
Hampton, William J.	5Oct1874		Wood, M. W.	Orphan. Consent of mother
Wilman, Wilburn	2Aug1875		Barnhill, W. P.	White
Kimble, J. T.	3Apr1876		Cody, A. H.	White
Jones, Katie	3July1876	15 yrs	Stockard, S. J.	White
Neal, Eliza Jane	4Sept1876	Abt 10 yrs	Hardin, J. W.	Until 21 yrs. Of color
Willoughby, Nerva	3June1878	Abt 9 yrs	Cherry, Edgar	Until 21 yrs. Of color
Carter, Jennie	4Oct1886		Sheffield, Rachel (Mrs)	
Carter, Samuel	4Oct1886		Sheffield, Rachel (Mrs)	
Carter, Alexander	4Oct1886		Sheffield, Rachel (Mrs)	
Harris, James Thomas	5Sept1887	9 yrs	White, John S.	Mother, Sallie Harris, unable to provide. Baseborn

Haywood County

Name	Date	Age	Master	Notes
Carter, Margaret	11Sept1826	15 yrs	Dodd, Willie	Illegitimate child. Spinster
Conner, William	14June1827		Hardwick, John	
Kinsey, John	14Mar1828		Wiatt, John	Taylor
Unnamed Male	14June1834	8 yrs	Fitzgerald, David	Mulatto. Cancelled 12Dec1834. Child now in Hardeman Co
Unnamed Female	14June1834	4 yrs	Fitzgerald, David	Until 18 yrs. Mulatto. Cancelled 12Dec1834. Child now in Hardeman Co
Brown, John	14Sept1835		Rutherford, Thomas	For 10 yrs. Orphan
Cruch, Jefferson	14Mar1836		Coxe, James	For 12 yrs
Glenn, John	7Aug1837		See, John	Orphan
Glenn, Kizzia	7Aug1837		Minor, Allen	Orphan
Glenn, Cassiah	7Aug1837		McWhirter, Isaac	Orphan
Glenn, Betsy	7Aug1837		Gridley, Chance	Orphan
Pevyhouse, Mable	1Jan1838	Abt 14 yrs	Lindsey, Caleb	Orphan. On 6Aug1838 Lindsey ordered to show cause why indenture (as Marble) should not be revoked for maltreatment
Pevyhous, Mavel	2Apr1838	Abt 7 yrs	McLeod, Neil	Consent of his mother. 3Sept1838*
Brown, William	1Oct1838		Cox, Thomas	Orphan
Glenn, Cassa	1Oct1838	Abt 13 yrs	George, Sr, Benjamin	Orphan
Mann, Gustavus	4Feb1839		Rutherford, Thomas & Rhoads, R. V.	Orphan of William Mann, Dcd
Jones, Elvy	5July1839		Willibee, James	On 1Oct1838 children of Rachel Jones over 8 yrs ordered to Court to be bound
Jones, Ann Eliza	2Dec1839		Mann, Samuel	Until 18 yrs. Dau of Betsy Jones. Of color
Jones, Mahala	2Dec1839		Mann, Samuel	Until 18 yrs. Dau of Betsy Jones. Of color
Jones, Lucinda	2Dec1839		Mann, Samuel	Until 18 yrs. Dau of Betsy Jones. Of color
Jones, John	2Dec1839		Mann, Samuel	Son of Betsy Jones. Of color
Pevyhouse,	3Feb1840		Hines, Charles C.	
Pevuhouse, Marble	6Apr1840		Hopper, John	

Child	Master/Guardian	Age	Date	Remarks
Burnett, George	Branch, Benjamin L.	Abt 2 yrs	3May1841	Orphan. Branch also apptd George's guardian and administrator of Daniel H. Burnet, Dcd. On 4July1842 Branch posts bond as guardian of George as well as of Frances, Martha Ann & John Burnett. Other sibs Eliza, James, & Thomas 4July1842
Burnett, James Thomas	Jennings, Robert	Abt 6 yrs	3May1841	Orphan
Williams, Joseph	Bowers, William E.		3May1841	Of color 1Aug1842. Rebound. On 2June1851 in Shelby Co Williams certified as free, his mother, also free, having been brought to Heywood Co from Virginia by Dr Joseph Jones
Williams, Alfred	Bowers, William E.		3May1841	Of color 1Aug1842. Rebound 2Dec1844
Williams, Samuel	Bowers, William E.		3May1841	Of color 1Aug1842. Rebound 2Dec1844
Smith, Littleton	Pettus, Albert H.		3Jan1842	Assent of Jane Smith, mother
Smith, Hulda	Pettus, Albert H.		3Jan1842	Assent of Jane Smith, mother
Briant, William [Henry]	Edwards, James G.	Abt 14 yrs	7Nov1842	Son of Louisa Bryant. Sibs Eli, Joseph, Martha, John Thomas, Benjamin & Nancy 3Oct1842
Statum, Charles	Purvis, William T.		2Jan1843	
Bennett, Bryant	Lanier, Lovick		7Aug1843	Orphan
Bennett, Mary M.	Lanier, Lovick		7Aug1843	Orphan
Bennett, William	Lanier, Lovick		7Aug1843	Orphan
Colwell, Elvira	Mahon, Francis E.	Abt 7 yrs	2Dec1844	Of color
Wren, William C.	Rhoads, William G.		6Oct1845	Orphan
Wren, John G.	Rhoads, John B.		6Oct1845	Orphan
James, Jordan	Bond, Thomas		5Jan1846	Mulatto. Rebound to Bond 1May1848. Mother appeals to Circuit Court
Wrenn, Thomas W.	Harrell, Ephraim	Abt 9 yrs	2Feb1846	Orphan
Unnamed male	Harget, George P.		2Nov1846	Cancelled 7Dec1846. "Harrison" (male) returned to his mother
Burnet, John	Jennings, Robert			Indenture made "some years ago" cancelled 2Aug1847
Belton, James Calvin	Smothers, Thomas	Abt 13 yrs	1Nov1847	
Redding, John Arthur	McIntosh, Daniel		7May1849	Assent of mother, Sarah Redding. Lately abandoned by father. Of color. Cancelled 9Jan1868. McIntosh left county
Redden, Sarah	McIntosh, D. F.			Data from cancellation entry 9Jan1868. Sarah dead. McIntosh left county

Name	Date	Age	Master	Notes
Redden, Margaret			McIntosh, D. F.	Data from cancellation entry 9Jan1868. McIntosh left county
Redden, Fannie			McIntosh, D. F.	Data from cancellation entry 9Jan1868. McIntosh left county
Lucas, John W.	2Dec1850		Brown, Samuel	
Lucas, Cebert	2Dec1850		Brown, Samuel	
Lucas, Louisa	2Dec1850		Brown, Samuel	
Lucas, William	2Dec1850		Brown, Samuel	
Lucas, Amanda	2Dec1850		Brown, Samuel	
Sally	6Jan1851	Abt 5 yrs	Taliaferro, Robert S.	Of color
Jane	6Jan1851	Abt 3 yrs	Taliaferro, Robert S.	Of color
James	6Jan1852		Womble, W. W.	Child of Lucinda Jones. Of color
Joe	6Jan1852		Womble, W. W.	Child of Lucinda Jones. Of color
Jones, Frances	2Feb1852		Smith, Samuel J.	Until 18 yrs. Child of Betsy Jones. Of color
McClellan, Louisa Frances	1Mar1852		Batchelor, Alexander	
McClellan, Elvira Lazenier	1Mar1852		Batchelor, Alexander	
Locus, Six children, unnamed	2Mar1852		Musgrave, James H.	Of color
Bousman, Hugh	5Apr1852	12 yrs	Wright, T. W. P.	Orphan
Susan Ann	4Oct1853	Abt 7 yrs	Jordan, John J.	Until 18 yrs. Art of serving. Of color. On 7Apr1856 Jordan ordered to show cause why indenture binding Susan Ann Mann should not be cancelled
Wright, Solomon Henry	6Nov1854		Keithly, John	Farming
Falkner, David	5Dec1854	13 yrs	Edwards, Silas	Son of Isaac Falkner, Dcd
Falkner, Henry	5Dec1854	11 yrs	Edwards, Joseph J.	Son of Isaac Falkner, Dcd
Fortum?, Jesse	7May1855	7 yrs	Potter, E. M.	
Mann, John	1Oct1855	18 yrs	Mann, Samuel H.	Farming. Of color
Bronte, William E.	1Dec1856	13 yrs	Robinson, Gabriel	
Clark, Ephraim	7Apr1857	14 yrs	Moody, William A.	
Jones, Sally	7Sept1857	12 yrs	Taliaferro, Lucy Jane	Of color
Jones, Amanda Jane	7Sept1857	10 yrs	Taliaferro, Lucy Jane	Of color
Joyner, William	5Jan1858	Abt 10 yrs	Whitehead, Richard	
Joyner, Richard	5Jan1858	Abt 8 yrs	Whitehead, Richard	

Name	Date	Term	Master	Notes
Lucas, Rhoda	6May1861	10 yrs	Whitehead, Richard	Of color
Lucas, Lizzie	6May1861	1 yr	Whitehead, Richard	Of color
Lucas, Zilpha	6May1861	5 yrs	Whitehead, Richard	Of color
Lucas, Silas	6May1861	6 yrs	Whitehead, Richard	Of color
Cotter, Dorsey	4July1866		Jones, J. C.	Orphan
Cogshall, Boyd	4July1866		Cogshall, J. C.	Orphan
Cogshall, Charlie	4July1866		Cogshall, J. C.	Orphan
Tyus, January	7Aug1866		Tyus, Thomas W.	Orphan
Tyus, Charlie	7Aug1866		Tyus, John E.	Orphan
Carrigan, Joe	7Aug1866		Scott, Thomas M.	Orphan
Graves, Tom	7Aug1866		Graves, E. A.	Orphan
Scott, Anthony	7Aug1866		Scott, Thomas M.	Orphan
Scott, Patrick	7Aug1866		Scott, Thomas M.	Orphan
Lyle, Lucy	3Sept1866		Lyle, W. J.	Orphan
Hotchkiss, Martha	3Sept1866		Hotchkiss, S. B.	Orphan. On 7July1868 Daniel Moody cited for harboring Martha. Cancelled 8July1868
Hotchkiss, George	4Sept1866		Hotchkiss, R. L.	Orphan
Hotchkiss, James	4Sept1866		Hotchkiss, R. L.	Orphan
Bond, Abram	4Sept1866		Bond, W. W.	Orphan
Bond, Cicily	4Sept1866		Bond, W. W.	Orphan
Smith, Edinborough	4Sept1866		McCoy, W. H.	Orphan. Consent of mother, Clarissa Smith
Smith, Wesley	4Sept1866		McCoy, W. H.	Orphan. Consent of mother, Clarissa Smith
Smith, Sarah E.	4Sept1866		McCoy, W. H.	Orphan. Consent of mother, Clarissa Smith
Smith, Henry	4Sept1866		McCoy, W. H.	Orphan. Consent of mother, Clarissa Smith
Barbee, Ben	1Oct1866		Barbee, John	Orphan
Barbee, Frances	1Oct1866		Barbee, John	Orphan
Burrough, Alice	1Oct1866		Turner, Joseph J.	Orphan
Case, Bettie	2Oct1866		Mann, John J.	Orphan
Case, Sarah	2Oct1866		Mann, John J.	Orphan
Currie, Nathan	2Oct1866	6 yrs (canc entry)	Currie, Harvy	Orphan. Of color (from canc entry). Cancelled 3Jan1877. Master died 6Nov1876.

Name	Date	Age	Master	Notes
Currie, Louisa	2Oct1866		Clark, James W.	Orphan
Drake, Thomas	5Nov1866		Drake, John	Orphan
Drake, Haywood	5Nov1866		Drake, John	Orphan
Coppedge, Mary	5Nov1866		Coppedge, T. C.	Orphan
Niblett, Alfred	5Nov1866		Niblett, J. T.	Orphan. Cancelled 6Dec1869 at request of father, Alfred Payne, who has returned from Texas
Niblett, July	5Nov1866		Niblett, J. T.	Orphan. Cancelled 6Dec1869 at request of father, Alfred Payne, who has returned from Texas
Cook, Jordan	5Nov1866		Cook, John W.	Orphan
Dunlop, Alex	5Nov1866		Dunlop, J. B.	Orphan
Burford, Pat	5Nov1866		Burford, S. C.	Orphan
Maclin, William	5Nov1866		Maclin, Lewis	Orphan
Maclin, Lucy	5Nov1866		Maclin, Lewis	Orphan
Hotchkiss, Lucy	6Nov1866		Hotchkiss, S. B.	Orphan. On 7July1868 Daniel Moody cited for harboring Lucy. Cancelled 8July1868
Wilson, Sam	3Dec1866		Wilson, James T.	Orphan
Livingston, Dilcey	3Dec1866		Livingston, J. L.	Orphan
Livingston, Nathaniel	3Dec1866		Livingston, J. L.	Orphan. Cancelled 3Jan1872 on application of Nathaniel & Mariah Livingston, his mother. No father living. Of color
Bond, Jackson	3Dec1866		Bond, W. T.	Orphan
Moses, William	3Dec1866		Moses, Nancy	Orphan
Sweet, Washington	4Dec1866		Sweet, S. M.	Orphan
Sweet, Araminter	4Dec1866		Sweet, S. M.	Orphan
Sweet, Ephraim	4Dec1866		Sweet, S. M.	Orphan
Thomas, Moses	4Dec1866		Thomas, John H.	Orphan
Buck, Laura	8Jan1867		Buck, Henry	
Davis, Gentry	4Feb1867		Davis, John C.	Orphan. Canc 3Apr1872. Gentry a runaway
Davis, Mary	4Feb1867		Davis, John C.	Orphan
Moore, Henry	4Feb1867		Kelsoe, J. F.	Orphan
Kirby, Allen	4Feb1867		Kirby, Eliza	Orphan

Name	Date	Master	Notes
Watson, Joel	4Feb1867	Dodd, W. T.	Orphan
Walker, Kate	5Feb1867	Walker, James	
Wilson, William	5Feb1867	Bond, William W.	
Wilson, Reuben	5Feb1867	Bond, William W.	
Drake, John	2Apr1867	Drake, John	Orphan
McCann, Horace	3June1867	Read, Isaac H.	Orphan
Lucas	3June1867	Read, Isaac H.	Orphan
Davis, Laura	5Aug1867	Tyns, Thomas W.	Orphan. Of color. Data from cancellation entry 2Feb1869
Winfield, Mary	6Aug1867	Winfield, Sr, James L.	Orphan. Cancelled 5Feb1868
Powell, Isabella	2Sept1867	Meux, T. R.	Orphan
Parker, Albert	7Oct1867	Parker, Mary A.	Orphan
Parker, Henry	7Oct1867	Parker, Mary A.	Orphan
Claiborne, Mary Frances	9Oct1867	Claiborne, F. A.	Orphan
Duncy, Jane	4Nov1867	Martin, A. H.	Orphan. Of color. Canc 3Nov1873, as Jane Conway, she having married Henry Carney
Clark, Green	4Nov1867	Clark, Hugh M.	Orphan. Of color
Shim, Nelson	4Nov1867	Shim, J. M.	Orphan. Of color
Shim, Richard	4Nov1867	Shim, J. M.	Orphan. Of color
George	4Nov1867	McFarland, John	Orphan
Elias	4Nov1867	McFarland, John	Orphan
Owen, Eugenia	2Dec1867	Watkins, John R.	Orphan
Owen, Edd	2Dec1867	Watkins, John R.	Orphan
Owen, Patrick E.	2Dec1867	Watkins, John R.	Orphan
Henry, Robert	2Dec1867	McFarland, John W.	Orphan
Smith, Sarah	3Feb1868	Johnson, D. B.	Orphan. Request of mother. Of color
Smith, Henry	3Feb1868	Johnson, D. B.	Orphan. Request of mother. Of color
Smith, Richard	3Feb1868	Johnson, D. B.	Orphan. Request of mother. Of color
Smith, Rachel	3Feb1868	Johnson, D. B.	Orphan. Request of mother. Of color
Stone, Thomas W.	3Feb1868	Whitehurst, B. A.	Orphan. Cancelled 2Mar1868, as Wesley Stone. To be bound to William A. W. Posey in Lauderdale Co
Stone, Asbury P.	3Feb1868	Johnson, Frank	Orphan

Name	Date	Age	Master	Notes
Newsom, Jack	4Feb1868		Newsom, William	Orphan. Of color
Winfield, Mary	5Feb1868		Winfield, George H.	Of color
Jeter, Thomas	2Mar1868		Jeter, J. C.	Orphan
Robbins, Bennett	2Mar1868	3 yrs in Sept1867	Lowery, Riley	Orphan. Has brother William Robbins & sister Laura V. 3Sept1867, 4Nov1867* Cancelled 6Mar1871
Campbell, Joseph	6Apr1868	17 yrs this August	Baker, Marmaduke	Request of Campbell
Bond, Angeline	7Apr1868		Irvin, Henderson	Orphan. Both of color
Bond, John	7Apr1868		Irvin, Henderson	Orphan. Both of color
Bond, Henry	7Apr1868		Irvin, Henderson	Orphan. Both of color
Moore, Daniel	5May1868		Avery, Wiley	Orphan. Of color
Wilbert, Frank	1June1868		Somerville, J. B.	Request of Wilbert. Orphan. Of color
Hotchkiss, Martha	8July1868		Nolen, H. C.	Orphan. Of color
Hotchkiss, Lucy	8July1868		Boyd, B. P.	Orphan. Of color
Taliaferro, Emma	8Sept1868	9 yrs	Moore, J. W.	Request of Sallie Taliaferro, mother. Of color. Canc 5May1873. Moore dead. Mother able to provide care. Age from cancellation entry
Tucker, Steven A. D.	5Oct1868		Tucker, W. E.	Orphan. Of color
Tucker, Hannah	5Oct1868		Tucker, W. E.	Orphan. Of color
Mann, Jordan	6Oct1868		Walker, Arron	Orphan. Of color
Mann, Levi	6Oct1868		Walker, Arron	Orphan. Of color
Mann, Mary	6Oct1868		Walker, Arron	Orphan. Of color
Mann, Nancy	6Oct1868		Fleming, A. W.	Orphan. Of color
King, Jennie?	8Dec1868		Wood, Gruneson?	Female orphan. Both of color
Batchelor, Jarnon?	6Jan1869		Clark, Jr, H. M.	Orphan. Of color
Batchelor, John	6Jan1869		Clark, Jr, H. M.	Orphan. Of color
Batchelor, Nancy	1Feb1869		Batchelor, John A. M.	Orphan. Of color
Davis, Laura	2Feb1869		McConico, W. E.	Orphan. Of color
Batchelor, Emma	3Feb1869		Randolph, Henry	Orphan. Both of color
Batchelor, Anthony	3Feb1869		Randolph, Henry	Orphan. Both of color
Batchelor, Lydia	3Feb1869		Randolph, Henry	Orphan. Both of color

Name	Date		Master	Notes
Batchelor, Louisa	3Feb1869		Randolph, Henry	Orphan. Both of color
Towns, Sam	1Mar1869		Compton, Jackson	Orphan. Both of color
Towns, Simuel?	1Mar1869		Compton, Jackson	Orphan. Both of color
Towns, Ulysses	1Mar1869		Compton, Jackson	Orphan. Both of color
Currie, Allin	1Mar1869		Midyett, Thomas H.	Orphan. Of color
Currie, James	1Mar1869		Midyett, Thomas H.	Orphan. Of color
Currie, Juda	1Mar1869		Midyett, Thomas H.	Female orphan. Of color
Currie, William	1Mar1869		Midyett, Thomas H.	Orphan. Of color
Currie, Andrew J.	1Mar1869		Midyett, Thomas H.	Orphan. Of color
Lee, Austin	1Mar1869		Taliferro, Simon	Orphan. Both of color
Lee, Henry	1Mar1869		Taliferro, Simon	Orphan. Both of color
Lee, Ellin	1Mar1869		Taliferro, Simon	Orphan. Both of color
Maclin, Charles	2Mar1869		Johnson, Henry	Orphan. Of color
Maclin, Sam	2Mar1869		Johnson, Henry	Orphan. Of color
Mann, Bell	2Aug1869		Mann, Austin	Orphan
Dudly, Stephen	2Aug1869		Read, W. B.	Orphan. Of color
Willie Ann	2Aug1869		Read, W. B.	Orphan. Of color
Owen, Parsons	2Aug1869		Owen, Thomas	Orphan. Previously apprenticed to Owen by FB. Now rebound by Court. Of color
Owen, William	2Aug1869		Owen, Thomas	Orphan. Previously apprenticed to Owen by FB. Now rebound by Court. Of color
Parter, Raymond	6Oct1869		Read, Seamon	Orphan. Both of color
Parter, John	6Oct1869		Read, Seamon	Orphan. Both of color
Jones, Charley	2Nov1869		Womble, W. W.	Orphan. Of color. Previously apprenticed (to Womble?) by FB. Now rebound by Court
Jones, John	2Nov1869		Womble, W. W.	Orphan. Of color. Previously apprenticed (to Womble?) by FB. Now rebound by Court
Beasley, Winney Ann	6Dec1869	Abt 8 yrs	Kavanaugh, James P.	Request of Harriet A. Beasley, mother
Holeman, John	7Dec1869		Austin, A. W.	Orphan. Of color
Halliburton, William	7Dec1869		Halliburton, A. J.	Orphan. Of color
Halliburton, Lindsey	7Dec1869		Halliburton, A. J.	Orphan. Of color

83

Name	Date	Age	Master	Notes
Coldwell, Joe	8Dec1869		Coldwell, VanBuran	Orphan. Both of color
Coldwell, Henry	8Dec1869		Coldwell, VanBuran	Orphan. Both of color
Coldwell, David	8Dec1869		Coldwell, VanBuran	Orphan. Both of color
Coldwell, Marshall	7Feb1870		Coldwell, Elias	Orphan. Of color
Jetton, Margret E.	7Mar1870		Jetton, J. B.	Orphan. Of color
Currie, Irvin	8Mar1870		Currie, Anderson	Orphan. Both of color
Ware, Annis	4Apr1870		Ware, Richard	Orphan. Of color
Ware, Roxey	4Apr1870		Ware, Richard	Orphan. Of color
Towns, Sam	2May1870		Howell, Madison	Orphan. Of color
Fleming, Peter	2May1870		Moses, Tom	Orphan. Of color
Towns, Nicey	2May1870		Howell, Madison	Orphan. Of color
Abernathy, Fannie	6July1870		Smith, Ceala	Orphan. Both of color
Abernathy, Sallie Ann	6July1870		Newbone, Tom	Orphan. Both of color
Grove, Julia	6July1870		Smith, Green	Orphan. Both of color
Grove, Isabella	6July1870		Grove, Annie	Orphan. Of color
Thomas, Lucy	6Sept1870		Longly, Jim	Orphan. Of color
Thomas, Richard	6Sept1870		Longly, Jim	Orphan. Of color
Thomas, Amanda	6Sept1870		Longly, Jim	Orphan. Of color
Thomas, Mary Jane	6Sept1870		Wills, Walstean	Orphan. Of color
Thomas, Hannah	6Sept1870		Wills, Walstean	Orphan. Of color
Harper, Charley	6Jan1871		Sherman, John L.	Orphan. Of color. Cancelled 3Sept1877, Charley having left Sherman
White, William	6Feb1871		Edwards, J. H.	Orphan
White, Leo A.	6Feb1871		White, Daniel	Orphan
Gregory, Albert	8Feb1871		Gregory, M.	Orphan. Of color. Cancelled 8Sept1874, Albert having absconded
Gregory, Henry	8Feb1871		Gregory, M.	Orphan. Of color
Gregory, America	8Feb1871		Gregory, M.	Orphan. Of color
Robbins, Bennett	6Mar1871		Burford, Mary (Mrs)	
Yelvington, Rachel	7Aug1871		Tucker, Jackson	Orphan. Of color

Name	Date	Age	Name	Notes
Taylor, Rallins	6Dec1871		Tayler, John A.	Orphan. Of color
McDonald, Ellen E.	2Apr1872		Moore, John W.	Orphan
Tanner, Wesley	2July1872		Tanner, William A.	Orphan. Of color
Little, Mary	5Aug1872		Lanier, Elizabeth	Orphan. Of color
James, Isam	5Aug1872		Green, Sarah A.	Orphan. Of color
Oldham, Stanton	4Feb1873	13 yrs	Anderson, H. C.	Orphan. Of color
Oldham, Richard	4Feb1873	11 yrs	Anderson, H. C.	Orphan. Of color
Oldham, Ralph	4Feb1873	9 yrs	Anderson, H. C.	Orphan. Of color
Buttler, Dennie	9Apr1873	14 yrs	Lea, Nash	Orphan. Both of color
Buttler, Cornelia	9Apr1873	9 yrs	Lea, Nash	Orphan. Both of color
Buttler, Cola P.	9Apr1873	5 yrs	Lea, Nash	Orphan. Both of color
Irvin, William	6May1873		Taylor, Edmond	Orphan. Both of color
Buttler, Elvira	6May1873		Austin, Annanias	Orphan. Both of color
Buttler, Annanias	6May1873		Austin, Annanias	Orphan. Both of color
Adams, John	4Aug1873		Newman, L. C.	Orphan
West, Allan	4Nov1873	11 yrs	West, W. B.	Farmer. Of color
Bond, John	6Jan1874		Henderson, William	Orphan. Of color
Bond, Henry	6Jan1874		Henderson, Scott	Orphan. Of color
Towey, Simeon	2Mar1874	17 yrs	Towey, Alexander	Farmer. Both of color
Towey, Vicious	2Mar1874	13 yrs	Towey, Alexander	Farmer. Both of color
Gill, Philus	3Mar1874	10 yrs	Gill, Julius	Farmer. Of color
Gill, Tom	3Mar1874	6 yrs	Gill, Julius	Farmer. Of color
White, Willie	9Sept1875	7 yrs	Jones, Burell	Farmer. Of color. Recorded Bond Bk p140
Smith, Rose	4Dec1875	3 yrs	Tibbs, Clara	Housekeeping, sewing and farming. Both of color
Smith, Charles	22Dec1883	b. 30Aug1882	Wilson, J. R.	Illegitimate son of Rachel Smith, who consents. Unable to support

Henry County

Name	Date	Age	Master	Notes
Gainer, William	6Mar1824		Miller, James	
Grace, John L.	16Sept1825		Davis, Archibald	Orphan. Tailor
Craig, James Mansfield	5Mar1827		Persise, John B.	Hatter. Re-recorded 13Mar1827. Orphan. Rescinded 11June1827
Mooney, Thomas	5Dec1827		Maxwell, John	Orphan
Williams, William Riley	2June1828	Abt 4 yrs	Gray, Thomas	Illegitimate son of Elizabeth Williams
Elkins, Claiborn	8Dec1828		Menus, Henry C.	For 4 yrs. Saddler
Watson, Leroy	8Dec1828		Menus, Henry C.	For 6 yrs 6 mo. Saddler
Elkins, William	8Dec1828		Davis, Archibald	For 7 yrs 9 mo. Tailor
Mooney, William	8Dec1828		Martin, Robert	For 11 yrs. Farmer
Dennis, Stephen	14Sept1829		Menus, Henry C.	For 10 yrs. Sadler. Cancelled 11Mar1833
Bracken, Isaac	7Dec1829		Bushart, John	For 4 yrs. Blacksmith
Withers, Elisha	7June1830		Palmer, John L.	For 9 yrs. Farmer
Dunn, Robert H.	6Dec1830		Roberts, Charles	For 3 yrs 6 mo. Tanner & curryer
Dunn, Thomas J.	6Dec1830		Roberts, Charles	For 3 yrs 6 mo. Tanner & curryer
Lamberth, Hezekiah	6Dec1830		Mix, George W.	For 3 yrs. Wool carder
Price, William	7Mar1831		Moore, John	For 15 yrs
French, Noah	7Mar1831		Johnston, William H.	For 7 yrs. Tanner
Rawls, Madison	8Mar1831		Eggers, John H.	For 10 yrs. Taylor
Watson, Elbert	14Mar1831		Davis, Archibald	Taylor. Cancelled 22Dec1834*. Same date Nathaniel Crockett apptd guardian. Orphan of Oran D. Watson, Dcd. Sibs Martha, Emanuel D. & Simeon
Brown, John	7Mar1832		Caldwell, Edward W.	Bricklayer
Cooksey, Mary Ann	4June1832		Green, John	For 10 yrs. Seamstress
Unnamed male	4June1832		Wimberly, William	For 14 yrs. Farmer
Millikin, Leander	11June1832		Swor, Robert	Farmer
Cooxey, Samuel	13June1832		McCorkle, Alexander	For 6 yrs. Blacksmith

Name	Date	Notes
Carter, Jerome	10Dec1832	For 6 yrs. Farmer
Smith, Betsy Ann	4Mar1833	For 8 yrs. Seamstress
Young, William A.	11Mar1833	For 17 yrs. Farmer
French, Berry	3June1833	For 11 yrs. Farmer
Williams, William	3June1833	For 10 yrs. Tanner. Cancelled 2Sept1833
Price, Terrell	24Dec1833	For 18 yrs. Wheel wright
Myrick George W.	30Dec1833	For 7 yrs. Boot & shoemaker. Same date Samuel Myrick appointed administrator of Harrison Myrick, Dcd
Norman, William	31Mar1834	For 16 yrs. Farmer
Guyman, Noah	31Mar1834	Tanner. Cancelled 6Nov1837
Guyman, John	31Mar1834	Tanner
Guyman, Thomas	31Mar1834	For 5 yrs. Farmer
Guyman, James	31Mar1834	For 8 yrs. Tanner
Price, Reuben T.	22Dec1834	For 17 yrs. Farmer
Buchanan, Henry F.	22Dec1834	For 14 yrs. Farmer. Cancelled 23Mar1835
Baker, Green N.	29June1835	For 14 yrs 9 mo
Baker, James McD.	29June1835	For 14 yrs 9 mo
Upchurch, Reuben	28Sept1835	Farmer
Baker, John	28Dec1835	For 7 yrs. Farmer
Guyman, Noah	6Nov1837	For 6 yrs. Farmer
Smoot, Elizabeth	6Nov1837	For 7 yrs. Seamstress
Ross, John G.	4Mar1839	For 14 yrs. Brick layer & plasterer
Sylvester, John	5Oct1840	For 12 yrs. Farmer
Yarbrough, William	6Dec1841	For 6 yrs 5 mo. Tanner & curier
Hening, Henry	7Mar1842	For 11 yrs. Farmer
Morgan, John	2May1842	Tailor
Williams, James R.	2May1842	Tailor
Herrin, Henry Clay	2Jan1843	Farmer
Muckling, Samuel	2Jan1843	For 11 yrs. Farmer
Bomar, Willis	1May1843	For 5 yrs 4 mo. Farmer. Rescinded 7June1847, as Willis Bonner
Wimberly, William P.	1May1843	Farmer. Cancelled 5June1843

Curlin, Hugh	
Watkins, James	
Young, George	
Lee, George	
Kendall, Richmond. G.	
Martin, Abraham	
Altom, Thomas B.	
Buchanan, Daniel	
Kendall, Richmond. G.	
Kendall, Richmond. G.	
Etheridge, David	
Waller, Ralph L.	
Edwards, Joseph	
Graham, Daniel	
Watkins, James	
Watkins, James	
Upchurch, John	
Davidson, Josiah	
Kilgore, James D.	
Jenkins, Robert M,	
Jackson, John F.	
Moore, John H.	
Kendall, Richmond. G.	
Crawley, William	
Brown, Jesse A.	
Brown, Jesse A.	
Crawley, William	
Poyner, Peter	
Aycock, James W.	
Wimberly, Noah	

Name	Age	Date	Master	Notes
Wimberly, Sarah		1May1843	Wimberly, Noah	Seamstress. Cancelled 5June1843
Grainger, William Henry Harrison		1May1843	Gibson, Elizabeth	For 19 yrs. Farmer
Rial, Thomas		1Jan1844	Corley, Catlet?	For 7 yrs. Farmer
Rial, James Calvin		5Feb1844	Watkins, James	For 13 yrs. Farmer
Rogers, William		5Feb1844	Peden, Cornelius	For 6 yrs. Cabinett maker
Hill, William		5Feb1844	Whitlock, Hardin	For 7 yrs. Farmer
Carter, Columbus L.		5Feb1844	Moore, James H.	For 18 yrs. Farmer
Williams, Gabriel James		2Dec1844	Williams, Zelia H.	For 10 yrs from 4Jan1845. Farmer. Canc 2Dec1850. To Dilliard R. Williams, Guardian
Williams, Susan		2Dec1844	Williams, Zelia H.	For 11 yrs from 3Jan1845. Spinster
Marberry, William		6Oct1845	Marberry, John	For 10 yrs. Farmer
Marberry, Pleasant		6Oct1845	Marberry, John	For 16 yrs. Farmer
Townley, Littleton		3Nov1845	Wafferd, John S.	Farmer
Townley, George		3Nov1845	Wafferd, John S.	Farmer
Kendall, William G.		3Nov1845	Hanry, John H.	Farming
Kendall, Peter		3Nov1845	Hanry, John H.	Farming
Dorch, Columbus		5Jan1846	Peden, Cornelius	For 3 yrs from 7Sept next. Cabnett workman. Rescinded 7Mar1846
Glass, Faranklin (Franklin?)		5Jan1846	Bond, James	For 16 yrs from Dec1845. Farmer
McAdoo, Bethomel P.		6Jan1846	Brown, Jesse A.	For 7 yrs. Taylor. Cancelled 4Sept1848
McAdoo, Robert B.		6Jan1846	Brown, Jesse A.	For 7 yrs. Taylor. Cancelled 4Sept1848
Spran?, William T.		2Feb1846	Harrison, William Henry	For 10 yrs from 25Aug1846. Farmer
Griffin, Thomas		6Apr1846	Foster, Robert A.	Sadler. Rescinded 7July1846
Bevill, John F.		6Apr1846	Peden, Cornelius	Cabinett workeman. On 6July1846 Oswell Potts apptd guardian to minor orphans of Martin Bevill, Dcd
Guin, Jacob		5May1846	Peden, Cornelius	Cabinett maker. Schooling requirement decreased to 5 mo 3Sept1849
McCarter, Andrew		1June1846	Guthrie, Robert	For 12 yrs from 16Jan1846
McArty, John		3Aug1846	Jones?, Gray	For 15 yrs from 1Sept1846. Farmer

Charlott	Durt?, W. J.		Of color. Rescinded 4Jan1847
Peter	Foster, Robert A.	1Mar1847	For 14 yrs. Of color. Sadler. Cancelled 7Aug1848
Charlotte	Foster, Robert A.	1Mar1847	For 7 yrs. Spinster & seamstress. Of color. Cancelled 7Aug1848
Smith, John J.	Lorell?, S. C.		Rescinded 3May1847
Coplinger, John S.	Coplinger, K. H.	7June1847	Farmer
Coplinger, Lucinda	Coplinger, K. H.	7June1847	Spinster
Coplinger, Tennessee	Coplinger, K. H.	7June1847	Spinster
Coplinger, Samuel?	Coplinger, K. H.	7June1847	Farmer
Deavlin, Charles	Sweat, John D.	2Aug1847	For 5 (4?) yrs. Farmer
Lewathen?, Richard	Peden, Cornelius	6Dec1847	Cabinant workeman
Hentry?, Miles B.	Derington, J. W.	6Mar1848	Wagon maker
Turbabille, James	Turbabille, William H.	1May1848	Farmer
Smith, Joseph	Avery, Elisha	3July1848	For 12 yrs. Farmer
Smith, Eliza	Kery, James P.	3July1848	For 12 yrs. Seemstress
Hudspeth, James Westley	Hudspeth, James W.	7Aug1848	For 11 yrs from 1Nov1848. Farmer. On 7May1849 Mary & Samuel C. Henderson asked that indenture be rescinded. No action recorded
Charlotte	Wright, Thornton F.	7Aug1848	For 6 yrs from 1Mar1848. Of color. Rescinded 4Sept1848
Peter	Wright, Thornton F.	7Aug1848	For 13 yrs from 1Mar1848. Of color. Rescinded 4Sept1848
Peter	Foster, Robert A., Edmunds, James T. & Cooney, John	4Sept1848	For 13 yrs from 1Mar1848. Of color. Sadler. Removed from Foster for inhumane treatment 10Jan1856
Charlotte	Foster, Robert A., Edmunds, James T. & Cooney, John	4Sept1848	For 6 yrs from 1Mar1848. Of color. Seamstress. On 4Sept1854 Charlotte, a mulatto woman now in her 22nd year, given certificate of freedom
Mcadoo, Bethuel P.	Alterie, Rowlern W.	4Sept1848	Shoe maker
Mcadoo, Robert B.	Newell, John W.	4Sept1848	For 5 yrs. Taylor
Ingram, James	Gold, John	6Nov1848	Farmer
Griffine, Calvin	Shunkle?, William	4Dec1848	Farmer
Macadoo, Pusa	Arnette, Andrew J.	5Mar1849	Blacksmith. Same date Thomas L. Dewell? apptd guardian of orphans of Alfred Mcadoo, Dcd

Name	Date	Age	Master	Notes
Trout, Calvin M.	5Mar1849		Bucey, John M.	Farmer
Shirley, Richard	2Apr1849		Gram, William F.	Farmer
Spencer, Sarah E.	7May1849		Midyett, Micajah	For 8 yrs. Orphan. Seamstress
Duffell, William B.	4June1849		Brizentine, William L.	Farmer
Griffine, William H.	4June1849		Wainscott, William	Farmer. Cancelled 1Dec1851, as Henry Griffin
Griffine, Richard C.	4June1849		Wainscott, William	Farmer. Cancelled 5Apr1852, as Richard Calvin Griffin
Spencer, John	4June1849		Leferur, William	Farmer. Cancelled 3Jan1853
Hudspeth, Jane	3July1849		Brown, Jesse A.	Spinster. On 2Sept1856, Jane, of color, now in her 22nd year, given certificate of freedom
Hudspeth, Peter	3July1849		Brown, Jesse A.	Farmer
Hudspeth, Isiah	3July1849		Pryor, William	Farmer
Hudspeth, Allis	3July1849		Pryor, William	Seamstress
McCarty, Elizabeth	3Sept1849		Culpepper, James H.	Pauper. Seamstress
Wellsone?, Rigella E	3Sept1849		Brooks, William H.	Spinster. Cancelled 3Mar1851, as L. E. Willson
McLane, Joseph	5Nov1849		Barton, James	Farmer. Cancelled 3Mar1851
McLane, John Westley	5Nov1849		Paschall, G. W.	Farmer
Snider, Samuel P.	5Mar1850		Peden, Cornelius	For 7 yrs. Cabinet maker
Snider, Thomas W.	5Mar1850		Peden, Cornelius	For 5 yrs. Cabinet maker
Ables, John	1Apr1850		Rateree, James E.	Farmer
Smoot, John	6May1850		English, James	Farmer
Richardson, Loving O.	1July1850		Swinney, William A.	Farmer
Mason, John	2Dec1850		Brizendine, Stephen A.	Farmer. Cancelled 3Oct1853
Gates, Mare A.	3Mar1851		Simpson, John	Seamstress
Mason, Wright	3Mar1851		Beard, Seivere?	Farmer
Griffin, Henry	1Dec1851		Wimberly, John	Farmer
Ashly, Nancy A. E.	6Dec1852		Mallard, Richard	For 11 yrs. Seamstress
Spencer, John	3Jan1853		Lefevre, John	Farmer
Alexander, William Henry	7Feb1853		Ethridge, J. A.	Farmer
Alexander, Joseph T.	7Feb1853		Alexander, Samuel W.	Farmer. Cancelled 7Mar1853
Alexander, Joseph T.	7Mar1853		Ethridge, Allen	Farmer

Name	Date	Term	Bound to	Notes
Derrington, Laura T.	4Sept1854		Metheney, John P.	Spinster
Mossman, William	6Nov1854		Hughes, C. T.	For 14 yrs. Farmer
Peter	5Feb1856		Kendall, Samuel	For 5 yrs. Sadler. "Yellow boy."
McCarty, James R. T.			Blythe, A. J.	Cancelled 2June1856
Davis, Julia Ann	10Apr1857		Wilson, Edward	For 11 yrs from 10Apr1857. Spinster
Thomas	2Feb1858		Hicks, A. J.	For 14 yrs. Of color
Asia	2Feb1858		Hicks, A. J.	For 13 yrs 8 mo or until 18 y/o. Of color
Williams, Henrietta	3May1858		Porter, Sr, J. D.	Spinster
Williams, Margaret	3May1858		Porter, Sr, J. D.	Spinster
Williams, Alice	3May1858		Porter, Sr, J. D.	Spinster
Adams, John Q.	2Aug1858		Jenkins, John L.	For 7 yrs 8 mo. Rescinded next day at request of mother, Rachel Adams
Henry	2Aug1858		Crutchfield, Charles B.	For 15 yrs. Of color
Henrietta	7Nov1859		Lewis, John C.	Bond renewed 5Mar1861. Of color. Spinster
Alace	7Nov1859		Lewis, John C.	Bond renewed 5Mar1861. Of color. Spinster
Margaret	7Nov1859		Moon, W. R.	Spinster. Of color
Simpson, James P. S.	6Feb1860		Davis, Lewis	For 9 yrs
Henrietta	5Aug1861	6 yrs	Walker, V. B.	Until 18 yrs. Of color
Alace	5Aug1861	Abt 3 yrs	Walker, V. B.	Until 18 yrs. Of color
Bayley, Henry L.	8Jan1863		Watkins, William	For 15 yrs from 8Jan1863
Jones, Alexander B.	2Feb1863		McKelvey, Meredith	For 20 yrs. Farmer
McCloud, Hardin	2Mar1863		Edmunds, James M.	For 14 yrs. Farmer
Beaver, Mary Jane	1Jan1866		Wharton, George B.	For 7 yrs
Atkins, Alexander	2July1867		Atkins, John D. C.	For 15 yrs from 2July1867. Of color
Dunlap, Manda	2July1867	Abt 11 yrs (from canc entry)	Dunlap, John H.	For 13 yrs from 2July1867. Of color. Cancelled 2Oct1871. "Susanah" having left
Dunlap, Mary Bell	2Sept1867		Dunlap, R. E.	For 6 yrs. Of color
Crumpton, David	3Sept1867		Fryor, Thomas C.	For 13 yrs. Of color
Kendall, Andy	7Oct1867		Kendall, R. A. (Mrs)	Of color
Kendall, Malinda	7Oct1867		Kendall, R. A. (Mrs)	Of color
Kendall, Alice	7Oct1867		Kendall, R. A. (Mrs)	Of color

Name	Date	Age	Master	Notes
Hicks, George F.	7Oct1867		Hardison, George W.	For 15 yrs
Loving, Mitty	4Nov1867		Loving, S.	Of color
Boyd, John A.	9Jan1868		Chilcutt, John M	
Hester, Clint	7Oct1868		Clark, A. J.	For 8 yrs. Of color
Jones, Watt	7Oct1868		Jones, A. B.	For 7 yrs. On 5Nov1868 Julius Burras & Mary Ann, his wife (Watt's mother), ask cancellation of indenture. Denied 6Feb1869. Appealed to Circuit Court 7June1869
Frazier, George	Nov18687	15 yrs	Frazier, Constantine	Cancelled 11Jan1869. Of color. Data from cancellation entry
Bowden, George	5Feb1869		Bowden, B. D.	Farming. Of color
Bowden, Ann	1Mar1869		Bowden, E. G.	Until 21 yrs. Of color
Haymes, Eliza	6Sept1869		Haymes, Charles	Until 20 yrs. Of color
Bush, Rheuben	6Sept1869		Dorns, Felix P.	
Church, Henry	6Sept1869		Tomlinson, W. J.	
Somers, Frank	4Oct1869		Wooddard, E.	Of color. Farming. Re-recorded 5Oct1869
Poyner, Joseph R.	1Nov1869		Poyner, J. C.	Farmer
Poyner, J. D.	1Nov1869		Poyner, J. C.	Farmer
Randle, George	2Nov1869		Campbell, Alex	Farmer
Steele, Polly	6Dec1869		Lovelace, H. H.	Housekeeping
Darnell, Charley	6Dec1869		Randle, W. G.	Farming
Darnell, Henry	6Dec1869		Randle, W. G.	Farming
Brizendine, Charley Edward	3Jan1870		Thompson, Matthew M.	
Trevathan, Susan	7Feb1870		Hurt, C. J. F.	Until 21 yrs. Of color
Ward, Leander	7Feb1870		Vaughn, W. F.	
Ward, Irvin	7Feb1870		Vaughn, Stephen	
Isley, James M.	4Apr1870	8 yrs	Ross, E. P.	Carpenter. Cancelled 3May1870
Thorpe, Isaac	5Apr1870	15 yrs	Thorpe, H. H.	Farmer. Cancelled 7Aug1874. Data from cancellation entry
Isley, James M.	3May1870		Green, William	
Cooper, William	6June1870	10 yrs	Duncan, E. H.	Farmer
Smith, Thomas	4July1870		Wilson, S. W.	
Lester, George	6Sept1870		Pryor, W. S.	Of color

Name	Date		Name	Notes
Loving, Mattie	4Oct1870		Birch, James	Until 21 yrs. Of color
Kirby, William R.	5July1871	Tender years	Douglass, W. A.	Farming. Parents, John & Rebecca Kirby, living apart. Consent of father. Mother takes pauper oath & appeals to Circuit Court
Merrell, Madona C.	7Aug1871		McKelvey, Meredith	Cancelled 21Aug1880, Madona having left McKelvey
Merrel, N. B.	7Aug1871		McKelvey, Meredith	Male
Polk, Coon Randolph	7Aug1871		Hudson, I. M.	
Randle, Bert	7Aug1871		Hudson, I. M.	
Turberville, Bob	7Aug1871		Turberville, Benjamin	
Turberville, Henry	7Aug1871		Turberville, Benjamin	
Dunlap, John	Jan1872		Sexton, Henry	Farming. Of color
Iseley, James	4Mar1872		Green, Samuel	
Carter, George	1Apr1872		Jones, Shelby	Until 21 yrs. Jones a freedman
Carter, Ada	1Apr1872		Jones, Shelby	Until 21 yrs. Jones a freedman
Turberville, Robert	6Aug1872		Turberville, J. D.	On 7Oct1872 John D. Turberville apptd guardian to Robert Turberville
Simpson, Clinton	4Nov1872		Hasting, J. M.	Farmer
Clark, John	5May1873		Cook, D. C.	For 8 yrs. Farming. Of color
Coleman, Loyed	2June1873		Cook, W. C.	Farmer
Darnell, Samuel	2Feb1874		Diggs, Jacob	Farmer
Presley, John W.	5Feb1874		Brown, Malindy J.	Farmer
Tharpe, Isaac	2Mar1874		Tharpe, John	Farmer. Both of color. Relinquished by H. H. Tharpe.
Todd, Charley	10Apr1874		Todd, J. M.	Farmer. Child of Hannah Todd, Dcd. 2Mar1874* Of color
Todd, Hannah	10Apr1874		Todd, J. M.	House servant. Child of Hannah Todd, Dcd 2Mar1874* Of color
Todd, Nicy	10Apr1874		Todd, R. H.	House servant. Prob child of Hannah Todd, Dcd 2Mar1874* Of color
Todd, Eliza	10Apr1874		Todd, J. M.	Farmer. Child of Hannah Todd, Dcd. 2Mar1874* Of color
Lucas, Docia	17Apr1874		McNeil, George	Seamstress
Lucas, Martha Ann	5July1874		Cox, John F.	Cancelled 30Aug1880, Martha having left Cox. Data from cancellation entry
Little, Margaret	6Oct1874		Smith, Sophronia	Seamstress

Name	Date	Age	Master	Notes
Owens, John N.	6Nov1874		Jackson, T. A.	Farmer. On 7Nov1874 A. J. Brown apptd guardian. Orphan of J. T. Owen
Cox, Alonzo	5Apr1875		Cox, Edmund	Farmer
Helms, Jefferson Dell	6Apr1875		England, W. F.	Farmer
Duff, George Washington Alexander Henderson	11Dec1875		Hastings, J. B.	At request of mother, Susanah America Maria Martha Duff. Farmer
Brake, Charley	7Aug1876		Clark, R. T.	Farmer
Sanders, William	4Dec1876		Bennett, E. (Mrs)	Farmer
Prince, Miles Morgan	4Dec1876		Lofon, A. M.	Farmer. Cancelled 1Nov1880. Prince gone
McNeill, Ben	18Feb1878		Bostic, J. S.	Farmer. Of color
Bonner, Walter N. R.	13May1878	6 yrs	Perry, Harberd	Farmer
Smith, Thomas J.	21Oct1878		Smith, Daniel	Farmer
Mellon, Elizabeth	12Dec1879		Wright, J. R.	Until 21 yrs. Of color
Calhoun, Toby	8Jan1880		McFadden, W. R.	Orphan. McFadden of color
Calhoun, Allen	8Jan1880		McFadden, W. R.	Orphan. Cancelled 1Mar1880. Unable to control. Both of color
Calhoun, Dora	8Jan1880		McFadden, W. R.	Orphan. Until 21 yrs. McFadden of color
Calhoun, Monroe	8Jan1880		McFadden, W. R.	Orphan. McFadden of color
Rogers, Charlie	24May1880		Rogers, Bob	Orphan. Both of color
Burris, Thomas Wyley	31Aug1880		Hicks, William Nelson	
Russell, James	31Mar1881		Marrs, John	Orphan
Burris, John	31Mar1881		Bagley, Timothy	Orphan

Lake County

Name	Date	Age	Master	Notes
Dorris, Laura	2Jan1871		Fowler, James R.	Daughter of ____ Dorris, Dcd. Housewifery
Dorris, Anna	2Jan1871		Fowler, James R.	Daughter of ____ Dorris, Dcd. Housewifery
Riley, Rob	2Jan1871		Riley, C. H.	Son of Rachael Riley, Dcd. Farming. Of color
Riley, Leroy	2Jan1871		Riley, C. H.	Son of Rachael Riley, Dcd. Farming. Of color
Fletcher, Francis M.	4Sept1871	11 yrs	Davis, W. A. J.	

Deberry, Sallie	7Oct1872		Deberry, W. W.	Daughter of Lucy Deberry, Dcd. Of color
Wallace, Martha	2Aug1875	12 yrs	Tipton, J. H.	Orphan
Hudgeons, Maggie	2Aug1875	10 yrs	Batt, Thomas A.	Orphan

Lauderdale County

Name	Date	Age	Master	Notes
Robison, Amandy Jane	4July1836		Chisum, Jemima	Orphan of Thomas Robison, Dcd
Robison, Elijah W.	4July1836		Chisum, Jemima	Orphan of Thomas Robison, Dcd. On 3Oct1842 William R. Chism (or Chisholm) named Administrator Of estate of Jemima
Robison, William T.	1Aug1836	11 yrs	Chisum, Henry T.	Planter and farmer. Orphan of Thomas Robison, Dcd. Cancelled 6Aug1838
Robison, Anna? N	1Aug1836	13 yrs	Chisum, William	Orphan of Thomas Robison, Dcd
Spain,	7Nov1836	11 yrs	Spain, Solomon D.	Pauper. Daughter of Solomon D. Spain, Dcd. Housewifery and spinster
Davis, William	7May1838	Between 13 & 14 yrs	Hooper, Samuel	Blacksmith. Cancelled 2July1838. To mother
Dyal, Mary Jane	2July1838	3 yrs	Dyal, Plesant G.	Cancelled 1Feb1841, as P. C. Dyal
Roberson, William T.	5Aug1838	13 yrs	Barnes, Nathaniel W.	Orphan. Farming
Bibb, Moses	4May1840		Farmer, Ezekial	Illegitimate son of Charlotte Bibb. Farming. On 1Feb1841 Farmer posted Bastardy Bond for an illegitimate child of Charlotte Bibb. Cancelled 6Nov1854, Farmer having left the county
Dyal, Mary Jane	1Feb1841		Elkins, Mary	Orphan
Robison, Elijah W.	7Nov1842	11 yrs on 12Mar1842	Meadows, Hiram	Orphan. Farmer
Wynns, Celia Ann	7Jan1845		Campbell, L. M.	Orphan of James Wynns, Dcd. Sibling John Wynns to be cared for by James A. Lackey
Wynns, James	7Jan1845		Williams, George R.	Orphan of James Wynns, Dcd. See above
Wynn, John	7July1845		Moore, John B.	Orphan of James Wynns, Dcd. Cancelled 5Oct1846, as Moore's wife now dead

Name	Date	Age	Master	Notes
Willis, John W.	3Nov1845	Under 14 yrs	Measles, Hardy	No father or mother. Son of John J. Willis, Dcd. 6Oct1845
Gilstrap, William	5Jan1846		White, John M.	Orphan. Son of Rebecca Gilstrap 7Nov1845. On 3May1847 allegation of brutal treatment made on 5April1847 rejected
Gilstrap, Susan	6Apr1846	9 yrs	Hagar, Steely	Orphan. Dau of Rebecca Gilstrap 7Nov1845
Winn, John	5Oct1846	Abt 4 yrs	Haynes, James A.	Orphan. Saddler
Gilstrap, Amanda	6Sept1847		Waddle, William	Orphan. 2Aug1847*
Gilstrap, Barnett	6Sept1847		Hall, Robert S.	Orphan. 2Aug1847*
Slater, John Perry	1Nov1847		Smith, John A.	Orphan. Has siblings Aubrey, Thomas, Harriet and Patsy 1Sept1847
Gilstrap, Barnett	3Feb1852		White, Samuel	Orphan
Langley, James	7June1852		Henderson, Hezekiah	Orphan of John Langley. On 5July1852 payment to Robertson Meadows for keeping infant child of John Langley, Dcd. for the remainder of the year .
Langley, William	7June1852		Patterson, Alvin C.	Orphan of John Langley. See above
Smith, Jefferson	6July1852		Barfield, Ira G.	Orphan. Stepchild of Thomas McPherson 5July1852
Smith, Alonzo	6July1852		Rush, Carroll B.	Orphan. Stepchild of Thomas McPherson 5July1852. Cancelled 2May1853
Smith, Alonzo	2May1853		Blankenship, J. W.	On 7June1858 ordered removed from Blankenship for abuse. Cancelled 6July1858
Pitchford, John C.	3July1854	6 yrs	Wakefield, Ezekiel S.	Bound at John's request. Orphan
Moses	6Nov1854		Oldham, Robert H.	Of color. See Moses Bibb. On 4Feb1861 "Moses alias Bibb" posted bond as a free man of color
Denny, Thomas	6Oct1856		Parker, William	Orphan of Alfred Denny, Dcd
Barber, James E.	6Jan1857	Abt 10 yrs	Jacobs, Mary	Orphan. On 3Oct1853 2 minor children of James Barber ordered brought to court
Phillips, Zach	3Aug1857		Quinn, John K.	Orphan. Cancelled 5Dec1859
Reynolds, Catherine	5Apr1858		Gillespie, James	Orphan of Henry Reynolds, Dcd. Has two siblings 6July1857. Cancelled 3Oct1859 due to Kate's weak intellect
Smith, Alonzo	5Oct1858		Barfield, Fred	Orphan
Ball, William	2May1859		Keltner, Jacob. B.	Orphan
Phillips, Zach	5Dec1859		Sumerow, Benjamin F.	Orphan

Name	Date	Age	Bound to	Notes
Rhinda	4Apr1860			Of color
Elln [sic]	7Apr1860			Of color
Titus, Dave	2Sept1861		Morrow, J. A.	Request of William Titus, father. Of color
Titus, Cris	2Sept1861		Henry, William A.	Request of William Titus, father. Of color
Titus, Isaac	2Sept1861		Henry, William A.	Request of William Titus, father. Of color
Titus, Joe	2Sept1861		Henry, William A.	Request of William Titus, father. Of color
Titus, Jess	2Sept1861		Henry, William A.	Request of William Titus, father. Of color
Titus, Lunsford	4Nov1861	17 yrs in Jan1861	Henry, William A.	Servant. Of color
Titus, Henry	4Nov1861	18 yrs in Mar1861	Henry, William A.	Servant. Of color
Kirkpatrick, Robert	4Nov1861	6 yrs on 3July last	Carlton, B. A.	Until 20 yrs. Farming
Kirkpatrick, Jackson	4Nov1861	5 yrs on 23Sept last	Carlton, B. A.	Until 20 yrs. Farming
Langley, F. N.	8Jan1862	12 yrs 10 mo 11 d	Paterson, Alvin C.	Until 20 yrs
Reynolds, Cate	4Aug1862	Abt 11 yrs	Reynolds, Nicholas	Orphan. Cancelled 5Mar1866 at request of Prudence Reynolds, administrator and widow of Nicholas Reynolds, Dcd
Akin, James	3Nov1862	Abt 6 yrs	Gudyer, M. W.	Cancelled 7Mar1864. To be cared for by Benjamin Kirby
Church	28Dec1865	10 yrs	Partee, Hiram	By FB. Farm labor. Orphan. Of color
Monroe	28Dec1865	10 yrs	Partee, Hiram	By FB. Farm labor. Orphan. Of color
Robert	28Dec1865	13 yrs	Partee, Hiram	By FB. Farm labor. Orphan. Of color
Gilley	28Dec1865	6 yrs	Partee, Hiram	By FB. Farm labor. Orphan. Of color
Robert	28Dec1865	13 yrs	Partee, Hiram	By FB. Farm labor. Orphan. Of color
Reynolds, Kate	5Mar1866		Crawford, J. S.	Cancelled 4Feb1867, Crawford having left the county
Eliza	3Apr1866	b. October 1854	Halliburton, R. L.	Freedman
Emma	3Apr1866	b. July 1858	Halliburton, R. L.	Freedman
David	3Apr1866	b. June 1860	Halliburton, R. L.	Freedman
Lucinda	3Apr1866	b. May 1862	Halliburton, R. L.	Freedman
Henry Thomas	4Apr1866	b. 2July1853	Wardlaw, J. N.	Orphan and freedman
Ellen	4Apr1866	b. 5Feb1855	Wardlaw, J. N.	Orphan and freedman
Emma	4Apr1866	b. 15Feb1857	Wardlaw, J. N.	Orphan and freedman
Anthony	4Apr1866	Abt 7 yrs	Cherry, Sarah A. (Mrs)	Freedman
Cobb, Alfred	7May1866		Cobb, Jesse	Freed person of color

Name	Date	Age	Master	Notes
Cobb, Martha	7May1866		Cobb, Jesse	Until 21 yrs. Freed person of color
Cobb, Paul	7May1866		Cobb, Jesse	Freed person of color
Cobb, Nancy	7May1866		Cobb, Jesse	Until 21 yrs. Freed person of color
Cobb, Mary	7May1866		Cobb, Jesse	Until 21 yrs. Freed person of color
Cobb, Henry	7May1866		Cobb, Jesse	Freed person of color
Hester	7May1866		Walker, Benjamin D.	Until 21 yrs. Freed person of color
Nina	7May1866		Walker, Benjamin D.	Until 21 yrs. Freed person of color
Fisher, Joseph	4June1866	11 yrs on 15Mar1866	Fisher, Bolling S.	Orphan. Plantation work. Of color
Fisher, Ned	4June1866	9 yrs on 1Mar1866	Fisher, Bolling S.	Orphan. Plantation work. Of color
Moorer, Ellen	4June1866	b. 30Oct1854	Moorer, William A.	Until 21 yrs. Orphan. Plantation work. Of color
Strain, Henry	4June1866	Abt 10 yrs	Strain, A. B.	Orphan. Freedman. Plantation work
Henry Bryant	2July1866	b. 1Aug1855	Coleman, John A.	Until 21 yrs. Freed orphan. Plantation work. On 8Feb1870 removal to Haywood Co allowed
Mary Eliza	2July1866	b. 16June1858	Coleman, John A.	Until 21 yrs. Freed orphan. Plantation work. On 8Feb1870 removal to Haywood Co allowed
Emma Etta	2July1866	b. 6June1861	Coleman, John A.	Until 21 yrs. Freed orphan. Plantation work. On 8Feb1870 removal to Haywood Co allowed
Arnold, Ella	3July1866	11 yrs 9 mo	Wilkerson, F. M.	Until 21 yrs. Freed orphan. Plantation work
Scott, Abner	6Aug1866	Abt 11 yrs	Jeffreys, Joseph	Orphan. Plantation work
Alston, Nancy	3Sept1866	7 yrs in May1866	Alston, Susannah (Mrs)	Orphan freedman
Currie, Joella	2Oct1866	b. 5Dec1860	Currie, Nancy	Freedman
Jordan, Edmend	2Oct1866	b. August 1853	Greaves, E. A. & Henrietta, his wife	Freedman
Jordan, Moses	2Oct1866	b. 1855	Jordan, John G.	Freedman
King	2Oct1866	b. March 1860	Ferguson, Felix G.	Freedman
John	5Nov1866	Abt 15 yrs	Glenn, N. C.	Freed orphan
Hancock, Tom	5Nov1866	Abt 15 yrs	Hancock, John	Freedman
Glenn, Malinda	5Nov1866	Abt 14 yrs	Glenn, Nancy (Mrs)	Until 21 yrs. Freedman

Child	Date	Age/Birth	Bound to	Notes
Fisher, Joseph	3Dec1866		Warren, Harriet S.	Orphan born & raised in this county. Appealed to Circuit Ct by Wills Thompson
Childress, James Washington	3Dec1866	b. 4May1852	Perkins, Levi	Orphan of Jesse Childress, Dcd.
Lewis, John Henry	9Jan1867		Dickerson, William E.	Freedman
Green, David	9Jan1867	13 yrs on 20Dec1865	Green, James L.	Freedman
Green, Claiborne	9Jan1867	10 yrs on 15Dec1865	Green, James L.	Freedman
Green, Henry	9Jan1867	5 yrs on 1July1865	Green, James L.	Freedman
Green, Delia	9Jan1867	3 yrs on 10July1865	Green, James L.	Until 21 yrs. Freedman
Terry, John	9Jan1867	Abt 15 yrs	Gaines, A. M.	Freedman
Webb, Joshua	9Jan1867	b. March 1854	Webb, W. A.	Freedman orphan
Moorer, Thomas	4Feb1867	Abt 18 yrs	Moorer, William H.	Freedman orphan
Reynolds, Cate	4Feb1867	Abt 13 yrs	Westbrook, P. H.	Orphan. Cancelled 2Nov1868
Blane, Celia Ann	4Feb1867		Rice, Shedrick	Freedman
Fortune, Dock	4Feb1867		McConico, W. C.	Freedman
Bym, Sarah Matilda	4Feb1867	b. 15Oct1859	Bym, Thomas J.	Freedman
Mann, Lea	5Feb1867	Abt 5 yrs	Mann, Joel B.	Freedman girl
Conner, Malinda	5Feb1867	Abt 6 yrs	Conner, William	Freedman
Andrews, Robert A.	4Mar1867	b. Abt 1855	Fisher, Ed	
Andrews, James M.	4Mar1867	Bet 14 & 15 yrs	Fisher, Thomas E.	
Reed, Ryley	5Mar1867	Abt 16 yrs	Webb, Miles D.	Orphan
Gingery, Israel	1Apr1867	b. 10Feb1860	Gingery, Jacob	Freedman orphan
Moorer, Frank	2Apr1867	b. January 1861	Moorer, William H.	Freedman orphan
Taylor, Jacob	3June1867	b. 8March1856	Machin, James S.	Freedman
Perkins, James	July1867	b. 14Feb1860	Chambers, John G.	Rescinded 4Nov1867. Mother living & able to support him. Data from Nov1867 entry
Somerow, Salina	5Aug1867	b. 15April1856	Tucker, William H.	Cancelled 2Sept1867. Returned to care of Robert & Rosetta Kennen? while mother out of the county. Of color

Name	Date	Age	Master	Notes
Wright, Almira	5Aug1867	b. 10Aug1857	Tucker, M. G.	
Fortune, William	2Sept1867	b. 25Dec1857	Henning, D. M.	Freedman orphan
Turner, Benjamin A.	8Oct1867	b. 7June1866	Shaw, J. W.	
Shaw, Prince	4Nov1867	b. 20Dec1860	Capelle, W. A.	Orphan
Walker, Ned	4Nov1867	b. July 1856	Henning, J. L.	Orphan. Of color
Powell, Sampson	3Dec1867	b. Abt 1855	Henning, D. M.	Orphan. Of color
Powell, Grant	3Dec1867	b. Abt 1853	Henning, D. M.	Orphan. Of color
Turner, Ellen	3Dec1867	b. 1857	Turner, William	Orphan. Of color
Turner, Susan	3Dec1867	b. 1860	Turner, William	Orphan. Of color
Turner, Bettie	3Dec1867	b. 1863	Turner, E. G.	Orphan. Of color
Turner, Peggy	3Dec1867		Turner, William	Orphan. Bond guaranteeing her care posted, but not formally apprenticed. Of color
Turner, Mariah	3Dec1867		Turner, William	Orphan. Bond guaranteeing her care posted, but not formally apprenticed. Of color
Turner, Harriet	3Dec1867		Turner, William	Orphan. Bond guaranteeing her care posted, but not formally apprenticed. Of color
Green, Mozela	4May1868		Green, A. A.	Freedman
Green, Louiza	4May1868		Green, A. A.	Freedman
Stone, Wesley	4May1868		Posey, A. W.	
Porter, Calvin	1June1868		Porter, Hiram	Freedman
Nelson, Henry	1June1868		Porter, Hiram	Freedman
Fitzpatrick, Mary Francis	1June1868		Jones, Edwinia (Mrs)	Orphan. Of color
Fitzpatrick, Ben	1June1868		Jones, Edwinia (Mrs)	Orphan. Of color
Davis, Tom	6July1868		Henning, Rachel (Mrs)	Freedman
Hardin, William	6July1868		Henning, Rachel (Mrs)	Freedman
Somerow, Georgeanna	3Aug1868	b. 1861	Somerow, J. M.	Freedman. 6Dec1869*
Alsabrook, Albert	3Aug1868	b. Abt 1859	Alsabrook, James C.	Freedman
Currie, Sophia	6Oct1868	b. April 1857	Currie, David B.	Freedman. Dau of Rebeca Green 3Aug1868
Green, Thomas	6Oct1868	b. 13May1862	Currie, David B.	Freedman. Son of Rebeca Green 3Aug1868
Richardson, Monica	2Nov1868		Burke, R. A.	Freedman

Name	Date	Birth	Guardian	Notes
Rice, Betsy	11Dec1868		Heaning, A. B.	Orphan freedman
Bibb, Richard Clay	1Feb1869	b. 15Feb1861	Bradford, W. R.	
Acuff, Leander	2Mar1869		Singleton, W. H.	Orphan. On 3Mar1869 B. F. Lackey ordered to sell personal property of James & Sarah Acuff, Dcd, for benefit of children. On 7June1869 Benjamin F. Boydston apptd guardian of Henry, Leander, Martha, Nedd, & Laban Acuff
Burks (Bucks?), Henry	5Oct1869	b. 1860	Jenkins, Jack	Of color
Jenkins, George	5Oct1869	b. 1867	Jenkins, R. G.	Of color
Porter, Wilson	1Nov1869	b. Abt 1Nov1859	Read, Laura E. (Mrs)	No parents living in county. Of color
Maclin, Robert	4Jan1870	b. Abt 1856	Oldham, Edward R.	Of color. On 7April1870 Oldham ordered to bring Maclin to Court. Cancelled 6July1870. Returned to grandmother, Sally Walker, who had had his care since his mother's death. Appealed to Circuit Court
Lucy	6June1870	b. Abt 1861	Partee, Hiram	Of color
Martin, William	5Sept1870	b. Abt 1865	Dunaway, S. H.	Orphan
Bond, James	4Oct1870		Wilkerson, W. D.	Of color
Butler, William	9Nov1870	b. 16Mar1854	Thurmond, O. L.	Cancelled 5May1875, William having left
Butler, Ben G.	9Nov1870	b. 1856	Thurmond, O. L.	
Gidcombe, John	5Dec1870	b. June 1863	Alston, Thomas P.	Cancelled 2Dec1872
Dunaway, Wesley	3Jan1872	b. November 1860	Parker, A. D.	Orphan. Of color
Porter, Anna	4Mar1872	b. 1867	Partee, Hiram	Of color
Scott, Orrang	6May1872	b. 1866	Groves, Thomas H.	No parents living in county. Of color
Bond, John	2Sept1872	b. 1867	Ruth, James V.	Of color
Bond, Eliza	2Sept1872	b. 1871	Ruth, James V.	Of color
Gidcombe, John	2Dec1872		Alston, A. B.	
Gidcombe, Samuel	2Dec1872		Alston, J. L.	
Chipman, Sam	8Jan1873	9 yrs in Nov 18??	Chipman, George	Of color
White, Joseph	3Nov1873	Abt 14 yrs	Craig, R. B.	Orphan
Nixon, Edward	7Jan1874		Wardlaw, J. H.	Of color
Nixon, Loiza	7Jan1874		Wardlaw, J. H.	Of color
Timms, Jeremiah	2Mar1874	b. Abt 1Feb1860	Lloyd, Claudius	Of color

Name	Date	Age	Master	Notes
Rice, Jonathan	3Aug1874	Abt 12 yrs	Harrison, A. J.	Orphan. 8 & 9July1874*
Goodman, James Vincen	6Sept1875	b. 14Mar1871	Carrigan, William	Cancelled 5Mar1878
Howard, Susan Jane	6Sept1875	b. June 1872	Keltner, M.	
Oldham, Mincie	6Oct1875		Jackson, James P.	Of color
Coleman, E. N.	6Jan1876	b. 1870	Young, G. W.	
Lowe, Willie	7Nov1876	b. 1871	Gouse, T. G.	No parents living in county. Of color
Lowe, Flerance	7Nov1876	b. 1872	Gouse, T. G.	No parents living in county. Of color
Colvin, Joseph L.	6Aug1877	b. October 1869	Jennings, G. C. C.	No parents living. On same date, William Paschall apptd administrator of estate of Rebecca Colvin, Dcd. Also, years support voted for minor children of V. L. Colvin, Dcd
Colvin, B. F.	6Aug1877	b. March 1871	Brown, R. C.	No parents living. See above
Goodman, James Vincen	5Mar1878		Jenkins, Dupree	
Howard, Nancy Jane	8Apr1880		Keltner, J. L.	Orphan. On same date year's provisions voted for Mrs. E. J. Howard, widow of L. D. Howard, Dcd
Partee, Berry	6Jan1881		Hunter, Anderson	Son of Lucy Partee, who consents. On 4Apr1882 Crowley Partee, of color, paid for burying Anderson Hunter, pauper, of color
Beard, Mattie	6Jan1881		Hunter, Anderson	Consent of Lucy Partee, mother. See above

Madison County

Name	Date	Age	Master	Notes
Osteen, William	16Sept1822	11 yrs	Baker (or Barker), Elijah	Making hats
Step, William F.	7Nov1825	Abt 16 yrs	McReynolds, Wilson O.	House carpenter
Step, John	7Nov1825	Abt 14 yrs	McReynolds, Wilson O.	House carpenter
Pulley, Henry	7Feb1829	Abt 15 yrs	Edwards, Francis C.	Orphan
Payne, Burwell Blackmon	2Nov1829	12 yrs	Hibbetts, Robert H.	For 9 yrs. Tanning. Orphan
McMillan, James	2Nov1829	8 yrs	Caison, James	Orphan
Haw, John Green	3Nov1829	Abt 13 yrs	Hutchings, Christopher	Orphan

Apprentice	Date	Age	Master	Notes
Payn, James	1Feb1830	14 yrs	Duty, Solomon	For 7 yrs. Orphan. Cancelled 7Feb1831
Harrison, Thomas	1Feb1830	11 yrs	Prendergrast, John B. & L. B.	For 10 yrs. Orphan
Unnamed female	2Aug1830	7 yrs	Bonner, Thomas	Until 17 yrs. Orphan
Drake, Jeremiah	3Nov1830	Abt 16 yrs	Cartmell, Martin	Orphan. Saddler. Cancelled 7Feb1831
Payne, James	7Feb1831	15 yrs	Huston, John	Orphan
Drake, Jeremiah	7Feb1831	Abt 16 yrs	Williamson, William L.	Orphan. Taylor
Skinner, Robert A.	5Nov1832		McKnight, James H.	Tayloring business
Statem, Charles	5Aug1833		Hopper, Turley	Forename "Louonia" in 6Aug1832 entry, when placed with William Hopper for 12 mo
Statem, Viney	5Aug1833		Hopper, Turley	For 14 yrs. Orphan"
Statum, Charles	4Nov1833	7 yrs	Anderson, Jacob	
Johnson, S. W.	5May1834	13 yrs	Johnson, West T.	
Sarah	5May1834		Johnson, West T.	
Johnson, Hugy	5May1834		Pate, Hartwell	
Branch, Levy	2Feb1835	Abt 11 yrs	Spivy, John	For 10 yrs. Orphan
Branch, William	2Feb1835	Abt 17 yrs	Barnes, Alexander B.	For 4 yrs. Orphan
Lary, Augustus	11May1835		Lary, James	Husbandry. James is grandfather of Augustus. Of color
Durden, Richard	11May1835		Givens, Samuel W.	Tanning. Illegitimate child
Henry, Charles	3Aug1835	Abt 15 yrs	McKnight, James H.	Orphan. Tayloring
Peach, Henderson	3Aug1835	Abt 13 yrs	Stepleton, Jonathan	For 8 yrs. Orphan. Farming
Futell, Richard	10Aug1835	Abt 17 yrs	Boles, John T.	Tanning
Croom, John	2Nov1835	Abt 13 yrs	Mooring, Wyatt	Orphan. Farming
Croom, Cullin	9Nov1835	Abt 13 yrs	Moore, William	Orphan. Tanning
Croom, Susan J.	9Nov1835	Abt 6 yrs	Simmons, John	For 11 yrs
Smith, William A.	9Nov1835		Robb, John	For 5 yrs. Cabinet maker
Collinsworth, Jesse	1Feb1836	Abt 15 yrs	Thompson, George	Orphan. Cabinet & joiner business. Cancelled 2Dec1839. Thompson not complying with contract
Anderson, William	5Dec1836		Thompson, George	For 5 yrs
Gannaway, Samuel Lancaster	4Sept1837		George Jenkins & Co	Until 20 yrs, on 10Mar1843. Assent of mother, May B. Gannawayr

Name	Date	Age	Master	Notes
Gannaway, James Walker	4Sept1837		George Jenkins & Co	Until 20 yrs, on 25Feb1845. Assent of mother, Mary D. Gannaway
Mary	2Oct1837	3 yrs	Taylor, Canellun	Consent of mother. Free born
Croom, Cullen	4Dec1837		Croom, Alexander	For 14 yrs. Farmer. Cancelled 5Nov1838
Dillingham, William H.	4Dec1837		Moody, John C.	For 11 yrs. Farming
Wright, James Pinckney	5Feb1838		Stark & Magevney	For 5 yrs. Consent of mother, Terry Wright. Tayloring. Son of Jacob Wright. Sibs Terry & George Washington Wright 5Sept1837
Parks, William	3Apr1838		Stewart, Henry T.	For 4 ys. Farming. Security released 3Feb1840
Dourtheage, William	7May1838		Freelan, William W.	For 15 yrs. Farming. Consent of Sarah Dourtheage, mother
Anderson, Robert	2July1838		Dorris, Henry P.	For 5 yrs from 6Nov1838. Tining. Consent of Nancy Anderson, mother
Jury	1Oct1838	11 yrs	McFarlan, Duncan	Spinstress. Consent of mother, Delly Artes. Of color
Adam	1Oct1838	17 yrs	Mooring, John	Farming. Consent of Delly Artes, mother. Of color
Morrison	1Oct1838	15 yrs	Mooring, John	Farming. Consent of Delly Artes, mother. Of color
Ellick	1Oct1838	13 yrs	Mooring, John	Farming. Consent of Delly Artes, mother. Of color
Rebecca	1Oct1838	9 yrs	Mooring, John	Spinstress. Consent of mother, Delly Artes. Of color
Alford	1Oct1838	4 yrs	Mooring, John	Farming. Consent of Delly Artes, mother. Of color. Cancelled 4Nov1850 as Alford Artist
Louisa	1Oct1838	2 yrs	Mooring, John	Spinstress. Consent of mother, Delly Artes. Of color
Haywood	1Oct1838	3 mo	Mooring, John	Farming. Consent of Delly Artes, mother. Of color. Cancelled 3Nov1851, as Heywood Artist, Mooring having left the State
Croom, Cullen	5Nov1838		Davis, David	For 13 yrs. Farming. Consent of Silva Croom, mother
Mullens, Robert	1Apr1839		Wynston, Arnold	For 10 yrs. Farming. Consent of Mary A. Mullen, mother
Mullen, Sidney D.	1Apr1839		Goodlow, George	For 8 yrs. Carpenter. Consent of Mary A. Mullen, mother. Cancelled 2Sept1839
Climer, Carroll	4May1840		Stewart, Leroy W.	For 11 yrs. Farming
Climer, Milton	4May1840		Jackson, William H.	For 10 yrs. Farming
Oliver, Polly Gennetta Jane	6July1840	2 yrs	Nolen, John	For 19 yrs. Spinstress. Consent of Mary Oliver, mother. Of color
Croom, Collen	7Sept1840		Ross, James C.	For 10 yrs

Name	Master	Date	Age	Notes
Williams, John F.	Houston, John	1Mar1841	Abt 19 yrs	For 2 yrs. Request of Williams & of Thomas M. Connally, Guardian. Taning. 5Apr1842*
Dinah	Hardage, John B.	6Sept1841	Abt 19 yrs	For 2 yrs. Spinstress. Of color
July Ann	Alison, Thomas	5Apr1842	2 yrs	For 19 yrs. Same date Mary Oliver, free woman of color, placed under control of Alison. On 2Oct1849 Judy Ann ordered returned to Court. Alison leaving county
Croom, Cullen	Bobbett, Samuel M.	6June1842	Abt 12 yrs	For 9 yrs. Farmer
Tyner, James	Dunaway, William M.	6Feb1843		For 3 yrs. Farming
Wilkerson, John W. F.	Bledsoe, Duncan C.	7Nov1843	Abt 12 yrs	For 9 yrs. Cabinet business. Consent by John
Heidleburg, Burwell	Cook, Archibald	7Nov1843	Abt 12 yrs	For 9 yrs. Farming. On 4Sept1843 commission apptd to lay off one yrs support to children of Richard Heidleburg, Dcd
Sam	Bachelor, John	2Jan1844	6 yrs in Dec1843	Child of Clarah Ash, of color, who assents
Prince	Bachelor, John	2Jan1844	3 yrs on 9Feb1843	Child of Clarah Ash, of color, who assents
Narcissa	Bachelor, John	2Jan1844	6 mo	Child of Clarah Ash, of color, who assents
Nowell, Thomas	Prendergast, Samuel	5Feb1844	9 yrs	For 11 yrs. Orphan of Barnibas Nowell, Dcd. Dempsy Nowell, Exec. Farming. Sibs Andrew & Elizabeth 7Dec1846
McGraw,	Parrish, John A. S.	2July1844		For 14 yrs
Carrington, Neal H.	Anderson, Robert	3Mar1845		For 4 yrs. Taner (or Tinner). Canc 8Feb1848
Wilkins, William	Curlin, John	7July1845	Abt 13 yrs	For 8 yrs. Farming
Nowell, Thomas	Henry, William	4Aug1845	10 yrs	For 11 yrs. Farming. Cancelled 2Mar1847. To mother
Artist, George Washington	McFarland, Duncan	2Dec1845		For 20 yrs. Of color. Cancelled 3Nov1846. George & his mother, Dury Artist, placed under control of Mosis Artist for 2 yrs
Climer, Harvey	Handley, John R.	3Aug1846		
Bratton, Milton	Johnson, Stephen	5Oct1846	Abt 9 yrs	Farmer
Belton, John	McMillan, Archibald C.	5Oct1846	15 yrs	Farmer
Williams, John	Forrest, George L.	5Apr1847		Brick mason
Vanderford, Richard B.	Murchison, William C.	8June1847	11 yrs	Orphan. Tanner & currier. On 5Feb1856 Murchison ordered to give new security
Maroney, Elizabeth Ann	Campbell, James	5July1847	12 yrs 11 mo	Orphan. Housekeeping. Indenture confirmed with new sureties 5Jan1848

Name	Date	Age	Master	Notes
Maroney, James T.	5July1847	11 yrs	Campbell, James	Orphan. Carpenter. Indenture confirmed with new sureties 5Jan1848, as a farmer
Redding, William T.	3Jan1848		Mason, E. B.	Request of mother, Emay K. Redding. On 7Dec1847 Mason apptd guardian of Lavina F., Elvina L., William T., & Mary L. Redding
Sullivan, John	7Nov1848	Abt 13 yrs	Fuller, Jeremiah	Farming
Loving, William	4Dec1848	Abt 14 yrs	Flaharty, James	Cabinet making. Cancelled 6Dec1848
Ellington, Edwin	4Dec1848	Abt 7 yrs	Childress, George W. S.	Farming. Cancelled 5Feb1855, Ellington having removed from the state
Loving, William	6Dec1848	Abt 16 yrs [sic]	Holliday, William	Farming
Heidleberg, Allen	6Feb1849	15 yrs	Lacy, Jr, Thomas	Farming. Cancelled 4Feb1850
Artiste, George	4June1849	Abt 5 yrs	Davie, Yarborough M.	Farming. Of color
Redding, Elvira L.	3Sept1849	Abt 8 yrs	McLeary, Frances	Until 21 yrs. Seamstress
Julian, John	3Sept1849	13 yrs	Drake, Jeremiah M.	Tailoring
Mower, George	4Sept1849	4 yrs	Delapp, Anderson	Son of Eliza Mower. Farming. Of color. Same date peace bond for 2 y/o sister, Laura, posted by Eliza
Wilson, Lafayette	7Jan1850	10 yrs	Jayne, Z.	To learn medicine by attending to Jayne
Heidleberg, Allen	4Feb1850		Shaw, James A.	Waggon making
McClish, Samuel	5Aug1850	12 yrs	Blythe, James	Orphan. Farming
McCain, George W.	7Aug1850	19 yrs	Hampton, David	Carpenter
Artist, Alford	4Nov1850	In 16th year	Fussell & Norwood	For 4 yrs. Born in Madison Co. Apprenticed to John Mooring 1Oct1838. Has resided with John & Henry Mooring since. Of color*
Mawers, Laura	2Dec1850	3 yrs	Delapp, Anderson	Bound by mother, Eliza Mawers. Of color
Vanderford, James	9Jan1851	12 yrs	Nobles, William A.	Farming
Artist, Haywood	3Nov1851	14 yrs	Mooring, Wyatt	Tanner. Of color. On 8Feb1853 Haywood returned to mother, Delilah Artist. * Granted Tennesse citizenship 9Feb1853
Jane	3Feb1852	11 yrs	Haynes, Richard J.	Farming. Of color
Calvin	3Feb1852	7 yrs	Haynes, Richard J.	Farming. Of color
Lewis	3Feb1852	5 yrs	Haynes, Richard J.	Farming. Of color
William	1Mar1852		Howlett, William R.	Of color

Hunt, Nancy	1Nov1852	10 yrs last July	Johnson, Cyrus	House & field servant. Of color
Hunt, Gilbert	1Nov1852	8 yrs last April	Johnson, Cyrus	Farming. Of color
Dickerson, Elvin Amariah	5Apr1853	Abt 10 yrs	Fussell, Wyatt	Ostler. Son of Mary, a freed woman of color, old, infirm & blind, who petitions for binding
Huntington, Sarah Ann	5Dec1853	b. 16June1838	Rice, Thomas H.	Orphan. House service. Of color
Huntington, William	5Dec1853	b. 30Oct1844	Rice, Thomas H.	Orphan. Farming. Of color
Huntington, Willis S.	5Dec1853	b. 11July1846	Rice, Thomas H.	Orphan. Farming. Of color
Huntington, Frances V.	5Dec1853	b. 5Oct1850	Rice, Thomas H.	Orphan. House service. Of color
Huntington. Mildred	5Dec1853	b. abt 10Jan1840	Lackey, Thomas	Orphan. House service. Of color
Huntington, Lewis C.	5Dec1853	b. 11Oct1848	Lackey, Thomas	Orphan. Farming. Of color
Robertson, Jane	7June1854	16 yrs this day	Reaves, Thomas C.	Req of Jane. Servant. Of color. 5Apr1854*
Pipkin, Francis	7Aug1854	14 yrs	Harrall, Thomas	Farming. Cancelled 3Sept1855, Pipkin having absconded
Wilson, James	7Feb1855		Ruffin, John B.	Mother deceased. Abandoned by father
Estes, Milton Brown	6Dec1858	12 yrs	Lawrance, Elisha P.	Orphan. Farming
Klink, William F.	9Nov1859	Abt 6 yrs	Spencer, William J.	Farming. Mother, the daughter of Spencer, married Frederick Klink abt 7 yrs ago. She died last July. Abandoned by father.* On 7Jan1861 Spencer allowed $80 for support of children of Jane Klink, Dcd
Klink, Tennessee A.	9Nov1859	Abt 4 yrs	Spencer, William J.	Housekeeping. See above
Klink, Martha	9Nov1859	Abt 3 yrs	Spencer, William J.	Housekeeping. See above
Klink, James Henry	9Nov1859	Abt 2 yrs	Spencer, William J.	Farming. See above
Tims, Franklin Pierce	8May1860	6 yrs	Woodall, Isaac P.	Orphan. Farming
Tims, James Buchanan	8May1860	3 yrs	Woodall, Isaac P.	Orphan. Farming
Trusty, George	4Dec1865	10 yrs	Morris, William T.	Orphan. Illegitimate
Meriwether, Martin	9Dec1865	9 yrs	Meriwether, H. A.	By FB. Orphan. Plantation work. Of color
Campbell, Emma	9Dec1865	9 yrs	Campbell, F. W.	By FB. Orphan. Plantation work. Of color
Robinson, Spencer	11Dec1865	10 yrs	Robinson, J. C.	By FB. Orphan. Plantation work. Of color
Shelton, Catherine	11Dec1865	10 yrs	Shelton, Henry W.	By FB. Orphan. Plantation work. Of color
Womack, Cora	19Dec1865	13 yrs	Womack, J. G.	By FB. Orphan. Plantation work. Of color
Bomar, Betty	21Dec1865	8 yrs	Bomar, Calvin C.	By FB. Orphan. Plantation work. Of color
Bomar, Phillip	21Dec1865	10 yrs	Bomar, Calvin C.	By FB. Orphan. Plantation work. Of color

Name	Date	Age	Master	Notes
Pyles, Carter	21Dec1865	10 yrs	Pyles, James M.	By FB. Orphan. Plantation work. Of color
Pyles, Bedford	21Dec1865	12 yrs	Pyles, James M.	By FB. Orphan. Plantation work. Of color
Bomar, Rins?	21Dec1865	10 yrs	Bomar, Calvin C.	By FB. Orphan. Plantation work. Of color
Paralee	23Dec1865	6 yrs	Johnson, Julius	By FB. Abandoned. Plantation work. Freed
Birdsong, Loan	1Jan1866	8 yrs	Birdsong, J. J. C.	By FB. Female. Orphan. Plantation work. Of color
Birdsong, Peter	1Jan1866	6 yrs	Birdsong, William	By FB. Orphan. Plantation work. Of color
Barnett, William	1Jan1866	9 yrs	McFee, William	By FB. Orphan. Plantation work. Of color
Sims, Malissa	1Jan1866	11 yrs	Sims, R. W.	By FB. Orphan. Plantation work. Of color
Tish	5Jan1866	10 yrs	Long, J. B.	By FB. Female. Orphan. Plantation work. Of color
Ann	5Jan1866	8 yrs	Lanier, John H.	By FB. Orphan. Plantation work. Of color
Wesley	5Jan1866	5 yrs	Lanier, John H.	By FB. Orphan. Plantation work. Of color
Hiram	5Jan1866	12 yrs	Long, J. B.	By FB. Orphan. Plantation work. Of color
Howlett, Bille	5Jan1866	6 yrs	Howlett, W. R.	By FB. Orphan. Plantation work. Of color
Granville	5Jan1866	11 yrs	Lanier, John H.	By FB. Orphan. Plantation work. Of color
De	5Jan1866	12 yrs	Long, J. B.	By FB. Orphan. Plantation work. Of color
Nance	5Jan1866	12 yrs	Long, J. B.	By FB. Orphan. Plantation work. Of color
Jane	5Jan1866	14 yrs	Irvin, John	Without parents. Of color. Once owned by Irvin
Joseph	5Jan1866	12 yrs	Irvin, John	Without parents. Of color. Once owned by Irvin
Alexander	5Jan1866	10 yrs	Irvin, John	Without parents. Of color. Once owned by Irvin
Lewis	6Jan1866	15 yrs	Brown, Milton	Once owned by Brown. Consent of father, Jarrett. Of color. Cancelled 5Sept1866. Illegally bound, per FB. To father
Susan	6Jan1866	13 yrs	Brown, Milton	Once owned by Brown. Consent of father, Jarrett. Of color. Cancelled 5Sept1866. Illegally bound, per FB. To father
Polly	6Jan1866	11 yrs	Brown, Milton	Once owned by Brown. Consent of father, Jarrett. Of color. Cancelled 5Sept1866. Illegally bound, per FB. To father
Cunningham, Patsy	10Jan1866	7 yrs	Cunningham, E. F. (Mrs)	By FB. Orphan. Plantation work. Of color
Cunningham, Billy	10Jan1866	9 yrs	Cunningham, E. F. (Mrs)	By FB. Orphan. Plantation work. Of color

Name	Date	Age	Bound To	Notes
Frank	11Jan1866	13 yrs	Woollard, James M.	Consent of mother, Jane Parish. Approved by FB 8Feb1866. Of color
Dick	11Jan1866	11 ys	Woollard, James M.	Consent of mother, Jane Parish. Approved by FB 8Feb1866. Of color
Andy	11Jan1866	9 yrs	Woollard, James M.	Consent of mother, Jane Parish. Approved by FB 8Feb1866. Of color
Sarah	11Jan1866	9 yrs	Woollard, James M.	Consent of mother, Jane Parish. Approved by FB 8Feb1866. Of color
Porter	11Jan1866	5 yrs	Woollard, James M.	Consent of mother, Jane Parish. Approved by FB 8Feb1866. Of color
Lambert, William	13Jan1866	11 yrs	Lambert, Delila (Mrs)	By FB. Orphan. Plantation work. Of color
Campbell, Susan	25Jan1866	8 yrs	Womack, James G.	By FB. Orphan. Plantation work. Of color
Chester, Charles	26Jan1866	5 yrs	Chester, John	By FB. Orphan. Plantation work. Of color
Chester, Charlotte	26Jan1866	9 yrs	Chester, John	By FB. Orphan. Plantation work. Of color
Chester, Maria	26Jan1866	7 yrs	Chester, John	By FB. Orphan. Plantation work. Of color
Elijah	5Feb1866	Abt 14 yrs	Jackson, Alexander	No father or mother. Of color. Formerly owned by Jackson. Cancelled 5Sept1866. Unable to control. Illegally bound, per FB
Silas	5Feb1866	13 yrs	Jackson, Alexander	No father or mother. Of color. Formerly owned by Jackson. Cancelled 5Sept1866. Unable to control. Illegally bound, per FB
Paul	5Feb1866	9 yrs	Jackson, Alexander	No father or mother. Of color. Formerly owned by Jackson. Cancelled 5Sept1866. Unable to control. Illegally bound, per FB
Harriet	5Feb1866	Abt 7 yrs	Jackson, Alexander	No father or mother. Of color. Formerly owned by Jackson. Cancelled 5Sept1866. Unable to control. Illegally bound, per FB
Buchanan, Ama	7Feb1866	13? yrs	Buchanan, Thomas N.	By FB. Female orphan. Plantation work. Of color
Weaver, Handy	8Feb1866	14 or 15 yrs	Weaver, Josiah H.	By FB. Orphan. Plantation work. Of color
Weaver, Franklin	8Feb1866	11 yrs	Weaver, Josiah H.	By FB. Orphan. Plantation work. Of color
Lacy, James K. P.	12Feb1866	16 yrs	Lacy, David	By FB. Orphan. Plantation work. Of color
Lacy, Margaret	12Feb1866	5 yrs	Lacy, David	By FB. Orphan. Plantation work. Of color
Lacy, Essex	12Feb1866	12 yrs	Lacy, David	By FB. Orphan. Plantation work. Of color
Lyon, Augustus	13Feb1866	6 yrs	Lyon, Wade W.	By FB. Orphan. Plantation work. Of color
Kent, George	15Feb1866	8 yrs	Lyon, Wade W.	By FB. Orphan. Plantation work. Of color

Name	Date	Age	Master	Notes
Ricketts, Lewis	19Feb1866	10 yrs	Jones, William F.	By FB. Orphan. Plantation work. Of color
Ricketts, Frances	19Feb1866	14 yrs	Jones, William F.	By FB. Orphan. Plantation work. Of color
Cock, Thomas	6Mar1866	13 yrs	Cock, John C.	Orphan. Of color
Cock, Dilla	6Mar1866	10 yrs	Cock, John C.	Orphan. Of color
George	8Mar1866	Abt 12 yrs	Lancaster, Edwin R.	Ex-slave of Lancaster. Without support
Emily	8Mar1866	Abt 8 yrs	Lancaster, Edwin R.	Ex-slave of Lancaster. Without support
William	8Mar1866	Abt 6 yrs	Lancaster, Edwin R.	Ex-slave of Lancaster. Without support
Perry, Jack	4Apr1866	6 yrs	Perry, Benjamin W.	Mother dead. Father left with Federal Army during war, not heard from since. Of color
Perry, Henry	4Apr1866	4 yrs	Perry, Benjamin W.	Mother dead. Father left with Federal Army during war, not heard from since. Of color
Eulalai	4Apr1866	10 yrs	McAdoo, Samuel	No father or mother. Of color
Nancy Louisa	4Apr1866	8 yrs	McAdoo, Samuel	No father or mother. Of color
Adam	4Apr1866	10 yrs	Vann, James R.	Orphan. Abandoned by mother. Of color
Hunt, Kate	1May1866	14 yrs	Hunt, Robert	By FB. Orphan. Work about dwelling house. Of color
James	7May1866	14 yrs	McKnight, Hugh	Orphan. Of color
Bob	7May1866	13 yrs	McKnight, Hugh	Orphan. Of color
Lizzie	7May1866	11 yrs	McKnight, Hugh	Orphan. Of color
Eliza J.	7May1866	9 yrs	McKnight, Hugh	Orphan. Of color
Harriet	7May1866	7 yrs	McKnight, Hugh	Orphan. Of color
James Andrew	7May1866		Cain, Andrew	Orphan. Of color
Wharton, Santeen	7May1866	12 yrs	Perkins, Josephus	Harriet Wharton, mother, consents. Of color
Wharton, Lydia	7May1866	9 yrs	Perkins, Josephus	Harriet Wharton, mother, consents. Of color
Wharton, Green	7May1866	7 yrs	Perkins, Josephus	Harriet Wharton, mother, consents. Of color
Wharton, George	7May1866	3 yrs	Perkins, Josephus	Harriet Wharton, mother, consents. Of color
James	8May1866	9 yrs	Crook, A. B.	Orphan. Of color
Tennessee	8May1866	7 yrs	Crook, A. B.	Orphan. Of color
Winchester, Wesley	24May1866	6 yrs	Winchester, William D.	By FB. Orphan. Plantation work. Of color
Winchester, Sambo	24May1866	4 yrs	Winchester, William D.	By FB. Orphan. Plantation work. Of color
Winchester, Henry	24May1866	8 yrs	Winchester, William D.	By FB. Orphan. Plantation work. Of color

Name	Date	Age	Apprenticed to	Notes
John	5June1866		McClanahan, Samuel	Orphan. Of color
Adeline	5June1866		McClanahan, Samuel	Orphan. Of color
Elizabeth	5June1866		McClanahan, Samuel	Orphan. Of color
Bob	5June1866		McClanahan, Samuel	Orphan. Of color
William	3July1866	15 yrs	Cock, Thomas A.	Ex-slave of Cock. Orphan
Alice	3July1866	13 yrs	Cock, Thomas A.	Ex-slave of Cock. Orphan
Christiana	3July1866	8 yrs	Cock, Thomas A.	Ex-slave of Cock. Orphan
Pleasant	3July1866	6 yrs	Cock, Thomas A.	Ex-slave of Cock. Orphan
Ella	3July1866	4 yrs	Cock, Thomas A.	Ex-slave of Cock. Orphan
Harriet	6Aug1866	15 yrs	Chester, Robert H.	Orphan. Ex-slave of Chester or of his sister. Cancelled 2Nov1868. Harriet Chester to marry Eli Gardner, of color
Robert	6Aug1866	Abt 11 yrs	Chester, Robert H.	Orphan. Ex-slave of Chester or of his sister
Edmond	6Aug1866	9 yrs	Chester, Robert H.	Orphan. Ex-slave of Chester or of his sister
Harriet	6Aug1866	7 yrs	Chester, Robert H.	Orphan. Ex-slave of Chester or of his sister
Millard	8Aug1866	Of tender years	May, Robert W. & wife, Mary C.	Orphan. Ex-slave of Mary C. May, formerly Mary C. Wilson
Lewis	3Sept1866	Abt 12 or 13 yrs	Murchison, D. J.	Mother dead. Father unknown. Living with Murchison since January. Of color
John	5Sept1866	Abt 8 yrs	Hudgings, Thomas	Abandoned by parents 4 yrs ago. Living with Hudgings for several years. Freed slave
Joseph	3Oct1866	10 yrs	Brooks, Benjamin S.	Ex-slave of Brooks. No father or mother
Simon	3Oct1866	8 yrs	Brooks, Benjamin S.	Ex-slave of Brooks. No father or mother
Langford, Willis J.	5Nov1866		Langford, William	Consent of mother
Langford, John W.	5Nov1866		Langford, William	Consent of mother
Polly	5Nov1866		Neeley, James B.	Orphan. Of color. Cancelled 9Apr1873, as Polly Weddell. "Neely ... getting old"
Randoph	5Nov1866	13 yrs	Pearson, Martha A.	Orphan. Of color
Ann	6Nov1866		Hicks, James	Orphan. Of color
Alice	7Nov1866	Abt 11 yrs	Hill, Leonidas S.	Orphan. Of color
Alfred	7Nov1866	Abt 11 yrs	Givens, Robert H.	Orphan. Of color
Sidney	6Dec1866	Abt 12 yrs	McClellan, John Q. A.	Orphan. Of color

Name	Date	Age	Master	Notes
Florence	7Dec1866		Lockard, Mary B.	Orphan. Of color. Cancelled 4Oct1869. Florance, now abt 13 yrs, agrees
Reid, John Henry	8Jan1867	8 yrs	Reid, James W.	Has neither father nor mother. Of color
Dick	8Jan1867	Abt 13 yrs	Scott, George R.	Has neither father nor mother. Of color
Charles	8Jan1867	Abt 11 yrs	Scott, George R.	Has neither father nor mother. Of color
Jennie	8Jan1867	Abt 10 yrs	Scott, George R.	Has neither father nor mother. Of color
Nathan	8Jan1867	Abt 7 yrs	Scott, George R.	Has neither father nor mother. Of color
Sanford	9Jan1867		Witherspoon, William	Of color
Martha	10Jan1867	9 yrs	Webb, Theodorick	Without father and mother. Of color
Bob	10Jan1867	Abt 7 yrs	Webb, Theodorick	Without father and mother. Of color
Billy	10Jan1867	Abt 5 yrs	Webb, Theodorick	Without father and mother. Of color
Dord	4Feb1867		Wilson, Henry B.	Female orphan. Of color
Alice	4Feb1867	Abt 10 yrs	Pearson, Henry J.	Orphan. Of color
Kaler	4Feb1867		Birdsong, William J.	Female orphan. Of color
Flora	5Feb1867		Alston, Sarah	No father or mother. Of color
Sarah	8Feb1867	9 yrs	Irvin, Daniel M.	Orphan. Of color
Baker, George	5Mar1867	8 yrs	Stobaugh, Robert	Consent of mother, Ceyley Baker. Of color
Baker, Rosella	5Mar1867	2 yrs	Stobaugh, Robert	Consent of mother, Ceyley Baker. Of color
Frank	5Apr1867	8 yrs	Williamson, Lewis T.	Orphan. Of color
Maria	5Apr1867	5 yrs	Williamson, Lewis T.	Orphan. Of color
Greer, Tilda	1May1867		Gates, John W.	Orphan placed with Gates by her uncle. Of color
Jesse	1May1867		Hicks, Benjamin M.	Orphan. Of color
Meriwether, Martin	5Aug1867		Meriwether, H. A.	Without means or friends to care for him. Of color
Emma	3Sept1867	10 yrs	Campbell, Francis W.	Orphan. Of color
Wallace	3Sept1867	6 yrs	Estes, R. A.	Orphan. Of color
Eliza	3Sept1867	7 yrs	Utley, William L.	Orphan. Of color
Susan	3Sept1867	9 yrs	Womack, James G.	Orphan. Of color
Jack	4Nov1867		Jones, Turner	Orphan. Of color. As Jack Jones, cancelled 2Mar1875. Turner Jones deceased
Maria	4Nov1867		Jones, Turner	Orphan. Of color

Name	Date	Apprenticed to	Age	Remarks
Yarbrough, Mary	4Nov1867	Yarbrough, David		Orphan. Of color
Yarbrough, Jasper	4Nov1867	Yarbrough, David		Orphan. Of color
Yarbrough, Chloe	4Nov1867	Yarbrough, David		Orphan. Of color
Thomas	5Nov1867	Fuller, Jeremiah		Orphan. Of color
George	5Nov1867	Fuller, Jeremiah		Orphan. Of color
Philip	5Nov1867	Fuller, Jeremiah		Orphan. Of color
Reeves, George	2Dec1867	Thornton, James R.		Orphan. Of color
Reeves, Thomas	2Dec1867	Thornton, James R.		Orphan. Of color
Meriwether, Emma	5Feb1868	Meriwether, M. D.		Father dead. Abandoned by mother. Of color
Charles	5Feb1868	Goff, John C.		Orphan. Of color
Jones, James A.	7Sept1868	Harris, C. R.	8 yrs	Only support is his mother, an idiot. Of color
Lackey, Sally	5Oct1868	Carter, Thomas L.	Abt 7 yrs	Without father, mother or relatives. Of color
Newby, Laura	6Oct1868	Bond, James W.	Abt 14 yrs	Child of Catherine Newby, Dcd. Of color*
Newby, James	6Oct1868	Bond, James W.	Abt 12 yrs	Child of Catherine Newby, Dcd. Of color*
Newby, Sallie	6Oct1868	Bond, James W.	Abt 10 yrs	Child of Catherine Newby, Dcd. Of color*
Newby, Catcy	6Oct1868	Bond, James W.	Abt 8 yrs	Child of Catherine Newby, Dcd. Of color*
Newby, Eliza	6Oct1868	Bond, James W.	Abt 6 yrs	Child of Catherine Newby, Dcd. Of color*
Newby, Martha	6Oct1868	Bond, James W.	Abt 5 yrs	Child of Catherine Newby, Dcd. Of color*
Newby, Wiley	6Oct1868	Bond, James W.	Abt 3 yrs	Child of Catherine Newby, Dcd. Of color*
Newby, Missy	6Oct1868	Bond, James W.	Abt 2 yrs	Child of Catherine Newby, Dcd. Of color*
McKinney, Joseph	9Dec1868	Hall, Jonathan	Abt 8 yrs	Orphan, without relatives or friends
Neely, Ellen	4Jan1869	Williamson, Anthony		Mother before her death asked Williamson to have both girls apprenticed to him
Neely, Ada	4Jan1869	Williamson, Anthony		Mother before her death asked Williamson to have both girls apprenticed to him
Jerry	7Oct1869	Crittenden, H. S.	9 yrs	Orphan. Of color
Peter	7Oct1869	Crittenden, H. S.	9 yrs	Orphan. Of color
Jane	7Oct1869	Crittenden, H. S.	8 yrs	Orphan. Of color
Randolph, Callie	7Feb1870	Pope, Joseph	7 yrs	Apprenticeship requested by mother. Of color
Randolph, Tom	7Feb1870	Pope, Joseph	3 yrs	Apprenticeship requested by mother. Of color
Bond, John	7Mar1870	Howlett, Isaac J.	Abt 14 yrs	Without parents or relatives. Of color

Name	Date	Age	Master	Notes
Bryant, Charley	7Mar1870	Abt 10 yrs	Howlett, Isaac J.	Without parents or relatives. Of color
Gordon, Fredonia	6Apr1870	8 yrs	Morgan, Isham	Orphan. Both of color
Gordon, Tennessee	6Apr1870	Abt 11 yrs	Lyon, Ed	Orphan. Request of stepfather. Both of color
Hargis, Richard M.	6June1870	Abt 9 yrs	Potts, J. C.	On application of mother
Newsom, Henry	1Aug1870	Abt 8 yrs	Phillips, J. L.	Left by mother to be apprenticed to Phillips. Of color
Rebecca	2Aug1870	Abt 14 yrs	Malone, B. J.	Orphan and child of Betsy Malone, who is old and unable to provide and requests the binding. Malone to care for Betsy also. Of color
Emily	2Aug1870	Abt 12	Malone, B. J.	Child of Betsy Malone. Of color. See above
Abe	2Aug1870	Abt 9 yrs	Malone, B. J.	Child of Betsy Malone. Of color. See above
Mary	2Aug1870	Abt 4 yrs	Malone, B. J.	Child of Betsy Malone. Of color. See above
Jane	2Aug1870	Abt 3 yrs	Malone, B. J.	Child of Betsy Malone. Of color. See above
John	2Aug1870	Abt 2 yrs	Malone, B. J.	Kin of Betsy Malone. Of color. See above
Mariah	2Aug1870	Abt 6 mo	Malone, B. J.	Kin of Betsy Malone. Of color. See above
Verser, Pleas	6Dec1870	11 yrs	Verser, James	Parents dead. James is uncle. Both of color
Verser, Arter	6Dec1870	13 yrs	Reid, Haywood	Parents dead. Reid is uncle. Both of color
Staton, Lezina	5Jan1871	11 yrs	Williamson, Rebecca C. (Mrs)	Orphan of Marsh Staton, Dcd. Bound per mother's death bed wish. Of color
Staton, Joseph	5Jan1871	9 yrs	Williamson, Rebecca C. (Mrs)	Orphan of Marsh Staton, Dcd. Bound per mother's death bed wish. Of color
Staton, Luke	5Jan1871	7 yrs	Williamson, Rebecca C. (Mrs)	Orphan of Marsh Staton, Dcd. Bound per mother's death bed wish. Of color
Staton, Paralee	5Jan1871	5 yrs	Williamson, Rebecca C. (Mrs)	Orphan of Marsh Staton, Dcd. Bound per mother's death bed wish. Of color
Staton, Rose	5Jan1871	4 yrs	Williamson, Rebecca C. (Mrs)	Orphan of Marsh Staton, Dcd. Bound per mother's death bed wish. Of color
Hart, Ranel	5June1871	12 yrs	Hicks, James W.	Mother died last March. Of color
Hart, Allen	5June1871	10 yrs	Hicks, James W.	Mother died last March. Of color
Evans, Joseph	2Oct1871	Abt 4 yrs	Dungan, W. A.	Listed in report of Poor House 6Apr1871 as 3 y/o, deserted by parents. White

Child	Bound to	Date	Age	Notes
Meriwether, Nellie	Meriwether, Elvira J. (Mrs)	6Nov1871	9 yrs	Orphan. Of color
Coleman, Silas	Gregory, John H.	4Dec1871	13 yrs	Petition of Ellen Coleman, mother. Of color
Coleman, George	Gregory, John H.	4Dec1871	11 yrs	Petition of Ellen Coleman, mother. Of color
Coleman, Charley	Gregory, John H.	4Dec1871	2 yrs	Petition of Ellen Coleman, mother. Of color
Langster, James	Pipkin, P. M.	4Mar1872	10 yrs	Neither father nor mother living. Of color
Day, Fanny	Perry, Marshall	6May1872	Abt 13 yrs	Orphan. Of color
Beaver, James F. B. F.	Hunter, James N.	4July1872	Abt 16 yrs	Orphan of John Beaver, Dcd
Beaver, Joseph R.	McKnight, Caleb	4July1872	Abt 11 yrs	Orphan of John Beaver, Dcd
Quin, Scylla	Newsom, John F.	10Oct1872	Abt 12 yrs	Minor with no one to care for her. Of color. Cancelled 6June1873 on petition of Thomas G. Edwards, next friend
Quin, Jim	Newsom, John F.	10Oct1872	Abt 8 yrs	Minor with no one to care for him. Of color
Quin, Judy	Newsom, John F.	10Oct1872	Abt 10 yrs	Minor with no one to care for her. Of color. Cancelled 4June1873, as Judith Fillmore. Reversed 5June1873 on petition of Newsom*
Adams, Thomas	Mayo, Jonas	10Oct1872	Abt 8 yrs	Mother dead. Father's whereabouts unknown
Phillips, George	Reid, James G.	4Dec1872	Abt 3 yrs	Bound at request of parents. Father a cripple. Of color
Lawler, Enoch	Trice, E. J.	9Jan1873	Abt 11 yrs	Request of Abner Lawler. Orphan of Manuel Lawler, Dcd. Trice married Enoch's aunt
Weddell, Polly	McCrory, H. W.	9Apr1873		Orphan. Of color
Fillmore, Judith	Goodell, Austin	6May1873	14 yrs	Consent of Judith. See Judy Quin. Cancelled 5June1873. Appealed to Circuit Court by Fillmore & Goodell 10Apr1874
Parks, Ella	Cole, M. A. (Mrs)	9July1873		Request of mother, Mary Parks, who has several children and no husband. Of color
Turner, Hannah	Henry, W. M.	4Aug1873	Abt 12 yrs	No father or mother living. Of color. Bryant Britton, her uncle, agrees
Utley, Billy	Reid, Nep	1Sept1873	Abt 7 yrs	No father or mother. Reid's wife is Billy's aunt. All of color
Redfearn, Eliza	Carpenter, Franklin	2Sept1873	Abt 6 yrs	Deserted by parents. Both of color
Redfearn, John	Carpenter, Franklin	2Sept1873	Abt 4 yrs	Deserted by parents. Both of color
Cooper, Homer B.	Gardner, William F.	4Nov1873	3 yrs	Orphan. In Gardner's care the past year at request of Homer's brother, who consents to binding

Name	Date	Age	Master	Notes
Burns, Maggie	2Dec1873	Abt 8 yrs	Lyons, Wade W.	Orphan. Of color
Stegall, William	8Jan1874	Abt 16 yrs	Temple, Thomas H.	Consent of mother. Father dead. Of color
Stegall, Thomas	8Jan1874	Abt 13 yrs	Hunter, R. P.	Consent of mother. No father. Of color
Ballard, Edmund	8Jan1874	Abt 13 yrs	Ballard, Ephraim	Bound to Ballard, his uncle, per father's dying request
Ballard, Wesley	8Jan1874	Abt 11 yrs	Ballard, Ephraim	Bound to Ballard, his uncle, per father's dying request
Cole, Ivie	4Feb1874	14 yrs	Reid, James G.	Farm laborer. Son of Rachel Cole, who consents. Of color
Cole, Allen	4Feb1874	12 yrs	Reid, James G.	Farm laborer. Son of Rachel Cole, who consents. Of color
Hawkins, Anna	5Feb1874		Barnett, Samuel D.	House girl & seamstress
Nelson, Henry	2Mar1874	9 yrs	Lawrence, John B.	Mother dead. Deserted by father 6 yrs ago. GM crazy & in Poor House. Of color
Jones, Jack	2Mar1875	Abt 12 yrs	Jones, J. D.	Orphan. Of color. J. D. only son of Turner Jones, Dcd, Jack's previous master
Andrews, Amanda	3May1875	Abt 11 yrs	Andrews, G. P.	Orphan. Of color. On 9June1875 appealed to Chancery Court by Jacob Jordan, next friend
Andrews, Lewis	3May1875	Abt 3 yrs	Andrews, G. P.	Orphan. Of color. See above
Reid, Mariah	3May1875	Abt 5 yrs	Reid, James G.	Bound by petition of mother. Of color
Willoby, Jim	4Jan1876		Sherrell, H. N.	Orphan
Eadleman, James N.	6Mar1876	Abt 3 yrs	Wood, Richard J.	Bound by petition of mother, Katie Eadleman. Deserted by father
Neely, Joseph	13Dec1876	14 yrs	Meriwether, James G.	Bound by request of grandmother. Of color
Neely, Henry	13Dec1876	12 yrs	Meriwether, James G.	Bound by request of grandmother. Of color
Moses, Henry	6Mar1877	Abt 14 yrs	Walker, P. H.	By request of father, John Moses. Of color
Baker, William Sampson	7Mar1877	Abt 8 yrs	Prewitt, Robert E.	Father dead. Mother, unable to support, requests apprenticing
Middleton, George Ellis	14May1878		Hays, Nick	Without father or mother. Hays is uncle
Simmons, William L.	3June1878	Under 17 yrs	Russell, George Mc.	No father or mother or other relative
Hart, Frank	7July1879	Abt 13 yrs	Trice, E. J.	Orphan. Mother living with or under care of Trice for 4 yrs before her death. She asked him to take & raise her children
Hart, Tom	7July1879	7 yrs	Trice, E. J.	Orphan. See above
Hart, Mat	7July1879	3 yrs	Trice, E. J.	Orphan. See above
Hart, Moses	7July1879	Abt 1 mo	Trice, E. J.	Orphan. See above

Name	Date	Age	Bound to	Remarks
Telpher, Frank	9Dec1879	Abt 9 yrs	Gill, Alexander	Orphan. Lived with Gill since death of his parents, in 1872. Both of color
Jones, James	16Dec1879	13 yrs	Sneed, R. A.	Alice, his mother, unable to support & asks he be bound. Of color
Cole, Roxie	14Jan1880	7 yrs	Whitfield, R. M.	Until 21 yrs. Mother requests binding. Of color
Hodge, John	2May1881	Abt 12 yrs	Hudson, J. H.	Illegitimate son of Martha Hodge, an "abandon" without means. Wandering around from place to place & badly treated
Chapman, William	2May1881	12 yrs	Harsten, Edgar	Orphan. 90 y/o GM requests binding. Of color
Chapman, Martin	2May1881	10 ys	Harsten, Edgar	Orphan. 90 y/o GM requests binding. Of color
Brown, Oliver	18Oct1881	12 yrs	Oliver, T. J.	Orphan. Released from confinement in jail for misdemeanor. Of color
Miles, James O.	18Oct1881	13 yrs	Oliver, T. J.	Orphan. Released from confinement in jail for misdemeanor. Of color
Smith, Caroline	6Dec1881	Abt 9 yrs	Parker, H. F.	Until 21 yrs. Orphan. Of color
Smith, Lun	6Dec1881	Abt 7 yrs	Parker, H. F.	Until 21 yrs. Orphan. Of color
Newbern, Jason	13Dec1881	Abt 9 yrs	Utley, W. L.	Mother requests binding. Of color
Haynes, Henry	2Jan1882	14 yrs	Freeling, J. H.	Mother dead. Father in penitentiary. Of color
Haynes, William	2Jan1882	10 yrs	Freeling, J. H.	Mother dead. Father in penitentiary. Of color
Haynes, Dinah	2Jan1882	8 yrs	Haynes, J. A.	Until 21 yrs. Mother dead. Father in penitentiary. Of color
Thatcher, Frank	6Feb1882	13 yrs	Hicks, William	Orphan. Mulatto. Hicks of color
Bond, Willie	10Oct1882	13 yrs	Bond, Freeman	Child of Frank Bond. Freeman Bond is GF. All of color*
Bond, Lovey	10Oct1882	11 yrs	Bond, Freeman	Child of Frank Bond. Freeman Bond is GF. All of color*
Bond, Eva	10Oct1882	9 yrs	Bond, Freeman	Child of Frank Bond. Freeman Bond is GF. All of color*
Bond, Clancy	10Oct1882	6 yrs	Bond, Freeman	Child of Frank Bond. Freeman Bond is GF. All of color*
Anthony, Lawson	9Jan1883	Abt 10 yrs	Ingram, Joseph (Rev)	Neither mother nor father living. Ingram is uncle. Of color
Carmickle, John	11Apr1883	12 yrs	Blackman, James W.	Mother dead. Father ?living. Of color
Merriwether, James	18Dec1883	3 yrs	Merriwether, Madison	Farming. Son of Gracy Brown, who agrees to binding. All of color
Baum, David	15Jan1884	12 yrs	Baum, Sr, H.	Father dead. Mother living in Europe. White
Patterson, Lizzie	7Apr1884		Not named	Mother of unsound mind & in Poor Asylum. Apprenticeship ordered, perhaps not completed

Name	Date	Age	Master	Notes
Cartwright, Bettie	7Oct1884	11 yrs	Cartwright, Jacob	Orphan. Cartwright is uncle. Both of color
Bond, Jesse	20Oct1885	8 yrs	Alexander, J. A.	Parents dead. Lived with Alexander past 2 yrs. Of color
Richardson, John William	11Jan1887	7 yrs	Hardin, J. P.	With approval of mother
Macon, Henrietta	15June1887	14 yrs	Gorman, Daniel	Until 21 yrs. Orphan. Of color
Northern, Henry	25Aug1887	Abt 18 mo	Northern, Jack	Before her death, Jane Fuller, mother, gave Henry to Northern's wife. All of color
Harris, Ida	11Oct1887	Abt 10 yrs	Williamson, John R.	Until 21 yrs. Orphan. Of color
Harris, Kelly	11Oct1887	Abt 8 yrs	Williamson, John R.	Until 21 yrs. Orphan. Of color

McNairy County

Name	Date	Age	Master	Notes
Fauler, George	1Feb1858		Sweat, Dollarson	Cancelled 4Jan1858, George having left
Rankin, David			Thompson, William	
Williams, Nancy Jane	1Mar1858		Jones, Mariah	House wifery
Miller, William	1Mar1858		Chambers, Samuel	Farmer
Leath, James Buchanan	3May1858		Leath, James W.	Farmer
Holeman, William P.	3May1858		Holeman, Mark M.	Orphan. Black smith
Holeman, Loisa	3May1858		Holeman, Mark M.	Orphan. Black smith
Watkins	3May1858	Abt 7 yrs 9Feb last	Riddle, Marquis L.	Orphan. Saddler. Of color
Nancy Ann	3May1858	3 yrs 31May1858	Riddle, Marquis L.	Orphan. Of color
Kizer, Sophia Ann	7June1858		Holyfield, Jacob	Orphan
Howell, J[ohn]. W.	2Aug1858	6 yrs on 6June1858	Chambers, Ziblin	Orphan. Farmer. Cancelled 3Sept1866
Howell, M. L.	2Aug1858	10 yrs on 10Apr1858	Forsyth, J. G.	Orphan. Farmer
Neill, Pinkney H.	2Aug1858	17 yrs last January	Neill, John M.	Orphan. Farmer. A prior apprenticeship to Asa Jones cancelled

Apprentice	Master	Date	Age	Notes
Smith, Aaron	Meek, Moses	1Nov1858	7 yrs	Orphan. Farmer. On 4Oct1858 payment made to coroner for an inquest over the body of Isaac Smith. Canc 2May1859. To mother
Deberry, Daniel	Pickett, J. H.	1Nov1858	9 yrs	Farmer
Smith, George	Fowler, R. J.	1Nov1858	12 yrs	Orphan. Farmer. See Isaac Smith
Starks, Elijah W.	Starks, Thomas W.	3Jan1859	12 yrs	Farmer
Howell, Marcus L.	Boatman, John G.	3Jan1859	12 yrs on 6Apr1859	Farmer. Orphan
Patridge, Vincy	Peery, Jackson A. J.	4Apr1859	5 yrs	Also spelled Perry. Cancelled 4Mar1861. Child never in Peery's custody
Ragsdale, James	Hurst, Elza	4July1859	14 yrs	Orphan. Farmer
Mandy	Harrison, W. L.	1Aug1859	3 mo this date	House wifery. Of color
Chamness, Mary	Sewell, E. B.	1Aug1859	4 yrs	Orphan. Housewifery
Pope, David M.	Morgan, John R.	7Nov1859	10 yrs last February	Orphan. Farmer. Cancelled 3Aug1868
Williamson, Jane	Crabtree, Abraham	2Jan1860	11 yrs	Housewifery
Vaughn, Elizabeth D.	Horn, John	6Feb1860	6 yrs	Housewifery
Chamness, E.	Chamness, J. H.	5Mar1860	6 yrs	Farmer
Fowler, Madison	Farnsworth, S. H.	5Mar1860	12 yrs	Farmer
Wist, Martha E.	Covey, J. C.	6Aug1860	6 yrs	House servant. Of color
Furlong, Viola	Blakeley, J. P.	5Nov1860	7 yrs	For 14 yrs. Housewife. Orphan. Entered into records twice. Race not stated
Miller, Jeremiah	Perkins, James D.	4Feb1861	10 yrs	Farmer. Cancelled 1July1867
Jones, Robert	Browder, J. J.	2Dec1861	9 yrs	Farmer
Amandy	Walker, Joseph	2Dec1861	2 yrs	Housewifery. Of color
Jones, James Guise	Browder, W. T.	6Jan1862	7 yrs	Orphan. Farmer
Garret, Mary Ann	Garret, McD.	6Jan1862	5 or 6 yrs	Orphan. Housewifery
Ellis, Joshua R.	Boon, D. M.	3Mar1862	17 yrs	Orphan. Farmer. A former apprenticeship to J. P. Roberson cancelled
Melton, James S.	Young, W. J.	7Aug1865		Orphan. Farmer. Hiram Melton, Security. Melton and B. J. Young appointed administrators of William W. Melton, Dcd

Name	Date	Age	Master	Notes
Melton, Sarah M.	7Aug1865		Young, W. J.	Orphan. Housewifery. Hiram Melton, Security. Melton and Young appointed administrators of William W. Melton, Dcd. Cancelled 6June1870 as M. E. Melton*
Melton, William S.	7Aug1865		Young, W. J.	Orphan. Farmer. Hiram Melton, Security. Melton and Young appointed administrators of William W. Melton, Dcd. Cancelled 6June1870*
Sally	1Jan1866	10 yrs	Lewter, Emily H.	Until 21 yrs. Orphan. Servant. Of color. Cancelled 4Dec1871. "Sarah" now gone. Emily Lewter now E. H. Roten
Rebecca	1Jan1866	7 yrs	Lewter, Emily H.	Until 21 yrs. Orphan. Servant. Of color
Amanda	5Feb1866	12 yrs	Pool, R. W. P.	Until 21 yrs. Orphan. Servant. Of color
Mariah	5Feb1866	10 yrs	Pool, R. W. P.	Until 21 yrs. Orphan. Servant. Of color. Cancelled 4Oct1869
Peggy	5Feb1866	Abt 11 yrs	Meeks, John H.	Until 21 yrs. Orphan. Servant. Of color. Cancelled 2Dec1867. Uncontrollable
Crocket	5Feb1866	10 yrs	Gorsell, F. W.	Male orphan. Servant. Of color
Huston, Julia			Warren, John	Cancelled 2Apr1866, Julia having left Warren.
Julia	2Apr1866	3 yrs	Adams, James M.	Until 21 yrs. Orphan. Servant. Of color
Mary	2Apr1866	16 yrs	Black, Narcisses	Until 21 yrs. Orphan. Servant. Of color
West, Samuel	4June1866	12 yrs	McCuller, Isaac	Orphan.
Winchester, Elizabeth	4June1866	13 yrs	Murry, S. J.	Orphan. Servant
Michie, Ann	4June1866	9 yrs	Michie, G. G.	Orphan. Servant. Of color
Michie, Sarah	4June1866	11 yrs	Michie, G. G.	Orphan. Servant. Of color
Michie, Phillis	4June1866	13 yrs	Michie, G. G.	Orphan. Servant. Of color
Douglas, Franklin	6Aug1866	10 yrs	McAnally, R. N.	Orphan. Farmer. Cancelled 6May1867
Flowers, Fanny	6Aug1866	7 yrs	McAnally, R. N.	Orphan. Servant. Cancelled 6May1867
Porter, George W.	3Sept1866	12 yrs	Simpson, William B.	Orphan. Farmer. Of color. Canc 3May1869
Barnes, Taylor			Littlefield, L. R.	Cancelled 1Oct1866, Barnes having left
Massey, Albert W.	3Dec1866	8 yrs	Worsham, Thomas J.	Orphan. Farmer
Massey, Nancy M	3Dec1866	12 yrs	Worsham, Thomas J.	Orphan. Cook & housewife
McCorkle, Paralee	3Dec1866	6 yrs	Ingraham, Alexander H.	Orphan. Cook & housewife. Of color. Also spelled Ingram

Name	Date	Age	Bound to	Notes
Woods, Samuel	3Dec1866	12 yrs	McCuller, Alexander	Orphan. Farmer. Of color. Cancelled 5Aug1872. Woods refuses to be governed
Patterson, Martin F.	3Dec1866	11 yrs	Patterson, Mary M.	Orphan. Farmer. Cancelled 6Sept1869 as F. M. Patterson
Hookey, Joseph	7Jan1867	15 yrs	Simpson, Willis H.	Orphan. Farmer. Of color. Canc 1Apr1867
Massey, Henry T.	7Jan1867	10 yrs	Massey, David P.	Orphan. Farmer
Milton	1Apr1867	10 yrs	Barnhill, John N.	Of color
Jeremiah	1Apr1867	9 yrs	Barnhill, John N.	Of color
Samuel	1Apr1867	7 yrs	Barnhill, John N.	Of color
Price, James	6May1867		Pettigrew, James M.	At request of Price. Cancelled 3June1867 at request of Louise Hobson, his mother by a former mariage
Merrill, Lewis	2Dec1867	Abt 16 yrs	Merrell, Nelson	Child of Margaret Scirratt. Of color. Merrell also appt'd guardian of Lewis, Aaron, & Marshall Merrell and of Robert Scirratt
Scirratt, Robert	2Dec1867	Abt 17 yrs	Merrell, Nelson	Child of Margaret Scirratt. Of color. Merrell also appt'd guardian. See above
Haro, John	2Mar1868		Haro, W. S.	Unrecorded bond cancelled 7Dec1868, John having left and refusing to return
Cardwell, William P.	1Mar1869	6 yrs on 6Dec1868	Plunk, Sidney	Consent of mother, Rachel Cardwell
Bourland, James			Cox, Anderson	Cancelled 1Mar1869
Cooper, George M.			Horn, John	Cancelled 7Jun1869
Raines, James F. M.	6Sept1869		Gooch, J. G.	
It appears that during the late 1860's some McNairy County apprenticeships were not recorded in the Court Minutes.				
Buggs, Charles B.	7Mar1870	9 yrs	Rogers, Jr, C. B.	Orphan
Buggs, Franklin	7Mar1870	8 yrs	Rogers, Jr, C. B.	Orphan
Buggs, Baker	7Mar1870	5 yrs	Rogers, Jr, C. B.	Orphan
Buggs, Ella	7Mar1870	3 yrs	Rogers, Jr, C. B.	Orphan
Channess, Martha J.	4Apr1870		Woolverton, John	A prior apprenticeship to R. F. Scott cancelled due to Scott's death
Cardwell, T. F.	2May1870	3 yrs	Williams, David	
Flowers, Francis			Carrol, C. C.	Female. Cancelled 6.June1870

Name	Date	Age	Master	Notes
Melton, M. E. [Sarah M.]	6June1870		Williams, James O. & M. E.	Williams intending to move to Texas, taking Melton. Called "Sarah M." when previously bound. Daughter of W. W. Melton, Dcd
Melton, W(illiam). S.	6June1870		Williams, James O. & M. E.	Williams intending to move to Texas, taking Melton. Son of W. W. Melton, Dcd
Goldsmith, Charles	4July1870		Goldsmith, Jessee	
Goldsmith, Francis	4July1870		Goldsmith, Jessee	
Tate, Fletcher	4July1870	13 yrs	Whitaker, John	
Patridge, John L.	1Aug1870	8 yrs	Whitaker, John	On 4Nov1872 Patridge ordered taken from McIntyre on suspicion of maltreatment
Mercer, Henry B.	5Sept1870	7 yrs	Fowlks, Jeptha	Of color
Serat, Aaron			Roberson, John C.	Of color. Cancelled Dec1870. Aaron gone
Reynolds, John	3Apr1871	16 yrs (from canc entry)	Hanm, John M.	Orphan. On 1Dec1873 Hanm applied to cancel bond, having complied with its terms
Burkhead, Andy	3Apr1871	7 yrs	Burkhead, Thomas O.	Of color
Burkhead, Peter	3Apr1871	9 yrs	Burkhead, Thomas O.	Of color
Burkhead, Alfred	3Apr1871	12 yrs	Burkhead, Thomas O.	Of color
Butler, William Leroy	5June1871	6 yrs	Kirby, John	White
Ross, James C.	3Feb1873		Plunk, Sidney	For 12 yrs
Roberson, Ben	3Feb1873		Ijams, B. C.	For 11 yrs
Spencer, Alex	3Feb1873		Farrell, C. F.	For 10 yrs
White, Susanah	7July1873	12 yrs	Whitten, George S. W.	Daughter of David White, Dcd
White, Malnda Jane	7July1873	13 yrs	Thompson, Doct E.	Daughter of David White, Dcd
White, William H.	7July1873	16 yrs	Richards, John	Son of David White, Dcd
White, Margaret E.	7July1873	14 yrs	Richards, John	Daughter of David White, Dcd
Allen, Nancy Jane	Oct1873		Wagoner, Robert	
Tucker, Jessee	1June1874		Cuningham, David	Bound at request of mother, Bordelia Moore. Cancelled March1878, Jessee refusing to stay with Cuningham
Davis, Isaac	3Aug1874		Mathes, Mark	Of color
Davis, Elizabeth	3Aug1874		Mathes, Mark	Of color

Name	Date	Age	Master	Notes
Murry, Bob	Oct1874	15 yrs	Stumph, John W.	
Gainess, Oscar	Oct1874	3 yrs	Rousey, James H.	Cancelled July1875. To mother, Mrs. Gainus
Gainess, Robert	Oct1874	6 yrs	Rousey, James H.	Cancelled July1875. To mother, Mrs. Gainus
Adair, James	Oct1874	8 yrs	Rousey, James H.	
Ball, Louis	7Nov1874	11 yrs	Ball, R. C.	
Ball, Fent	7Nov1874	9 yrs	Ball, R. C.	
Adams, Rufus M.	7Nov1874	4 yrs	Cox, Caleb	
Ivy, Mary E.	1Feb1875		Hendrix, R. J.	
Rutherford, Charles	5Apr1875		Crasky, John	Of color
Rutherford, Jack	5Apr1875		Kirlen, Bernard	Of color
Eurton?, Sarah Jane	5Apr1875		Walker, Clark	
Dunn, Sarah Lewellen	3May1875		Hodges, J. C.	
Mitchel, Hannah	July1875		Baker, W. H.	White
Stewart, Lilly	Sept1875		Randoph, John G.	Of color
Moon, Grant			Whitsides, Alex	Cancelled Sept1875. Moon now with his grandfather, George W. Kemp, of Hardin Co
Beck, Robert			McKenzie, David	Of color. Cancelled April1876
Ivy, Molly	July1876		Franklin, Josiah	
Patridge, John			Moore, H. C.	Cancelled 2Apr1877, John having left Moore
Smith, Mary Susan	3Dec1877	6 yrs	Romine, J. H.	Canc 7July1879, Mary having left Romines
Wesham, Heny	7Jan1878	10 yrs	McKenzie, D.	
Wesham, Frank	March1878	6 yrs	Roberson, Beverly	
No court minutes recorded April through August, 1878				
Morgan, Fannie	7Oct1878		Sherrell, W. A.	
Morgan, Lee	7Oct1878		Sherrell, W. A.	
Hair, William Bell	1Sept1879		Beard, Mary J. (Mrs)	
Shields, Archabald	6Oct1879		Roark, J[ames]. P.	Cancelled 3Mar1880. Court rules apprenticing obtained by fraud. Recorded with February 1880 minutes
Grimes, Flora L.	2Aug1880		Franklin, J. D.	Bound at req of mother, Mrs. E. J. Nichols

Name	Date	Age	Master	Notes
Butler, Billy	6Dec1880		Adams, James	Infant of Cath Butler, Dcd. Taken from poor house. Forename from 4Oct1880 entry
Roberts, Cagia	4July1881		Henderson, W. C.	Child of John M. & Mary Roberts, Dcd. Cagia to have wearing apparel of his parents
Callicut, Ella	6Nov1882		Mitchel, Josh	Taken from Poor House. No bond required
Batey, Jane	4Jan1883	3 yrs	Daley, John	Daughter of Eliza Pate, who consents
Harp, Fred	1Apr1889		Carter, J. N.	Orphan. Bound previously, entered this date
Webster, Charley	1Apr1889		Wagoner, Jacob	Orphan. Bound previously, entered this date

Obion County

Name	Date	Age	Master	Notes
Harriss, Thomas	18Oct1824		, Bedford, Jonas	Bound by County Court of Jackson. Of color. On 4Jan1836* Thomas Harriss, a 25 y/o brickmason born free in Jackson County, registered as a free negro
Biggs, John	5Oct1827	13 yrs on 17Sept last	Jones, John	Bound by father, Francis Biggs
Smith, Andrew	6July1829	14 yrs on 8Apr1829	Pankey, John	Panky also chosen Guardian
Rodgers, John Wesley	6Mar1837	Abt 4 yrs	Bright, George W.	Son of Nathaniel Rodgers, died Feb1837. John T. Abington, Adm. 1May1837* On 5July1841 Rodgers ordered taken from Bright. William Rodgers, next friend alleges abuse. Motion denied 4Oct1841. Bright apptd guardian 6Aug1849
Rodgers, [Mary] Mariah	6Mar1837	Abt 13 yrs	Taylor, Jefferson	Daughter of Nathaniel Rodgers, died Feb1837, John T. Abington Adm.1May1837* On 6May1839* Jefferson Taylor, her uncle, apptd guardian of Mary Mariah Rodgers
Rodgers, Alexander	6Mar1837	Abt 10 or 11 yrs	Nelms, Richard	Son of Nathaniel Rodgers, died Feb1837, John T. Abington, Adm. 1May1837*
Robinson, Elizabeth	1Oct1838	5 yrs in April last	Calhoon, Samuel S.	Spinstress & seamstress. County charge since 4Jan1836 as Elizabeth Robertson. Mulatto

Name	Date	Age	Master	Notes
Zellers, Mary Jane	5May1840	Abt 9 yrs	Mitchell, John B.	Orphan of Thomas Zellers, Dcd
Zellers, Issabella	5May1840	Abt 6 yrs	Mitchell, John B.	Orphan of Thomas Zellers, Dcd
Zellers, Olivia Bartlett	5May1840	Abt 6 mo	Mitchell, John B.	Orphan of Thomas Zellers, Dcd
Ezell, Sylvanus	6July1840	Abt 12 yrs	Wright, Moses	Orphan of Zacherus Ezell, died 1840. Agriculture. Father called Ezachius Ezell 4Jan1841. Cancelled 6Nov1843, as Sylvester. To his brother, Lewis E. Underwood, of Weakley Co
James, Sarah Jane	4Jan1841	Abt 12 yrs	Bright, George W.	Orphan of William Bright, Dcd. Seamstress & spinster. Had been supported for several years by Bright, her brother-in-law
James, Elizabeth	4Jan1841	Abt 10 yrs	Bright, George W.	Orphan of William Bright, Dcd. Seamstress & spinster. Had been supported for several years by Bright, her brother-in-law
Williams, Michael C.	?		Morgan, John	On 5Dec1841 apprentice given to care of William Caldwell. Morgan died Nov1841
Boston, Sandy	7Feb1842	8 yrs on 26Dec1841	Farris, Thomas J.	Orphan. Son of Hannah Boston, who agrees
Ray, William F.	?	Abt 19 in May1842	Duff, James M.	Orphan. On 2May1842 apprentice asks protection of court. Duff ordered to appear.
Davis, Martha Jane	4Oct1842		Davis, Lewis	Orphan
Davis, James William	4Oct1842		Davis, Lewis	Orphan
Sapp, Samuel	7Aug1843		Davis, James	Orphan. Bound at Samuel's request
Margaret Ann	1Apr1844		Purvis, Starkey	Until 20 yrs. Orphan
Loyed, Nancy	3June1844		Hart, James	Orphan of "widow Loyd, Dcd" 5May1844. Archibald Crockett, Administrator
Loyed, Elizabeth	3June1844		Legate, Jefferson H.	Orphan of "widow Loyd, Dcd" 5May1844. Archibald Crockett, Administrator
Young, Joseph	3Dec1844	7 yrs	Stansbury, William	
Young, John	7Jan1845		Crockett, John P.	
Walton, Edmund	4Feb1845		Nants, Peter R.	
Fields, James F. M.	7Apr1845		Murphey, Nathaniel G.	
Bostick, Samuel Alexander	5May1845		Bright, David	
Nichols, James H.	2June1845		Fare, James H.	Orphan of William Nichols, Dcd
Nichols, Sarah	2June1845		Fare, James H.	Orphan of William Nichols, Dcd

Name	Date	Age	Master	Notes
Pounds, Thomas	5July1847	11 yrs	Reeves, Bethel	Orphan. Cancelled 4Oct1847, request of mother, Jane Pound
Pounds, William H.	5July1847		McNeely, W. W.	Cancelled 4Oct1847, request of mother, Jane Pound
Pounds, Samuel	5July1847		McNeely, Ansalam H.	Cancelled 4Oct1847, request of mother, Jane Pound
Far, John H.	5Mar1849		Far, John	Child of James Far
Far, Francis M.	5Mar1849		Far, John	Child of James Far
Jones, William	1Oct1849		Hogue, J. B.	Orphan. Bound at wish of relatives
Oar, Gilbert	5Aug1850		Lane, James	
Oar, John Hawkins	5Aug1850		Lane, James	
Neal, Sidney G.	6Jan1851	Abt 14 yrs	Harper, James B.	Orphan
Hood, Salina	6Dec1853	7 yrs the 2nd instant	Harper, John	Orphan
Neal, James W.	2Jan1854	14 yrs	Neal, Richard M.	Orphan
Joyner, Mary L.	3Apr1854	2 yrs	Bright, George W.	Orphan
Powell, John Alexander	2May1854	10 yrs	Harper, William B.	Orphan
Jones, Mary Elizabeth	5Feb1855	6 yrs	Crockett, Silas C.	Until 21 yrs. Orphan
Jones, Nancy Jane	5Feb1855	5 yrs	Crockett, Silas C.	Until 21 yrs. Orphan
Jones, Washington	5Feb1855	8 yrs	Wheeler, John H.	Orphan
Jones, Millie Ann	5Feb1855	10 yrs	Wheeler, John H.	Until 21 yrs. Orphan
Jones, Ferdinand	2Apr1855		Wilson, Hugh	Of color. Wilson released from bond 1Feb1869
Ross, David	2Apr1855	19 or 20 yrs	Moser, Joseph	
Buckley, Solomon O	2Apr1855	8 or 10 yrs	Macham, James H.	
Buckley, Joseph Brooks	2Apr1855	7 yrs	Harper, James B.	
Buckley, John T	8May1855	Some 13 yrs	Hampton, Thomas	Orphan
Lee, Sarah Jane	1Oct1855	2 yrs	Glover, John M	Orphan. Rescinded 6Nov1855. Mother living in county
Jones, George W.	6Mar1856		Coldwell, John P.	
Jones, Mary Ann	6Mar1856		Coldwell, John P.	
Jones, Nancy J.	6Mar1856		Coldwell, John P.	
Wright, Melissa (?Melina) J.	7April1856		Lewis, Robert N.	Orphan
Wright, William P.	7April1856		Lewis, Robert N.	Orphan

Name	Date	Age	Bound to	Notes
Crockett, David	2June1856	Abt 16 yrs	Curtner, Williamson	Orphan. Same date Curtner apptd guardian. Son of Jane Clark, formerly Jane Crockett. Cancelled 7Sept1857. David left Curtner
Mayberry, William	2Sept1856		Wright, John R.	Orphan. Cancelled 2May1859
Mayberry, John W.	2Sept1856		Wright, John R.	Orphan. Cancelled 2May1859
Bettisworth, Lousdale	5May1857	8 yrs	Fowlkes, Nathan G.	Until 20 yrs. Orphan. Farming business
Maberry, John W.	2May1859		Simpson, John	Orphan
Maberry, William	2May1859		Duncan, P. W.	
Parker, Thomas M.	4June1860	14 yrs 2 mo	Hickman, James M.	Orphan
Parker, Robert	1Oct1860	12 yrs	Welbern, John	Orphan
Bettis, Dick	4Dec1860		Calhoun, Oceana	Of color
Wallis, Charles	2Sept1861	14 yrs	Hendrix, Thomas P.	
Smith, Isaac	7Oct1861	9 yrs	Dunagan, J. D.	Cancelled 7Apr1862. Smith had fits before being bound
Gibson, Felix	7Oct1861	3 yrs	Pierce, Felix	
Smith, Deliah	7Oct1861	8 yrs	Burris, J. B.	
Hines, David	7Oct1861	14 yrs	Waldroup, James G.	
Hines, Jane	7Oct1861	6 yrs	Waldroup, James G.	
Smith, George	7Oct1861	4 yrs	Morris, T. P.	
Smith, Robert	7Oct1861	4 yrs	Morris, T. J.	
Hines, Thomas	7Oct1861	13 yrs	Cole, James M.	
Hines, Louisa B.	7Oct1861	3 yrs	Green, Sally	
Fluty, Neel S. B.	7Nov1865		Pryor, Henry	On 6Apr1870 Pryor ordered to answer charge he was not teaching Fluty properly. Fluty released 7June1870
Caldwell, James A.	5Dec1865	11 yrs	Whipple, David H.	Orphan. Cancelled 4Jan1866
Carroll (or Carreway), James M.	6Feb1866	17 yrs	Carpenter, Martha J.	Orphan
Brice, Lucy	6Feb1866	Abt 13 yrs	Brice, Walter	Orphan. Of color
Frank	6Feb1866	Abt 13 yrs	Marberry, P. H.	Orphan. Of color
Lucy	6Feb1866	11 yrs	Marberry, P. H.	Orphan. Of color
Peyton	6Feb1866	9 yrs	Marberry, P. H.	Orphan. Of color
Henry, Henry	6Mar1866	14 yrs	King, James H.	Orphan. Of color

Name	Date	Age	Master	Notes
Dougherty, Polly	6Mar1866	14 yrs	Dougherty, James F.	Orphan. Of color
Dougherty, Eliza	6Mar1866	8 yrs	Dougherty, James F.	Orphan. Of color
Dougherty, Emma B.	6Mar1866	6 yrs	Dougherty, James F.	Orphan. Of color
Dougherty, George Ann	6Mar1866	4 yrs	Dougherty, James F.	Orphan. Of color
Alexander, Abraham	6Mar1866	Abt 12 yrs	King, William D.	Of color. Cancelled 5Nov1866 on petition of mother, Sarah Alexander
Farris, Betty Lucy	6Aug1866		Farris, Isaac N.	Of color
Farris, Tom	6Aug1866		Farris, Isaac N.	Of color
Farris, Jim	6Aug1866		Farris, Isaac N.	Of color
Farris, Clem?	6Aug1866		Farris, Isaac N.	Of color
Harris, Solomon	6Aug1866	10 yrs	Harris, M. V.	Orphan. Of color
Harris, Martha	6Aug1866	12 yrs	Harris, M. V.	Orphan. Of color
Lewallen, George M.	4Sept1866	9 yrs	Stephens, Jeremiah	Orphan
Wright, Abe	5Nov1866	10 yrs	Wright, Jr, P. A.	Orphan. Of color
Wade, James	5Nov1866	13 yrs	Wade, W. B.	Orphan. Of color. Cancelled 7Jan1869. Illegally bound. To mother, Sarah Wade
Wade, John	5Nov1866	15 yrs	Wade, W. B.	Orphan. Of color. Cancelled 7Jan1869. Illegally bound. To mother, Sarah Wade
Wade, Matt	5Nov1866	13 yrs	Wade, W. B.	Female orphan. Of color
Gum, Boyd	6Nov1866	15 yrs	Gum, W. N.	Orphan. Of color
Gum, Feby	6Nov1866	11 yrs	Gum, W. N.	Orphan. Of color
Gum, Fillis	6Nov1866	13 yrs	Gum, W. N.	Orphan. Of color
Yeagan, Wallace	3Dec1866		Lippard, C. T.	Orphan. Of color
Mabery, William	5Aug1867		Duncan, P. W.	Orphan in destitute circumstances
Coleman, Joshua	2Sept1867		Mitchell, J. W.	Canc 2Dec1867. To mother, Martha Mitchell
Mitchell, Alice	2Sept1867		Mitchell, J. W.	Canc 2Dec1867. To mother, Martha Mitchell
Haynes, T.	8Oct1867		Cloar, John E.	Orphan
Maubly, Henry	9Jan1868		Nall, R. C.	Of color
Crockett, Narcis	9Jan1868	Abt 7 yrs	Crockett, Lean	Orphan
Green, William N.	2Mar1868		Key, L. C.	Canc 8Sept1868. To mother, Mary A. Green

Name	Date	Age	Guardian	Remarks
Oseteen, Harvey	2Mar1868		Walker, W. Y.	Orphan. On 4May1868 Walker awarded $4 for making a coffin for Elizabeth Oseteen, a pauper
Oseteen, Zacariah T.	2Mar1868		Walker, W. Y.	Orphan. See above
Gardner, Mary	2Mar1868		Gardner, D. S.	
Gardner, Miles	2Mar1868		Gardner, D. S.	
Gardner, Andrew	2Mar1868		Gardner, D. S.	
Gardner, Mark	2Mar1868		Mooring, Wyatt	
Gardner, Sally	2Mar1868		Mooring, Wyatt	
Gardner, Sidney	2Mar1868		Mooring, Wyatt	
Dollins, Jesse E.	2Mar1868	7 yrs	Watson, John S.	Orphan. Cancelled 8Jan1878, Jessee havig become helpless & unable to be instructed
Kirby, Charles	6Apr1868	8 yrs (from canc entry)	Jackson, Squire	Cancelled 6Jan1868. Taken by mother, Betsy Jane Kirby. All of color
Dabney, Munroe	4May1868		Peacock, J. N.	Of color
Letitia	7Sept1868		Rogers, S. J.	Daughter of Viney
Demington?, James A.	7Dec1868		Hummas, John N.	Orphan
Alexander, John	6Jan1869	9 yrs	Farkinton, J. C.	Orphan. Entry X'd out. "Bond rejected"
Alexander, Abraham	6Jan1869	12 yrs	Blair, A. B.	Orphan. Entry X'd out. "Bond rejected"
Alexander, Mary	6Jan1869	13 yrs	Hampton, T. B.	Orphan. Entry X'd out. "Bond rejected"
Alexander, Mark	6Sept1869	10 yrs	Cooper, S. M.	Orphan. Entry X'd out. "Bond rejected"
Wheatley, Bill	6Sept1869		Williams, C.	
Haley, Betty	1Nov1869	12 yrs	Moonig, Wyatt	Of color
James, Jennie	2Nov1869		Hickman, Michael	Of color
King, Charles	2Nov1869		Hickman, Michael	Of color
Demmington, Jesse	2Nov1869		Williams, J. S.	
Gwynne, A. J.	8Feb1870		Bright, David	
Bull, H. F.	8Mar1870	10 yrs	Bradford, R. S.	
Glover?, Joshua	4Apr1870		Glover, Jesse T.	
Unnamed	3Apr1871		Wilson, L. G.	
Henry	1May1871		Callicott, W. F.	Of color
Caroline	1May1871		Callicott, W. F.	Of color

Name	Date	Age	Master	Notes
Bradford	1May1871		Callicott, W. F.	Of color
Wright, J. H.	3July1871		Hall, John B.	Cancelled 3Oct1871
Unnamed	7Aug1871		Cloar, T. C.	
Knight,	7Aug1871		Harrison, Jesse W.	Cancelled 4Feb1872. Name from canc entry
McCairy, A. B.	6Nov1871		Roberts, T. J.	
Unnamed	6Nov1871		Cole, J. M.	
King, Thomas	4Dec1871	12 yrs	C___s, John G.	White
Halloway, William	1Jan1872		Wright, S. P.	
Halloway, Edward	1Jan1872		Wright, S. P.	
Hicks, Benjamin	1Jan1872		Wright, S. P.	Cancelled 4Apr1881
Crockett, John D.	1Apr1872	17 yrs	Brown, Hiram R.	
Phipp, Mary	3June1872		Meacham, Willey (Mrs)	Of color. Cancelled 3Apr1878, Mary having left Meacham
Hayes, Albert	2Sept1872	6 yrs	Parsons, George	
Turner, Henry	2Sept1872	15 yrs	Turner, David	Both of color
Dunavant, James	4Nov1872	Abt 14 yrs	Field, W. R.	Orphan. Farming & stock raising. Of color
Louallen, Pinkney	5Aug1873	3 yrs	Loudon, Thomas N.	Taken from the County Assylum
King, Jennett	2Sept1873	8 yrs	Brown, Silas	Both of color
Mott, Mollie	187_		Mott, P. W.	Cancelled 3Nov1873. To mother in Illinois
Mott, Andy	2Feb1874	12 yrs	Caldwell, L. O.	Of color
Turner, May	4May1874	13 yrs	Turner, Dave	Both of color
Whitaker, John Walter?	6July1874	5 yrs	Lawson, Phillip	
Carnatzor, M. J.	1Mar1875		Board, John	Probably female
Carnatzor, W. E.	1Mar1875		Board, John	Probably male
Farris, Newman	2Aug1875	Abt 11 yrs	Board, G. F.	Of color
Farris, Clara J.	7Sept1875	11 yrs	Hardison, H. A.	Of color
Branham, Annie	1Nov1875	7 yrs	Gardner, W. H.	Of color
Branox, Lucy	6Nov1876	8 yrs	Chambers, J. W. & Mariah	Consent of mother. Of color
McWherter, Henryetta	4Dec1876	Abt 10 yrs	Moore, J. B.	Of color
McWherter, Willie	4Dec1876	Abt 5 yrs	Chiles, J. T.	Of color

Name	Date	Age	Bound to	Remarks
McWherter, John M.	4Dec1876	6 1/2 yrs	Miller, Milton	Of color
McWhorter, Malinda	4Dec1876	Abt 3 yrs	Miller, A.	Of color
Patton, Robert J.	4Dec1876	Abt 6 yrs	Wallis, Isham	
Patton, Thomas J.	5Feb1877	Abt 10 yrs	Milner, R. T.	
Littleton, Enoch Franklin	5Feb1877	6 1/2 yrs	Jackson, B. J.	Probable son of W. R. Littleton & wife, who died early 1876. See adoption of Emily Parley Littleton by S. B. Dunbar 6Mar1876*
Armor, J. H.	5Mar1877	5 1/2 yrs	Pollock, J. H.	Cancelled 4June1877, Pollock now having care of two grandchildren due to death of their father
Nailling, Isham	3Apr1877	Abt 10 yrs	Ford, William & M. E.	Of color
Armer, J. H.	5June1877	Abt 5 1/2 or 6 yrs	Boyett, B.	
Connelly, Guss	6Aug1877		Tanner, F. H.	Of color
Frazier, John W.	3Sept1877		Mahan, L. M.	
Maho, Lind	3Sept1877		Stovall, B. L.	Of color
Cross, Sallie	1Nov1877		Prather, John W.	
Taylor, Jerry	3Dec1877	11 yrs (from canc entry)	Stovall, B. W.	Canc 3June1878 for mistreatment. Stovall mentally incapable of raising apprentice
Vick, John	3Mar1879	Abt 2 yrs	Laney, E. F.	
Moss, Willie	6Oct1879		Bonner, C. H.	Son of L. J. Moss, Dcd. Mother not able to provide 2Sept1879*. Sibs Christina, Maggie & John sent to Poor House
Hargrove, William	6Oct1879	Abt 10 yrs	Leppard, C. T.	
Hargrove, Harry V.	6Oct1879		Campbell, David	
Moss, Christina	3Nov1879	Abt 7 yrs	Noah, F. L.	See Willie Moss
Moss, Margaret E.	1Dec1879		Donnell, R. A.	See Willie Moss
Tilghman, Willie	2Aug1880	Abt 6 or 7 yrs	Ramsey, A. M.	Of color
Shipman, Exeline	2Aug1880	Abt 14 yrs	Foster, R. H.	Mulatto
Tilghman, W.	4Jan1881	Abt 8 yrs	Pollock, J. H.	Of color
Ferguson, Ellsworth	4Apr1881		Foster, R. H.	Of color
Ferguson, Frank	4Apr1881	Abt 10 yrs	Foster, R. H.	Of color
Robertson, James Erwin	6June1881	Abt 4 yrs	Meadows, James B.	Of color
McKenzie, Grand	4July1881	Abt 6 yrs	Clement, R. H.	Of color
Patton, Tom			Milner, A. T.	Cancelled 2Oct1882

Name	Date	Age	Master	Notes
Stovall, David	2Oct1883	7 yrs	Hughlett, R. W.	Of color. Consent of Milly Stovall, mother
Wadlington, Franklin	2Oct1883	3 yrs	Hughlett, R. W.	Of color. Consent of grandmother
Davis, Ida Bell	4May1885	1 yr 2 mo	Davis, Blake	
Phillips, Joseph	7Dec1885	Abt 7 yrs	Johnson, J. W.	Farming
Barker, Thomas	1Nov1886	Abt 9 yrs	Orrell, W. T.	Farming

Shelby County

Name	Date	Age	Master	Notes
Taylor, Charles	7Feb1826	12 yrs	Bunch, Elijah	Orphan. Shoe maker
Vickers, John	20Oct1828		Wilcox, William	Orphan
Goyne, Aaron	22Oct1828	17 yrs	Kincaid, William	Orphan
Liston, Anthony	21Jan1829	15 yrs	Simpson, Lawrence	Orphan
Kirk, Polly	21Jan1829	12 yrs	Ralston, John	Orphan. On 19Jan1828 Constable ordered to bring 5 oldest children of Thomas Kirk, Dcd
Kirk, Catharine	21Jan1829	14 yrs	McDaniel, Clement	Orphan. See above
Kirk, John	21Jan1829	Abt 10 yrs	Robbins, Benjamin	Orphan. See above
Price, John	21Jan1829	6 or 7 yrs	Manning, John W.	Orphan
Newsom, Thomas	20Apr1829	Abt 12 yrs	Graham, John D.	Orphan
Newson, Sarah	20Apr1829		Powers, John	Orphan
Miles, John	22Apr1829	5 yrs	Rennolds, Renold	Orphan. On 20Apr1829 orphans of Mrs Miles ordered brought to court to be bound
Miles, Matildy	22Apr1829	12 yrs	Abbott, James	Orphan. See above. Revoked 23Apr1829
Miles, Jane	22Apr1829	2 yrs	Jameson, Jame	Orphan. See above
Miles, Polly	23Apr1829	Abt 9 yrs	Bowles, James	Orphan. See above
Nusum, John	22July1829	8 yrs	Williams, William	Orphan
Pritchard, David L.	21Oct1829		Shobell, John F.	For 3 yrs. Orphan.
Mills, William	19July1830		Dickens, John	Orphan. Of color
Weatherford, Eliza	18Apr1831	8 yrs	Ervin, Matthew	Orphan
Powel, Lucy M.	18July1831	13 yrs	Bryant, William A.	Orphan

Name	Date	Age	Name	Notes
Powel, James	18July1831	4 yrs	Bryant, William A.	Orphan
Kelley, John	21July1831		Montgomery, William H.	Orphan
Not named	17Oct1831		Vanhook, Larchus	Polly Hicks a party to indenture
Powel, James	16Apr1832		Messick, Jeferson	Orphan
Walker, Joseph	16Apr1832	Abt 18 yrs	Jordan, Thomas	
Walker, Joseph	21Jan1833		Ammon, Peter	Orphan
Harris, William	18Apr1833	14 yrs	White, Eppy	Orphan. Cancelled 6Dec1836
Harris, H.	18Apr1833	12 yrs	Davis, Willis	Orphan
Ward, James W.	15July1833	Abt 8 or 10 yrs	Kelley, John	Orphan
Vicus, William Carson	21July1834	6 or 7 yrs	Vaughan, William	Orphan
Fips, William	19Jan1835		Montgomery, William H.	Orphan
Fips, Mary Ann C.	19Jan1835		Jimerson, James	Orphan. Cancelled 23Oct1835
Fips, M. C.	23Jan1835		Jameson, James	Bond posted. Orphan female. Probably same as Mary Ann Fips
Givens, Rebecca	20Apr1835		Foley, John	Orphan. On 20July1835 James Harrol was paid for support of Moses Givens, a pauper
Given, John	24Apr1835		Flipps, John	Orphan. See above
Harris, Albert	19Oct1835		Lundy, Joshua C.	Farming. Probably one of three or four children of William Harris, Dcd 24Apr1835
Harris, Paity	19Oct1835		Lundy, Joshua C.	See above
Phipps, Mary Ann	23Oct1835	Abt 12 yrs	Banks, Enoch	Orphan
Meredith, William	18Jan1836		Gant, John H.	Cancelled 7Aug1843 as William Maryweather
Meredith, Jane	18Jan1836		Gant, John H.	Cancelled 7Aug1843 as Sarah Jane Maryweather
Vickers, John	21Jan1836	Abt 12 yrs	Hale, Meshac	
Playway, Levy	21Jan1836	Abt 17 yrs	Hornsby, Roseland	
Harris, Ewell	August1836	14 to 16 yrs	Montgomery, W. H.	Orphan. Probable son of William Harris, Dcd 24Apr1835. A prior indenture with W. Speckernagle cancelled
Walker, Moses C.	August1836	10 yrs	Huddleston, William C.	Orphan
Rayburn	August1836	17 yrs	Johnson, William	Mulatto
Cardozo, Edward S.	7Nov1836	12 yrs	Seckernagle, William	Orphan
Aiken, Pleasant	2Jan1837	Abt 10 yrs	Murray, Charles B.	
Phillips, Zaecheus	2Jan1837	Abt 17 yrs	Murray, Charles B.	Cancelled June1840

Name	Date	Age	Master	Notes
Starns, William	June1837	Abt 16 yrs	Queen, David C.	
Reyborn	August1837	18 yrs 2 mo 23 d	Williams, Joseph	Mulatto
Walker, Rachel	August1837	10 yrs	Epperson, Caro	
Harris, Stephen	Sept1837		Midgett, Nathan	
Harris, Geraldine	Sept1837		Midgett, Nathan	
Hale, Rebecca	January1838		Owen, Travis	Mulatto. Bound 12 yrs ago, term served. Indenture recorded and Rebecca released.
Bettis, John	3Sept1838		Bettis, William	
Bettis, James F.	3Sept1838		Bettis, William	
Joseph	5Oct1840		Connell, William	Until 20 yrs
Printz, William	5Oct1840		Jungclos, John	
Joice, Mary	3May1841		Blickly, T. C.	Orphan. On 4Aug1845 Blakely ordered to court on allegation of mistreatment. Cancelled 7Oct1845. Mary to remain with her brother, William Joice
Joyce, Thomas J.	3May1841		Crawford, J. C.	
Maryweather, William	7Aug1843		Reaves, John	
Maryweather, Sarah Jane	7Aug1843		Reaves, John	
House, James W.	6Nov1843	Abt 9 yrs	Gant, J. H.	Of color
House, John W.	6Nov1843	Abt 6 yrs, later corrected to 4 mo	Gant, J. H.	Of color. Cancelled & rebound 6Oct1857, at which time age at binding corrected to 4 mo
House, Erasmus	6Nov1843	Abt 5 yrs	Abernathy, J. S.	Of color
House, Pleasant	6Nov1843	Abt 2 yrs	Hamner, Hezekiah F	Of color. On 5May1845 ordered returned to court, Hamner having absconded
House, Margaret	6Nov1843		West, James F.	Of color
Cross, Mary E.	1Jan1844		Lewis, J. P.	
Cordozo, Willlam H.	5Feb1844		Lynch, William	
Hall, Esther Narcissa Manerva Jane	1Apr1844	12 yrs	Sappington, Mark Brown	Of color. Cancelled 6Jan1846 for mistreatment. Indentrure restored 6Apr1846
Catherine	3Feb1845	9 yrs	Collins, R. A.	Of color
Stephen	3Feb1845	11 yrs	Richards, Walter	Orphan. Of color

Name	Date	Age	Master	Notes
House, Pleasant	2June1845	3 yrs	Robins, William J.	Of color. On 6Mar1854 to temporary custody of Uriah Keller. Robins now deceased
Jackson, Elijah	7July1845	7 yrs	Paynter, H. H.	
Sweeney, Jerome P.	7July1845	12 yrs	Williams, Samuel C.	
Sweeney, Lorena J.	7July1845	10 yrs	Williams, Samuel C.	Until 21 yrs
Sweeney, Lewis C.	7July1845	13 yrs	Riley, L. C.	
Sweeney, Willie W.	7July1845	6 yrs	Riley, L. C.	
Harrison, Mary Jane	6Oct1845	8 yrs	Brown, Martha	Of color
Harrison, Harriet	5Jan1846	4 yrs	Hawthorn, John W.	Of color
Hall, Esther	6Jan1846	14 yrs	Harrell, E. B.	Of color. Cancelled 6Apr1846. Returned to M. B. Sappington, former master
Bright, James	7Apr1846	12 yrs	Sloan, John	Orphan
Bright, Thomas L.	7Apr1846	11 yrs	Robinson, Alexander M.	Orphan
Bright, Thomas L.	4May1846	8 yrs	Reese, H. J.	At request of Bright's mother
Young, John	7Sept1846		Morris, Silas M.	
Young, Jasper	7Sept1846		Morris, Silas M.	
Lewiscott, Lycargus	4Jan1847		Allen, Joseph D.	For 3 yrs
Manuel	7June1847	15 yrs	Gonzales, Manuel Farina	Orphan
Sisba, Lorenzo	5July1847	Abt 14 yrs	Farina, Manuel	Orphan. Lorenzo Mexican by birth
Richard	2Aug1847	7 yrs	Aikin, W. A.	Of color
Jane	2Aug1847	4 yrs	Aikin, W. A.	Of color
Hutchens, Patton	2Aug1847	10 yrs	Hutchens, Clem	Orphan
Rawlings, Kitty	6Sept1847	Abt 16 yrs	Whitsett, W. W.	Of color
Branchee, Joawe	7Sept1847	Abt 12 yrs	Dunahoo, John	
Henry, James	1Nov1847	2 yrs	Howcott, Lewis	Of color. Consent of mother. New indenture entered 2Dec1850
Peres, Antonio	6Dec1847	15 yrs	Farinas, Manuel	Orphan. Antonio Mexican by birth
Hadley, Lemuel	3Jan1848	Abt 16 yrs	Allen, J. D.	Orphan
Frances	3Apr1848	Abt 14 yrs	Owen, F. A.	Of color
Washington	3Apr1848	Abt 12 yrs	Owen, F. A.	Of color

Name	Date	Age	Master	Notes
Peter	3Apr1848	Abt 9 yrs	Owen, F. A.	Of color
Montgomery	3Apr1848	Abt 7 yrs	Owen, F. A.	Of color
Daniel	3Apr1848	Abt 5 yrs	Owen, F. A.	Of color
Fowler, Mary Catherine	1May1848	Abt 12 yrs	McKnight, Leonides P.	Orphan
Franklin	8Nov1848		Huffman, James	Bond entered 4Dec1848. Cancelled 7Nov1853 & assigned to Isaac D. Wesson
Collister, James	1Jan1849		Cowley, William	
Ed	4Nov1850		Harrel, E. B.	Of color
General	4Nov1850		Harrel, L. D.	Of color
Margaret	4Nov1850	3 yrs	Harrell, Jacob D.	Of color
Alice	4Nov1850	1 yr	Harrell, Jacob D.	Of color
Armstrong, John	2June1851		Whitworth, P. G.	Cancelled 7July1851
Hudenburg, James I.	7July1851	16 yrs	Harper, W. H.	Farmer
Lynch, James	1Sept1851	8 yrs	Evans, H. C.	White
Hidiburg, James I.	1Dec1851		Shelton, John F.	
Bright, Thomas L.	2Feb1852	14 yrs	Yarbrough, William H.	
Berry, William	4May1852	Abt 14 yrs	McCollum, Malcolm	Servant. Of color
Berry, Ann	4May1852	Abt 12 yrs	McCollum, Malcolm	Servant. Of color
Berry, Doty	4May1852	8 yrs	McCollum, Malcolm	Servant. Of color
Berry, Wesley	4May1852	Abt 6 yrs	McCollum, Malcolm	Servant. Of color
Mary	3May1853	Abt 7 yrs	Eanes, William H.	Servant. Of color
Caroline	3May1853	Abt 6 yrs	Eanes, William H.	Servant. Of color
Walker, Susan	4July1853	Abt 10 yrs	Robinson, Robert	Until 21 yrs. White orphan
Moody, Tillman Fox	1Aug1853	Abt 10 yrs	John L. Saffanans & Co	Carpenter
Franklin	7Nov1853		Wesson, Isaac D.	Orphan. Previously bound to James Huffman
Wright, Richard H.	3Apr1854		Stout, Isaiah	Cancelled 9Feb1859. To mother at her request
Wright, Andrew J.	3Apr1854		Stout, Isaiah	Cancelled 5July1859. To mother at her request
House, Pleasant	4Apr1854	Abt 11 yrs	Robins, Mary E.	Of color
Anderson, James	7Aug1854	13 yrs	White, John	Orphan
Linn, Jane	7Aug1854	3 yrs	Hawthorne, J. W.	Until 21 yrs. Orphan. Of color

Name	Date	Age/Term	Notes
Holt, Susan	Hill, Hume F.	7Aug1854	10 yrs	Until 21 yrs. Orphan
House, Pleasant	Robins, Thomas D.	4Sept1854	11 yrs	Orphan. Of color
Riley, Franklin	Hardaway, Franklin	5Feb1855	13 yrs	Orphan
Hank, Christian	Specht, Joseph	4June1855	15 yrs	Orphan
Schmetzer, John	Specht, Joseph	4June1855	19 yrs	Orphan
Thiele, August	Pante, D.	2July1855		Child of Joseph Thiele, Dcd
McGee, Thomas	Adams, William S.	3Dec1855	5 yrs	Orphan
Schmitzer, Christiana	Arlt, F. W.	3Dec1855	6 yrs	Orphan.
Owen, Elijah A.	Steelman, James	3Dec1855	10 yrs	Orphan
Preston, Rachel Ann	Preston, Martha	3Dec1855	10 yrs	Both of color. Martha's child
Preston, David	Preston, Martha	3Dec1855	7 yrs	Both of color. Martha's child
House, James W.	Coleman, James M.	8Apr1856	Abt 14 yrs	Of color. Entry crossed out
Stocks, Jr., Cullen	Stocks, Cullen	10Apr1856	18 yrs	Orphan
Bently, G. B.	Spencer, Zachariah T.	5May1856	Abt 10 yrs	Orphan
Laberque, Vincent	Specht, Joseph	3Nov1856	17 yrs	Until 20 yrs
Stone, Martha Angelina	McClellan, Thomas	6July1857	7 yrs	
Woods, Rachel	Foster, William	7July1857		Both of color. A previous apprenticeship to Martha Preston rescinded for maltreatment
House, John W.	Wilson, E. H.	6Oct1857	4 mo on 6Nov1843	Of color
Madden, Augustus N.	Sherry, P.	6Jan1858	9 yrs	Orphan
Madden, Mary	Sherry, P.	6Jan1858	7 yrs	Orphan
Adams, James	Bivins, Lewis C.	7Mar1859	Abt 13 yrs	Orphan
Shrimpf, Charles	Specht, Joseph	3Oct1859	Abt 17 yrs	Until 19 yrs 9 mo. White
Copperwhite, Julia	Tighe, Edward	4Jan1860	14 yrs	
Copperwhite, Elizabeth	Tighe, Edward	4Jan1860	3 yrs	
Copperwhite, John	Tighe, Edward	4Jan1860	2 yrs	
Albert	Allen, W. H.			Previously apprenticed to Allen, who is now deceased. On 5Nov1860 executors testify that Albert has served his apprenticeship & is now free. Of color
Toney, Christopher	Hickle, David	5Feb1861	13 yrs	Of color

Name	Date	Age	Master	Notes
Toney, Matthew	5Feb1861	11 yrs	Hickle, David	Of color
Toney, David	5Feb1861	9 yrs	Hickle, David	Of color
Toney, William Henry	5Feb1861	7 yrs	Hickle, David	Of color
Matlock, James	3June1861	14 yrs	Giles, T. L.	Orphan
Dean, William Henry	17Aug1865	7 yrs	Dean, S. S.	By FB. Twin child of Joahanes Dean, mother, who consents to have him taken to Marshal Co, Mississippi. Of color
Dean, Henrietta	17Aug1865	7 yrs	Dean, S. S.	By FB. Until 21 yrs. Twin child of Joahanes Dean, mother, who consents to have her taken to Marshal Co, Mississippi. Of color
Ridley, Robert	6Nov1865	13 yrs	Craighead, William A.	By FB. Farm work. Orphan. Craighead a planter of Mississippi Co, AK. Of color
Harding, Mary	8Nov1865	12 yrs	Harding, T. (Mrs)	By FB. Farm work. Orphan. Of color
Harding, Julia	8Nov1865	8 yrs	Harding, T. (Mrs)	By FB. Farm work. Orphan. Of color
Harding, Lydia	8Nov1865	7 yrs	Harding, T. (Mrs)	By FB. Farm work. Orphan. Of color
Harding, Ben	8Nov1865	12 yrs	Harding, T. (Mrs)	By FB. Farm work. Orphan. Of color
Harding, Nisa	8Nov1865	8 yrs	Harding, T. (Mrs)	By FB. Farm work. Orphan. Of color
Mitchel, Edward	8Nov1865	6 yrs	Scanlan, W. E.	By FB. Farm work. Orphan. Scanlan a planter of Crittenden Co, Ark. Of color
Johnson, George	8Nov1865	7 yrs	Scanlan, W. E.	By FB. Farm work. Orphan. Scanlan a planter of Crittenden Co, Ark. Of color
Wall, Francis	8Nov1865	7 yrs	Scanlan, W. E.	By FB. Farm work. Female orphan. Scanlan a planter of Crittenden Co, Ark. Of color
Miller, Foster	8Nov1865		Scanlan, W. E.	By FB. Farm work. Orphan. Scanlan a planter of Crittenden Co, Ark. Of color
Scanlan, Rachall Gibbs	8Nov1865	11 yrs	Scanlan, W. E.	By FB. Farm work. Orphan. Scanlan a planter of Crittenden Co, Ark. Of color
Scanlan, Angeline Gibbs	8Nov1865	9 yrs	Scanlan, W. E.	By FB. Farm work. Orphan. Scanlan a planter of Crittenden Co, Ark. Of color
Funk, Peter	8Nov1865	12 yrs	Scanlan, W. E.	By FB. Farm work. Orphan. Scanlan a planter of Crittenden Co, Ark. Of color
Miller, George	8Nov1865	13 yrs	Scanlan, W. E.	By FB. Farm work. Orphan. Scanlan a planter of Crittenden Co, Ark. Of color

Brown, William	8Nov1865	12 yrs	Scanlan, W. E.	By FB. Farm work. Orphan. Scanlan a planter of Crittenden Co, Ark. Of color
Scanlan, Henrietta	8Nov1865	8 yrs	Scanlan, W. E.	By FB. Farm work. Orphan. Scanlan a planter of Crittenden Co, Ark. Of color
Scanlan, Maria Gibbs	8Nov1865	12 yrs	Scanlan, W. E.	By FB. Farm work. Orphan. Scanlan a planter of Crittenden Co, Ark. Of color
Scanlan, Horace	8Nov1865	13 yrs	Scanlan, W. E.	By FB. Farm work. Orphan. Scanlan a planter of Crittenden Co, Ark. Of color
Scanlan, Sara Gibbs	8Nov1865	8 yrs	Scanlan, W. E.	By FB. Farm work. Orphan. Scanlan a planter of Crittenden Co, Ark. Of color
Johnson, Lewis	10Nov1865		Gray, John	By FB. Farm work. Orphan. Of color
Johnson, Randall	10Nov1865	7 yrs	Gray, John	By FB. Farm work. Orphan. Of color
Lewis, Edwin	10Nov1865	8 yrs	McNeal, J. H.	By FB. Farm work. Orphan. McNeal a planter of Crittenden Co, Ark. Of color
Sims, George	10Nov1865	3 yrs	McNeal, J. H.	By FB. Farm work. Orphan. McNeal a planter of Crittenden Co, Ark. Of color
Harris, Margaret	10Nov1865	8 yrs	McNeal, J. H.	By FB. Farm work. Orphan. McNeal a planter of Crittenden Co, Ark. Of color
Sims, Nancy	10Nov1865	8 yrs	McNeal, J. H.	By FB. Farm work. Orphan. McNeal a planter of Crittenden Co, Ark. Of color
McNeal, Henry	10Nov1865	8 yrs	McNeal, J. H.	By FB. Farm work. Orphan. McNeal a planter of Crittenden Co, Ark. Of color
Taylor, James	10Nov1865	8 yrs	McNeal, J. H.	By FB. Farm work. Orphan. McNeal a planter of Crittenden Co, Ark. Of color
Vaultz, Thomas	10Nov1865	7 yrs	McNeal, J. H.	By FB. Farm work. Orphan. McNeal a planter of Crittenden Co, Ark. Of color
Ayrs, Charles	10Nov1865	5 yrs	McNeal, J. H.	By FB. Farm work. Orphan. McNeal a planter of Crittenden Co, Ark. Of color
Ransom, John	10Nov1865	8 yrs	McNeal, J. H.	By FB. Farm work. Orphan. McNeal a planter of Crittenden Co, Ark. Of color

Name	Date	Age	Master	Notes
Winfield, Augustus	10Nov1865	9 yrs	Davis, Richard S.	By FB. Farm work. Orphan. Davis a planter of Tippah Co, Miss. Of color
Cummings, Laura	11Nov1865	6 yrs	Fishback, George	By FB. House servant or cook. Fishback a publisher of St Louis. Mo. Orphan of color
Carraway, Maggie	11Nov1865	6 yrs	Buckingham, H. G.	By FB. Farm work. Orphan. Of color
Theasus, Robert	11Nov1865	11 yrs	Buckingham, H. G.	By FB. Farm work. Orphan. Of color
Carraway, Betsy	11Nov1865	10 yrs	Buckingham, H. G.	By FB. Farm work. Orphan. Of color
Brown, Mary	11Nov1865	8 yrs	Batchelor, F. Y.	By FB. Farm work. Orphan. Of color. Batchelor permitted to move Mary to Cincinnati, OH
Sharp, Bidwell	14Nov1865	5 yrs	Stewart, H. M.	By FB. Farm work. Orphan. Of color
Sharp, Horace	14Nov1865	7 yrs	Stewart, H. M.	By FB. Farm work. Orphan. Of color
Eddins, Frank	15Nov1865	8 yrs	Eddins, M. J. (Mrs)	By FB. Farm work. Orphan. Of color
Rodgers, Lucinda	15Nov1865	10 yrs	Rodgers, H. E. (Mrs)	By FB. Farm work. Orphan. Of color
Maxey, John	15Nov1865	7 yrs	Davis, R. W.	By FB. Farm work. Orphan. Davis a planter of Mississippi Co, Ark. Of color
Shirley, Virginia Ann	16Nov1865		Shirley, J. T & wife	By FB. Seamstress. Consent of mother, Harriet Green
McFarland, Peter	16Nov1865		Shirley, J. T & wife	By FB. Porter. Consent of mother, Harriet Green
Selby, Dora	16Nov1865	4 yrs	Anderson, M. A. (Mrs)	By FB. Farm work. Orphan. Of color
Anderson, Parthenia	16Nov1865	10 yrs	Anderson, M. A. (Mrs)	By FB. Farm work. Orphan. Of color
Shelton, Eliza	17Nov1865	7 yrs	Shelton, R. W. (Mrs)	By FB. Farm work. Orphan. Of color
Hamlin, Laura	20Nov1865	10	Hamlin, William B.	By FB. Farm work. Orphan. Of color
Powers, Emma	22Nov1865	10 yrs	Powers, John	By FB. Farm work. Orphan. Of color
Jones, Peter	22Nov1865	8 yrs	Avery, William T.	By FB. Farm work. Orphan. Of color
Green, Jacob	23Nov1865	7 yrs	Green, Fannie (Mrs)	By FB. Farm work. Orphan. Of color
Lynch, Emma	23Nov1865	6 yrs	Holman, Edward M.	By FB. Farm work. Orphan. Of color
Lynch, Benjamin	23Nov1865	8 yrs	Holman, Edward M.	By FB. Farm work. Orphan. Of color
Lynch, Ann	23Nov1865	10 yrs	Holman, Edward M.	By FB. Farm work. Orphan. Of color
Green, Margaret	23Nov1865	11 yrs	Green, Fannie (Mrs)	By FB. Farm work. Orphan. Of color
Stewart, James	24Nov1865	8 yrs	Stewart, Andrew	By FB. Farm work. Orphan. Of color
Stewart, Georgiana	24Nov1865	7 yrs	Stewart, Andrew	By FB. Farm work. Orphan. Of color

Name	Date	Age	Bound To	Remarks
Stewart, Alex	24Nov1865	10 yrs	Stewart, Andrew	By FB. Farm work. Orphan. Of color
Billie	24Nov1865	14 yrs	Hicks, Sarah A. (Mrs)	By FB. Farm work. Female orphan. Of color
Farron, Minnie	25Nov1865	13 yrs	Farron, Lemuel	By FB. Farm work. Orphan. Of color
Farron, Josephine	25Nov1865	8 yrs	Stewart, Andrew	By FB. Farm work. Orphan. Of color
Farron, Alice	25Nov1865	9 yrs	Stewart, Andrew	By FB. Farm work. Orphan. Of color
Dix, Fayette	27Nov1865	12 yrs	Mariner, E. J.	By FB. Farm work. Orphan. Of color
Farron, Melvina	27Nov1865	10 yrs	Farron, E. S. (Mrs)	By FB. Farm work. Orphan. Of color
Farron, Rodgers	27Nov1865	2 yrs	Farron, E. D. (Mrs)	By FB. Farm work. Orphan. Of color
Farron, Rhoda	27Nov1865	10 yrs	Farron, E. D. (Mrs)	By FB. Farm work. Orphan. Of color
Farron, Amanda	27Nov1865	11 yrs	Farron, E. D. (Mrs)	By FB. Farm work. Orphan. Of color
Williams, Alexander	27Nov1865	7 yrs	Taylor, Enoch	By FB. Farm work. Orphan. Of color
Farron, Delia	27Nov1865	9 yrs	Farron, E. D. (Mrs)	By FB. Farm work. Orphan. Of color
Williams, Lucinda	27Nov1865	9 yrs	Taylor, Enoch	By FB. Farm work. Orphan. Of color
Green, Jacob	30Nov1865	7 yrs	Green, Frances (Mrs)	By FB. Farm work. Orphan. Of color. Mrs Green allowed to take Jacob to Texas
Green, Margaret	30Nov1865	11 yrs	Green, Frances (Mrs)	By FB. Farm work. Orphan. Of color. Mrs Green allowed to take Margaret to Texas
Nelms, Joanna	30Nov1865	10 yrs	Nelms, Kate (Mrs)	By FB. Farm work. Orphan. Of color. Mrs Nelms a planter of De Soto Co, Miss
Nelms, Clinda	30Nov1865	6 yrs	Nelms, Kate (Mrs)	By FB. Farm work. Orphan. Of color. Mrs Nelms a planter of De Soto Co, Miss
Nelms, Sandy	30Nov1865	9 yrs	Nelms, Kate (Mrs)	By FB. Farm work. Orphan. Of color. Mrs Nelms a planter of De Soto Co, Miss
Nelms, Calvin	30Nov1865	6 yrs	Nelms, Kate (Mrs)	By FB. Farm work. Orphan. Of color. Mrs Nelms a planter of De Soto Co, Miss
Gillam, Phebe	1Dec1865	7 yrs	Gillam, P. A. (Miss)	By FB. Farm work. Orphan. Of color. Miss Gillam a planter of De Soto Co, Miss
Carrel, Jesse	2Dec1865	7 yrs	Carrel, James	By FB. Farm work. Orphan. Of color
Carrel, Benjamin	2Dec1865	11 yrs	Carrel, James	By FB. Farm work. Orphan. Of color
Kennedy, Oscar	2Dec1865		Partee, Hiram A.	Bound by father, Peter Kennedy, in FB Court.
Kennedy, Trenton	2Dec1865		Partee, Hiram A.	Bound by father, Peter Kennedy, in FB Court. Female

141

Name	Date	Age	Master	Notes
Dixon, Kate	2Dec1865	12 yrs	Atkinson, Sarah (Mrs)	By FB. Farm work. Orphan. Of color
Dixon, Betsey	4Dec1865	14 yrs	Dixon, George	By FB. Farm work. Orphan. Of color. Entry overwritten "Cancelled"
Dixon, Millie	4Dec1865	10 yrs	Dixon, George	By FB. Farm work. Orphan. Of color
Mary Emma	12Dec1865	7 yrs	Monroe, L. E. (Mrs)	By FB. Farm work. Orphan. Of color
Raynor, Rose	13Dec1865		Raynor, Mary A. (Mrs)	Bound by mother, Eliza Jane Raynor, in FB Court
Crenshaw, Kate	21Dec1865	6 yrs	Crenshaw, F. B.	By FB. Farm work. Orphan. Of color
Crenshaw, Martin	21Dec1865	12 yrs	Crenshaw, F. B.	By FB. Farm work. Orphan. Of color
Jefferson, Ann	2Jan1866	12 yrs	Brown, Benjamin C.	By FB. Cook & house servant. Orphan. Of color. Brown a lawyer of Crittenden Co, Ark.
Wallace, Mary	Prob 1866	10 yrs	Poyner, William	Abandoned by father, Randall Wallace. Mother, Hester Wallace, unable to support, consents. Only petition found. Of color.
Wallace, Rosa	Prob 1866	8 yrs	Poyner, William	Abandoned by father, Randall Wallace. Mother, Hester Wallace, unable to support, consents. Only petition found. Of color.
Cole, Mittie	4Jan1866	7 yrs	Cole, Sue (Miss)	By FB. Farm work. Orphan. Of color
Munson, Joseph	8Jan1866	9 yrs	Munson, Amos	By FB. Farm work. Orphan. Of color
Mansfield, Georgia	8Jan1866	11 yrs	Mansfield, Samuel	By FB. Farm work. Orphan. Of color. Mansfield a druggist of Shelby Co
Maltravers, Ernest	10Jan1866	13 yrs	Martin, C. M. (Dr)	By FB. Farm work. Orphan. Of color. Martin, a physician, given permission to remove Ernest to Fulton Co, Ill
Liewallen	10Jan1866	13 yrs	Grant, J. E.	By FB. Farm work. Orphan. Of color. Grant a planter of De Soto Co, Miss
Thompson, Anderson	12Jan1866	6 yrs	Thompson, Florida C. (Mrs)	By FB. Farm work. Orphan. Of color
Mary	17Jan1866	12 yrs	Caraway, P. B. (Mrs)	By FB. Farm work. Orphan. Of color
Emeline	17Jan1866	10 yrs	Caraway, P. B. (Mrs)	By FB. Farm work. Orphan. Of color
Felts, Evaline	24Jan1866	9 yrs	Felts, J. E.	By FB. Farm work. Orphan. Of color
Watson, Patsy	27Jan1866	10 yrs	Chalmers, James R.	By FB. House servant. Orphan. Chalmers a lawyer of Shelby Co. Of color
Newell, Florence	29Jan1866	10 yrs	Newell, Jane (Mrs)	By FB. Seamstress or house servant. Orphan. Of color
Smith, Elisa	7Feb1866	10 yrs	Cuningham, Phillip	By FB. Sewing, washing & ironing. Orphan. Of color

Name	Date	Age	Bound to	Notes
Taylor, Phillip	16Feb1866	9 yrs	Taylor, Samuel T.	By FB. Farm work. Orphan. Of color. Taylor a planter of Washington Co, Miss
Eliza	Feb1866	9 yrs	Crook, George W. L.	By FB. Household work. Orphan. Of color
Hunt, William	10Mar1866	6 yrs	Hunt, T. W. (Mrs)	By FB. Farm work. Orphan. Of color. Indenture signed by Judith P. Hunt as mistress
Hunt, Anna	10Mar1866	8 yrs	Hunt, T. W. (Mrs)	By FB. Farm work. Orphan. Of color. Indenture signed by Judith P. Hunt as mistress
Walker, Charles	3Apr1866	10 yrs	Henderson, A. M.	By FB. Farm work. Orphan. Of color. Henderson a planter of Coahoma Co, Miss
Lind, Jenny	6Apr1866	13 yrs	Henderson, A. M.	By FB. Farm work. Orphan. Of color. Henderson a planter of Coahoma Co, Miss
Tanner, Henry Clay	11Apr1866		Rutter, George R. (Esq)	Bound in FB court by mother, Mary Louisa Tanner. Rutter a banker of Shelby Co
Worthy, Mary	16Apr1866	6 yrs	Sims, Clifford Stanley	By FB. House servant. Orphan. Of color. Sims a planter of Desha Co, Ark
Rice, Jacob	17Apr1866	12 yrs	Bethel, Pinckney C.	By FB. Farm work. Orphan. Of color. Indenture not signed by Bethel or his surety
Rice, Jinsey	18Apr1866	10 yrs	Bethel, Pinckney C.	By FB. Farm work. Orphan. Of color. Indenture not signed by Bethel or his surety
Dickson, Adeline	25Apr1866	7 yrs	Hunt, William Richardson	By FB. House servant. Orphan. Of color. Note appended that Adeline's mother may have custody if she makes her appearance
Dickson, Ella	26Apr1866	6 yrs	Hunt, William Richardson	By FB. Farm work. Orphan. Of color. Note appended that Ella's mother may have custody should she make her appearance
Washington, George	15May1866	8 yrs	Jones, J. E. (Dr)	By FB. Farm work. Orphan. Of color. Jones a planter of Mississippi Co, Ark
Allen, Diisey	16May1866	10? yrs	Allen, John R.	By FB. House servant. Orphan. Of color
Codswell, John	1June1866	8 yrs	Cogswell, A. M.	Until 18 yrs. By FB. Farm work. Orphan. Of color
Ford, Albert	6Aug1866	14 yrs	Stout, J.	Farm work. Parentage unknown. Of color
Butler, John	6Aug1866	11 yrs	Stout, J.	Farm work. Parentage unknown. Of color
Daniels, Kate	6Aug1866	4 yrs	Stout, J.	Until 21 yrs. House work. Of color

Name	Date	Age	Master	Notes
Brown, Wilbourne	6Aug1866	6 yrs	Stout, J.	Farm work. Of color
Brown, Ben	6Aug1866	4 yrs	Stout, J.	Farm work. Of color
White, Peter	6Aug1866	14 yrs	Perkins, William M.	Farming. Of color
Johnson, Sibby	6Aug1866	12 yrs	Perkins, William M.	Until 21 yrs. House work. Orphan. Of color
Andrew	6Aug1866	10 yrs	Chester, Robert I.	Parents dead. Of color
Alec	6Aug1866	8 yrs	Chester, Robert I.	Parents dead. Of color
Price	6Aug1866	5 yrs	Chester, Robert I.	Parents dead. Of color
Fred	10Sept1866		Jones, Nancy C. (Miss)	Of color
Tannehill, Tommie	10Sept1866		Lewis, Eliza	Consent of Jane Tannehill, mother. Of color
Amos	9Oct1866	8 yrs	Robertson, Mary	In SCA. Taken from Colored Orphan's Asylum. Robertson of McNairy Co. Of color
Roberta	19Oct1866	Abt 11 yrs	Ruffin, James D.	House servant. Orphan. Of color
Williams, Amanda	19Oct1866	Abt 5 yrs	Taylor, J. R.	House servant. Orphan. Of color
Amanda	29Oct1866	Abt 10 yrs	King, Elias	Orphan. Of color
Jones, Frederick	5Nov1866		Jones, George M.	From bond in SCA
Hannah	8Mar1867	10 or 11 yrs	Johnston, W. J.	Until 1Jan1874. Mother died several yrs ago. Abandoned by father. Of color
Madison, Joseph	6May1867		Judge, Margaret	Until 25Feb1888. In care of Judge since 25Feb last. Servant
Wallace, William	12June1867	8 yrs	Robertson or Robinson, P. A.	House servant. Of color. Without father or mother. Taken from orphan asylum. To be removed to White Co, Arkansas
Emaline	6Aug1867	Abt 8 yrs	Mosby, S.	Orphan. With Mosby since mother's death 4 yrs ago. Only petition found. Of color
Rice, Adam	10Oct1867	13 yrs	Wesley, John	No father of mother. Wesley is uncle. Both of color. Permitted to be removed from Shelby county
Rice, Samuel	10Oct1867	11 yrs	Wesley, John	No father of mother. Wesley is uncle. Both of color. Permitted to be removed from Shelby county
Samples, Emma	11Oct1867	Abt 8 yrs	Avery, William T.	Consent of mother, Sarah Hawkins. Father dead
Clark, Susan	5Dec1867	12 yrs	Gay, William	Orphan. Nurse & chambermaid. Of color
Redditt, Mack	6Dec1867	9 yrs	Redditt, Starkey	Orphan. Born a slave of Redditt. Farmer. Of color. SCA

Name	Date	Age	Bound to	Notes
Ike	14Dec1867	Abt 8 yrs	Powell, J. V.	With Powell for past 6 or 8 months. Neither father nor mother. Only petition found. Of color
Brown, Mary Jane	5Feb1868	10 yrs	Magiveny, Eugene	Orphan. Nurse & chambermaid. Of color
White, Henry	3Mar1868	6 yrs	Hunt, Eliza T. (Mrs)	Farming. Parents dead. Of color. Inmate of the Canfield Colored Orphan Asylum. To be taken to Mississippi
Johnson, Fannie	10July1868	10 yrs	Vinson, F. M.	Orphan, living with Vinson's family since her mother's death 3 yrs ago. Of color. Housekeeping
Emily	1Feb1869	Abt 10 yrs	Forrest, N[athan]. B.	Orphan. House keeping. Of color
Bleckley, Calvin		Abt 10 yrs	Bleckley, T. C.	Bound Jan1866. Consent of Milley Bleckley, mother. Calvin dead by 20Jan1869. See SCA. Of color.
Bleckley, Malvina	2Feb1869		Bleckley, T. C.	Bound Jan1866. Consent of Milley Bleckley, mother. Calvin dead by 20Jan1869. See SCA. Of color.
Bleckley, James	2Feb1869		Bleckley, T. C.	Bound Jan1866. Consent of Milley Bleckley, mother. Calvin dead by 20Jan1869. See SCA. Of color.
Thompson, Fannie	13Feb1869	13 yrs	Hanbury, T. E.	Orphan. House keeping. Brother is Robert Thompson. Of color. SCA
Shelton, Eliza	11Mar1869		Shelton, R. W.	Orphan. House keeping. Of color
Rogers, Mary H.	6Oct1869	Abt 10 yrs	Rogers, William E. (Dr)	No father or mother. Mary & her mother former slaves of Rogers. Mother died in Mary's infancy. No apprenticeship order or bond found
Rinz, Johannes	17Jan1870	14 yrs 10 mo	Specht, Joseph	For 4 yrs or until 21 yrs [sic]. Orphan. Confectioner
Hertel, Lena	8Mar1870	b. 28Sept1859	Laski, R. L. (Dr)	An apprentice indenture dated 13Oct 1860 in Shelby Co between William Hertel, father, and Dr. Laski entered as exibit in adoption of Lena by Laski. Name changed to Lily Laski. Mother dead when bound
Taylor, Sarah	10Mar1870	8 yrs	Taylor, Washington S. & Ann E. (his wife)	Orphan. Mulatto
Brooks, Mann	18Apr1870	13 yrs	Trigg, Henry	Orphan. Of color
Brooks, Philip	18Apr1870	11 yrs	Trigg, Henry	Orphan. Of color
Brooks, Jerry	18Apr1870	8 yrs	Trigg, Henry	Orphan. Of color
Dolan, Catherine	7June1870		Foley, Thomas	

Name	Date	Age	Master	Notes
Lynch, Maggie	16Aug1870	Abt 8 yrs	Humphreys, J. H.	Orphan. House servant. Consent of mother, Mrs. Ann Foley
Garrett, Martin Lee	6Sept1870	Abt 7 yrs	Sweatt, F. T.	Orphan. Carpenter. Consent of Mrs. Ann M. Sweatt, Martin's half sister
Allison, Oscar	21Oct1870	Abt 10 yrs	Rogers, S. C.	House servant. Of color
Steinkuhl, Herman	21Oct1870		Branner, John	For 3 yrs, 1Sept1870 - 1Sept1873. Boot & shoe maker.
Osborn, Josephine	22Oct1870		Pickett, W. S.	Until 21 yrs. Ladies maid & house servant. Of color
Wilson, Henry	9Nov1870	Abt 10 yrs	Douglas, George T.	Of color
Wilson, Alice	9Nov1870	Abt 13 yrs	Godwin, D. Y. (Dr)	House keeping & cooking. Of color
Fazzi, Charles	7Dec1870		Wolf, Frederick	Until 18 yrs 2 mo (one year). Barber. Consent of father, Lorenzo Fazzi, who has failed to provide
Lee, Henry	8Dec1870		Lee, Burrell	Farming
Massey, Sie	4Apr1871		Massey, W. J.	Farming. Of color
Land, William L.	13June1871	21 y/o in 1876	Converse, Elam	Orphan of Jeremiah Land, Dcd
Land, John A.	13June1871	21 y/o in 1879	Converse, Elam	Orphan of Jeremiah Land, Dcd
Hill, Christopher	7Aug1871	9 yrs	Perkins, William M.	Orphan. General farm work. Of color
Hill, Jessie	7Aug1871	13 yrs	Perkins, William M.	Orphan. General farm work. Of color
Hill, James	7Aug1871	11 yrs	Perkins, William M.	Orphan. General farm work. Of color
Farrar, Francis	4Sept1871		Farrar, J. J.	Orphan. Housework. Of color
Farrar, William	4Sept1871		Farrar, J. J.	Orphan. Farming. Of color
Frankling, Joseph	4Sept1871		Perkins, William M.	Farming
Saffarrans, Callie	5Sept1871		Williams, J. N.	Until 21 yrs. Housework. Of color
Thomas, McWilliams	8Dec1871		Stocks, Lux	Farming.
Thomas, George Anderson	8Dec1871		Stocks, Lux	Farming.
Shaw, Sarah Francis	3Jan1872	11 yrs	Taft, Frank	Orphan. Of color
Palmer, James	7Feb1872		Broom, Jeremiah	Farming
Guthrie, Warner	19Feb1872		New, W. H.	Farming
White, John W.	12Mar1872	8 yrs	Nelson, William R.	Schoolteacher
Saffarrans, Eliza	20Apr1872	12 yrs	Mitchell. W. Z.	Of color
Mosby, Aaron	20Apr1872		Law, A. C.	Cooking & house servant. On 25Mar1872 mother (unnamed) ordered to show cause why he should not be bound

Name	Date	Age/Birth	Master	Occupation/Notes
Dixon, Adeline	20May1872		Hunt, William R.	House servant
Dixon, Ella	20May1872		Hunt, William R.	House servant
Gaynor, Isaac	28Oct1872		Treven, John	Carpentering
Wallace, Mary			Joyner, William	Cancelled 28Oct1872, request of Randel Wallace, father. Of color
Wallace, Rosa			Joyner, William	Cancelled 28Oct1872, request of Randel Wallace, father. Of color
Baker, Fannie	11Nov1872	Abt 9 yrs	Pearson, Doyle	Orphan
Polk, Isaac	27Dec1872	10 yrs	Dunn, Caroline	Illegitimate son of Lucinda Knowland, who consents to apprenticeship. Dunn is Lucinda's mother. Of color
Robinson, William	20Jan1873		Horsfall, T. M.	Harness making
Kerr, German	6Mar1873	Abt 12 yrs	Hicks, Anderson	Planter or farmer. No parents living. Reared & supported since about 2 mo by Hicks
Glease, German	13Mar1873	13 yrs	Williams, Philip	Farmer
Hill, Mollie	2Sept1873	Abt 8 yrs	Douglass, Henry L.	Orphan
Person, Katie	16Dec1873		Trainor, James	Until 21 yrs. House keeping
Burke, Amanda	17Dec1873	15 yrs	Laws, M. J. (Mrs)	Baseborn orphan. Mulatto
Dabney, Dick	17Dec1873		Puryear, W. W.	Farming. The mother and two of the three children bound to Puryear are deaf & dumb
Williams, Judy	17Dec1873		Puryear, W. W.	Farming. See above
Coly (or Cody), George	17Dec1873		Puryear, W. W.	Farming. See above
Adams, Samuel	12Jan1874		Nelson, A. W.	Farming
Stringfellow, Lillie	4Feb1874		Treadwell, B. D.	House keeping
Pruden, John	14Mar1874	b. April 1860	Pruden, Thomas	Agriculture. John is Thomas' nephew. Both of color
Harris, Malinda	20May1874		Austin, Ann	Housekeeping. Of color
Harris, John	20May1874		Austin, Ann	Blacksmithing. Of color
Schlosser, John	22June1874	b. 4Feb1864	Ottman, W. F.	No father or mother living. Mercantile business
Carter, Rachel	29June1874	8 yrs	Rice, Jesse & Mary	Housekeeping. Of color
Carter, Henry	29June1874	4 yrs	Rice, Jesse & Mary	Farming. Of color
Carter, Amanda	29June1874	11 yrs	Shepherd, I. N.	Housekeeping. Of color
Mitchell, Jefferson Davis	3Aug1874	b. abt 25Dec1860	Ward, J. C.	Agriculture. Surname "Mitchell" on bond in SCA

Name	Date	Age	Master	Notes
Butcher, Alice	14May1875		Venable, Joseph	Housekeeping
Caldwell, Joseph	3June1875	11 yrs on 12Apr1875	Elliott, Isaac	Consent of mother
Hughes, Lucinda Jane	3July1875		Brown, W. A.	
Tidwell, Mary	10Apr1876	Abt 11 yrs	Taylor, Eliza	Of color
Cook, Mary	19Aug1876	5 yrs	Weaver, Jane E. (Mrs)	Of color
White, Mack	11Jan1878	Abt 11 yrs	White, Clark C.	Until 16 yrs. Of color
Shepherd, Mark	3May1879	13 yrs	Gragg, J. W.	No father or mother. Of color
Stewart, Robert	10May1879	14 yrs	Stewart, James	No father or mother
Stewart, James	10May1879	12 yrs	Stewart, James	No father or mother
Gregory, Charles T.	26May1879	15 yrs	Stewart, James	Had been in Church Orphan's Home for several years. Petition of Mrs Helen S. Harris, President of Home
McGrath, Patrick	26May1879	12 yrs	Stewart, James	Had been in Church Orphan's Home for several years. Petition of Mrs Helen S. Harris, President of Home
Bohannan, Lizzie	20Nov1879	13 yrs		From Ladies Christian Association. Mother & stepfather accused of being poor, dissolute and immoral & summoned to court. No further record. Probably not bound
Statum, Annie	19Dec1879		Lamb, S. R.	On 18Dec1879 Annie Dowley ordered to bring child, of color, to Court & present objection, if any, to apprenticeship
Crooms, Lizzie	11Aug1883	11yrs on 17Sept1882	Ward, Joe O.	Until 16 yrs. Consent of Catherine Crooms, mother, who is in poor house and ?insane. Housekeeping. Indenture completed 28Nov1887. Of color
Munn, Edward Alexander	10Nov1883	Abt 10 yrs	Oldham, Joe R.	Until 19 yrs. Farming.

Tipton County

Name	Date	Age	Master	Notes
Oldon, Charles T.	1June1829		Cooper, William D.	Orphan. Tailoring
McGaha, William	1June1829		Cooper, William D.	Orphan. Tailoring
Greer, Joseph	9Sept1830		Hopper, Joel	Orphan. House carpenter. On 8June1831, on complaint of Lucinda Greer, court ordered Hopper to bring Joseph to court next day. Action not recorded
Mitchell, William	8Mar1831		Burnett, Thomas M.	Orphan son of Thomas Mitchell, Dcd. Tin smith
Neale, Crawford	7June1832		Clark, Hamilton & Fulshen, William	Orphan. Tailoring
Neale, Thomas	7June1832		Clark, Hamilton & Fulshen, William	Orphan. Tailoring. Cancelled 3Sept1839
Hill, Charles Harry	4Mar1833		Hill, Thomas B.	Minor of Martha Hill, Dcd. Tanning. Thomas Hill also appointed guardian of Charles. On 8Mar1833 David S. Hill, minor heir of Martha Hill, Dcd chose John Postlethwail as his guardian
Myers, Robert	2June1834		Feizor, Henry	Tanning & currying. Orphan. Cancelled 5Apr1837
Myers, William	2June1834		Smithial, Tobias	Blacksmithing. Orphan
Norman, Jackson	7Sept1835	Abt 8 yrs	Hunt, Anderson	Orphan
Pickle, Washington J.	Oct1836		Horn, Josiah	Farming. Orphan
Pickle, James W.	Oct1836		Horn, Josiah	Farming. Orphan
Linvill, Elizabeth Jane	7Nov1836		Thomas, John D.	
Weatherford, Louisa	7Nov1836		Wiseman, William	
McGowan, Thomas	7Nov1836		Land, Williamson	
McGowan, Joseph	7Nov1836		Land, Williamson	
McGowan, Eliza	7Nov1836		Land, Williamson	
Norman, Rhoda	5Dec1836		Moore, Charles	
Norman, Sarah	5Dec1836		Boarding, Sr, John	
Norman, Dilly	2Jan1837		Wiseman, John B.	
Sneed, James T.	2Jan1837		Taylor, James W.	

Name	Date	Age	Master	Notes
Sneed, Mary A.	2Jan1837		Taylor, James W.	
Name not stated	2Jan1837		Vaught, Dan	Of color
Name not stated	2Jan1837		Vaught, Dan	Of color
Benjamin, Robert J.	Sept1837		Robinson, Harry R.	Shoemaking. Of color
McGowan, Joseph	2Oct1837	Abt 7 yrs	Turnage, William A.	Orphan
McGowan, Eliza	2Oct1837		Turnage, Henry	Orphan
Sneed, Caroline			Taylor, James W.	Cancelled 6Nov1837
McNeu?, Julius	6Nov1837		Vaught, Dan	Orphan. Of color
McNeu?, Arabella	6Nov1837		Vaught, Dan	Orphan. Of color
Jonathan, John	1Oct1838		Bearden, John	
Wooton, Nancy	1Oct1838		Bearden, John	
Neal, Thomas	3Sept1839		Wood, Oliver H. P.	Orphan. Tailoring.
Swann, Nick	2Mar1840		Newman, Nelly C.	Child of Anna Swann. Of color
Swann, Milley	2Mar1840		Newman, Nelly C.	Child of Anna Swann. Of color
Swann, Peggy	2Mar1840		Newman, Nelly C.	Child of Anna Swann. Of color
Swann, Charity	2Mar1840		Newman, Nelly C.	Child of Anna Swann. Of color
Swann, Jim	2Mar1840		Newman, Nelly C.	Child of Anna Swann. Of color
Swann, Kitty	2Mar1840		Newman, Nelly C.	Child of Anna Swann. Of color
Swann, Addison	2Mar1840		Newman, Nelly C.	Child of Anna Swann. Of color
Swann, Sally Ann	2Mar1840		Newman, Nelly C.	Child of Anna Swann. Of color
Ivey, Anderson	6Oct1840	21 yrs on 5Mar1845	Gardner, Thomas	Orphan. Shoe & boot maker. Cancelled 4July1842
Barless, Shedrick	3Jan1842	Abt 14 yrs	McMillan, Malcolm G.	Orphan. Farming & planting
Ivey, Anderson	4July1842		Hill, Charles H.	Orphan. Shoe & boot maker
Pearson, Polly Ann	2Sept1844	Abt 12 yrs	McCreed, Gabriel	Until 21 yrs .Orphan
Gardner, Marcus Lafayette	3June1850	Abt 10 yrs	Cullum, James	Orphan of Thomas Gardner, Dcd
Starnes, William	1Sept1851	12 yrs on 18June	Fry, Henry	Farming. Orphan of Wesley Starnes, Dcd. Consent of Martha Selfridge, mother
Starnes, Harvey	1Sept1851	9 yrs on 3Aug last	Fry, Henry	Farming. Orphan of Wesley Starnes, Dcd. Consent of Martha Selfridge, mother

Name	Date	Age	Bound to	Remarks
Duhon, David	6Jan1852	12 yrs on 19Nov last	Brown, Jordan	Farming. Consent of July Duhon, mother. Of color
Wilson, Francis	4Sept1854	15 yrs	Jones, Edward W.	Until 20 yrs. Orphan of David P. Wilson, Dcd. Farming & husbandry
Demsey, A.. W.	1Dec1856	9 yrs	Forbiss, J. H.	Orphan. Wheel wright
Solomon, James	5May1857	Abt 13 yrs	Dacus, W. C.	Orphan. Farming & husbandry
Mitchell, Joan	7Mar1859	10 yrs	Billings, Henry Y.	Orphan. Housewifery
Mitchell, James E.	7Mar1859	14 yrs on 8Jan1859	Hill, Daniel	Orphan. Farming & husbandry
Mitchell, Bennett	7Mar1859	7 yrs	Hill, Daniel	Farming & husbandry
Brown, Whit	4Sept1860	Abt 11 yrs	Douglas, John T.	Laborer. Of color. Starting 1Sept1863, Douglas to support Whit's mother, Matilda, until $100 expended
Greggs, John	4Sept1860	Abt 15 yrs	Densford, James	Laborer. Of color
Brown, Hollis	4Sept1860	Abt 16 yrs	Densford, James	Laborer. Of color. Densford to support Hollis' mother, Matilda, until $100 expended
Childers, William J.	5Nov1860	Abt 11 yrs	Brown, Elijah	Farming & husbandry. Orphan child of Harriet McCraw
Childers, James W.	5Nov1860	Abt 8 yrs	Brown, Elijah	Farming & husbandry. Orphan child of Harriet McCraw
Searcy, Mary	3Apr1861	Abt 13 yrs	Boswell, N. H.	Orphan. House wifery
Celia	7May1861	Abt 12 yrs	Hill, Lafayette (Dr)	Of color
Wright, William B.	7May1866	6 yrs	Wood, David H.	Laborer. Of color
Wright, Andrew J.	7May1866	9 yrs	Wood, David H.	Laborer. Of color
Trimble, Robert S.	8May1866	Abt 6 yrs	Boyd, James W.	Orphan. Laborer. White
Cotherane, Dickson	1Oct1866	Abt 13 yrs	Cotherane, Jesse S.	Orphan. Laborer. Of color
Cotherane, Buck	1Oct1866	Abt 11 yrs	Cotherane, Jesse S.	Orphan. Laborer. Of color
Cotherane, Betsy	1Oct1866	Abt 7 yrs	Cotherane, Jesse S.	Orphan. Laborer. Of color
Cotherane, David	1Oct1866	Abt 11 yrs	Cotherane, Jesse S.	Orphan. Laborer. Of color
Wilson	3Oct1866	Abt 10 yrs	Whitley, Henrietta E. (Mrs)	Orphan. Former slave of A. J. Whitley
Cherry	3Oct1866	Abt 8 yrs	Whitley, Henrietta E. (Mrs)	Orphan. Former slave of A. J. Whitley

Name	Date	Age	Master	Notes
Haywood	3Oct1866	Abt 6 yrs	Whitley, Henrietta E. (Mrs)	Orphan. Former slave of A. J. Whitley
Pickard, Lafonso	5Nov1866	Abt 14 yrs	Pickard, J. H.	Orphan. Child of Peggy Pickard. Farming & husbandry. Of color
Pickard, Fannie	5Nov1866	Abt 8 yrs	Pickard, J. H.	Orphan. Child of Peggy Pickard. Farming & husbandry. Of color
Pickard, Ester Ann	5Nov1866	Abt 5 yrs	Pickard, J. H.	Orphan. Child of Peggy Pickard. Farming & husbandry. Of color
Tipton, Frankie	5Nov1866	12 yrs	Tipton, Nat	Female orphan. Of color. Entry X'd out
Tipton, Willy	5Nov1866	9 yrs	Tipton, Nat	Orphan. Of color. Entry X'd out
McCallum, Ann	5Nov1866	14 yrs	McCallum, Daniel	Orphan of Emily McCallum, Dcd. Of color
McCallum, George	5Nov1866	7 yrs	McCallum, Daniel	Orphan of Emily McCallum, Dcd. Of color
Cothron, Betsy	5Nov1866	Abt 7 yrs	Cothron, Jesse S.	Orphan. Of color
Cothron, Dickson	5Nov1866	Abt 13 yrs	Cothron, Jesse S.	Orphan. Of color
Cothron, Buck	5Nov1866	Abt 11 yrs	Cothron, Jesse S.	Orphan. Of color
Cothron, David	5Nov1866	Abt 11 yrs	Cothron, Jesse S.	Orphan. Of color
Beadles, Malinda	3Dec1866		Beadles, D. J.	Orphan. Farming & husbandry
Rivers, Frederick	3Dec1866	8 yrs	Rivers, William B.	Orphan. Farming & husbandry. Of color
Rivers, Henry	3Dec1866	10 yrs	Rivers, E.	Orphan. Farming & husbandry. Of color
Rivers, Dolly	3Dec1866	6 yrs	Rivers, E.	Orphan. Farming & husbandry. Of color
Hooks, Emily	3Dec1866	8 yrs	McCall, James R.	Orphan. Child of E. Hooks, Dcd. Farming & husbandry. Of color
Hooks, Amy	3Dec1866	10 yrs	McCall, James R.	Orphan. Child of E. Hooks, Dcd. Farming & husbandry. Of color
McDill, Bell	3Dec1866	8 yrs	McDill, R.	Orphan of Caroline McDill, Dcd. Farming & husbandry. Of color
McDill, Henry	3Dec1866	6 yrs	McDill, R.	Orphan of Caroline McDill, Dcd. Farming & husbandry. Of color
Peete, Kiziah	3Dec1866	11 yrs	Peete, E. R.	Orphan of Martha Peete, Dcd. Farming & husbandry. Of color
Peete, Amy	3Dec1866	8 yrs	Peete, E. R.	Orphan of Martha Peete, Dcd. Farming & husbandry. Of color
Tipton, Frankie	5Dec1866		Tipton, Nat	Female orphan. Husbandry & farming. Of color
Tipton, Willis	5Dec1866		Tipton, Nat	Orphan. Husbandry & farming. Of color
Tipton, Hager	6Dec1866	Abt 15 yrs	Lauderdale, Thomas S.	Orphan. Laborer. Of color
Elkan, Elizabeth	8Jan1867	8 yrs	Ellison, Y. R.	Orphan. Of color
Lauderdale, John	8Jan1867		Stone, J. J.	Orphan. Laborer. Of color
Onelia	4Feb1867	Abt 4 yrs	Harris, Paul T.	Orphan. Of color
Heiss, Frank	6Mar1867	Abt 9 yrs	Malone, W. P.	Farming & husbandry. White

Nelson, Jane	Wilson, Joel E.	1Apr1867	11 yrs	Orphan
Sandford, Martha	Sandford, Richard	3Apr1867	Abt 12 yrs	Orphan. Domestic servant. Of color
Saunders, Sarah	Bell, M.	6May1867	Abt 12 yrs	Illegitimate orphan. Domestic. Of color
Collier, Violet	Feezor, William H.	3June1867	Abt 12 yrs	Orphan. Domestic servant. Of color
Cotheran, Bettie	Cotheran, Jesse S.	3June1867	Abt 7 yrs	Orphan. Domestic servant. Of color
White, Joe Ann	White, Hugh E.	5Aug1867	12 yrs	Orphan. Farm & house hand. Of color
White, Jacob M.	White, Hugh E.	5Aug1867	10 yrs	Orphan. Farm & house hand. Of color
Lindsey, Martha	Brooks, William W.	7Oct1867	11 yrs	Orphan
Shankle, Simon	Walk, Alfred	3Dec1867	4 yrs	Orphan. Husbandry & farming. Of color
Shankle, Caroline	Murphy, James	3Dec1867	10 yrs	Orphan. Husbandry & farming & household work. Of color
Stitt (or Still), Samuel	Sherrill, M. A. (Mrs)	3Dec1867	Abt 10 yrs	Orphan of Sallie Stitt (or Still). Farming & husbandry. Of color
McDonald, Mariah	Sadberry, J. R.	7Jan1868	Abt 12 yrs	Orphan of Joanna (or Jonah) Shelton (or Sheton). Farming & husbandry
Dunday, John	Mitchell, J. H.	9Jan1868	Abt 12 yrs	Orphan. About to become a county charge. Of color
Porter, Sarah Carter	Roane, Thomas W.	1Mar1868	Abt 9 yrs	Orphan. Farming & husbandry
Goodman, Isaac	Harris, L. J.	5May1868	2 yrs	Orphan. Farming or husbandry
Goodman, Jane	Harris, L. J.	5May1868	8 yrs	Orphan. Farming or husbandry
Lewis, Matha Ann	Wynne, G. W.	3Aug1868	Abt 11 yrs	Orphan. Farming & husbandry
Feizor, Nancy	Miller, W. F.	7Oct1868	9 yrs	Orphan of Peter L. Feizor, Dcd. Farming & husbandry. Indenture dated 1June1868
Feizor, Leonard	Miller, W. F.	7Oct1868	12 yrs	Orphan of Peter L. Feizor, Dcd. Farming & husbandry. Indenture dated 1June1868
Vaughan, Noah	McIntosh, James S.	7Dec1868	Abt 14 yrs	Orphan. Child of Ambers Vaughn. Farming & husbandry
Sanford, Nancy	Sanford, James R.	5Jan1869	Abt 10 yrs	Orphan. Farming & husbandry. Of color
Black, Alfred	Floyd, B. R.	2Feb1869	Abt 14 yrs	Orphan. Farming or husbandry. Of color
Palmer, Berry	Palmer, John R.	3May1869	16 yrs	Orphan. Child of Brandon Palmer.
Palmer, George	Palmer, John R.	3May1869	13 yrs	Orphan. Child of Brandon Palmer.
Palmer, Quinley	Palmer, John R.	3May1869	11 yrs	Orphan. Child of Brandon Palmer.
Hall, Martha	Hall, Elam	4May1869	12 yrs	Orphan. Child of Lucy & Isham Hall
Hall, Sallie	Hall, Elam	4May1869	10 yrs	Orphan. Child of Lucy & Isham Hall
Hall, Isham	Hall, Elam	4May1869	9 yrs	Orphan. Child of Lucy & Isham Hall

Name	Date	Age	Master	Notes
Taylor, Lela	6Sept1869	10 yrs	Burrel, Taylor	Child of Susan Maclin or (Machin)
Rose, Catherine	6Sept1869	12 yrs	Coleman, W. A.	Orphan. Mother also dead. Farmer's girl or house servant
Newton, William	1Nov1869	11 yrs	Moore, Melvi A.	Orphan. Child of Sarah Newton. Cancelled 3Jan1877. Moore leaving Tennessee
Hutchison, John	3Jan1870	8 yrs	Moore, John G.	Child of Martha Hutchison, who asserts. On 19April1873 John David Hutchinson ordered returned to Court, Moore having died
Currie, Sallie	7July1870	13 yrs	Curry, S. S.	Child of Alex and Caroline Currie. Sallie consent's. Of color
Wiseman, Tennessee	7Dec1870	13 yrs	Warr, S. S.	Illegitimate orphan
McDill, Belle	6Feb1871	13 yrs	McDill, Nancy	Orphan child of Caroline McDill. Belle consents
McDill, Henry	6Feb1871	11 yrs	McDill, Nancy	Orphan child of Caroline McDill. Henry consents
Baird, Isaac	3Apr1871	Abt 10 yrs	Marshall, John L.	Orphan. Child of Martha Baird
McCain, Elizabeth	6June1871	Abt 9 yrs	Tisdale, L. T.	Orphan
Jones, Mary C.	3July1871	4 yrs	Johnson, M. T. & Sue E.	Orphan. Child of Harriet J. Weaver
Williams, Wesley	2July1872		Reed, George	Orphan. Child of Nancy Williams
Williams, Moses	2July1872		Reed, George	Orphan. Child of Nancy Williams
Williams, Doc	2July1872		Reed, George	Orphan. Child of Nancy Williams
Williams, Nancy	2July1872		Reed, George	Orphan. Child of Nancy Williams
Dale, Thomas Tipton	4Nov1872	8 yrs	Cothran, Jesse S.	Orphan. Child of Charles Dale. On 3Feb1873 James S. Mayes appointed administrator of estate of Charles Dale. 6May1873*
McCraw (McCrun?), Josephine	6Jan1873	10 yrs	Bowen, W. A.	Child of Kate McCraw (McCrun?)
McCraw (McCrun?), William	6Jan1873	3 yrs	Bowen, W. A.	Child of Kate McCraw (McCrun?)
Green, Minnie	2June1873	3 yrs	Sherill, C. E.	Orphan. Child of Nice Green. Same day Thomas S. Hall appointed administrator of estate of Nice Green (Fe)
Green, John	2June1873	5 yrs	Sherrill, Frances I.	Orphan. Child of Nice Green. See above
Green, Lee	2June1873	9 yrs	Sherrill, Frances I.	Orphan. Child of Nice Green. See above
Green, Victoria.	2June1873	6 yrs	Hall, Thomas S.	Orphan. Child of Nice Green. See above
Hutchinson, John	1Sept1873	11 yrs	Yancy, J. B.	Child of Martha Hutchinson.
Owen, James	8Oct1873		Owen, Isaac	Child of Peter Owen
Owen, Melia	8Oct1873		Owen, Isaac	Child of Peter Owen

Name	Date	Age	Master	Notes
Owen, Dora	8Oct1873		Owen, Isaac	Child of Peter Owen
Owen, Peter	8Oct1873		Owen, Isaac	Child of Peter Owen
Owen, Willie	8Oct1873		Owen, Isaac	Child of Peter Owen
Owen, Mary	8Oct1873		Owen, Isaac	Child of Peter Owen
Eckford, Martha	3Feb1874	7 yrs	McGregor, Ned	Child of Ben Eckford. Martha consents
Green, John	1June1874	6 yrs	Smith, Leroy	Child of Nice Green
Green, Lee	1June1874	9 yrs	Sherrill, Sarah E.	Child of Nice Green
Droffin, Jesse John Calhoun	2Aug1875	10 yrs	Droffin, Elizabeth	Orphan
Washington, George	5Mar1877	11 yrs	Orr, James H.	George consents
McCram, William	5May1889	12 yrs	Bowers, H. C.	

Weakley County

Name	Date	Age	Master	Notes
Williams, Joseph	July1826	21 yrs on 28Jan1838	Rogers, John W.	Orphan. On 14Jan1830 Rogers ordered to return Williams to court. Mistreatment alleged. Cancelled 14Jan1831. Data from cancellation entry
Cassilman, James H.	8Oct1827	8 yrs on 4Jan last	Ore, William C.	Farmer
Cassilman, Arthur L.	8Oct1827	12 yrs on 22Jan last	Morgan, Samuel	Farmer
Sims, John J.	16July1828		Buckner, Virgil	Bricklayer. Bound by Alexander Sims
Mitchell, John	15Jan1830	Abt 7 yrs when bound	Jenkins, John	Now 21 yrs, released. Had been bound in Granville Co, NC, by father, David Mitchell for $14. Of color
Usenem?, George	11Oct1830		Raulhoe?, George G.	Orphan
Williams, Joseph	12July1831		Parker, Gideon	Cabinet maker. Parker also apptd guardian
Dillon, Jackson	9July1832	21 yrs on 10Dec1837	Parker, Lorenzo D.	Orphan. Cabinet maker
Baldridge, Jr, Charles	14Oct1833	6 yrs on 10Oct inst	Baldridge, William	Orphan.
Baldridge, Charles W.	1Jan1834	6 yrs on 10Oct1833	Baldridge, William	Orphan. Mother appealed to Circuit Court

Name	Date	Age	Master	Notes
Fulton, William	15Oct1834	5 yrs on 3June last	Vincent, Oren	Orphan. Son of William Fulton, Dcd. Younger sibs Susan, Joseph & John 13Oct1834 & 16Oct1834
Boulton, William	11Jan1836		Shrum, Mary	Orphan
Gilmore, Robert	4July1836	14 yrs on 15Apr last	White, Pheland?	Orphan. Farmer
Parker, Nancy	1May1837	18 yrs on 23Jun1846	Redick, Lewis W.	Orphan of William T. Parker, Dcd. Sibs Polly, William T., Seralda, & Jane 3Apr1837
Parker, Polly	1May1837		Gunter, Charles	Orphan of William T. Parker, Dcd. Cancelled 6Aug1838. Taken away by George Ward
McElray, Andrew J.	5June1837	21 yrs on 15Jan1841	Smith, Daniel	
Box, Elizabeth	4Sept1837		Cavett, George W.	House keeping. Cancelled 4Feb1839
Box, Isaac	4Sept1837		Cavett, George W.	Cancelled 4Feb1839
Parker, Melinda Jane	6Nov1837		Jimmerson, James	Jimmerson promises to adopt her as his daughter. See Nancy Parker
Barnard, Martha Ann	7Jan1839		Smith, Jonathan	Same date allowance voted for Jane Barnard, a pauper, to be drawn by Jonathan Smith
Box, Elizabeth	4Feb1839		Cavett, William A.	
Box, Isaac	4Feb1839		Cavett, William A.	
Russel, Jonah	1Apr1839		Frizell, Asa	Ordered brought by sheriff 4March1839*
Russel, James Petty	1Apr1839		Russel, Majah William	Ordered brought by sheriff 4March1839*
Russel, Hannah	1Apr1839		Ward, John	Ordered brought by sheriff 4March1839* Until 21 yrs 6May1839. Heir of Buckner Russell, Dcd 2May1842*
Russel, Rachel	1Apr1839		Ward, George M.	Ordered brought by sheriff 4March1839.* On 6May1839 term specified 21 yrs. Heir of Buckner Russell, Dcd 2May1842.* Cancelled 4July1843
Reaves, Henderson	1Apr1839	21 yrs in Dec1845	Brooks, Michel	Ordered brought by sheriff 4March1839* On 6May1839 term specified 21 yrs
Reaves, Catharine	1Apr1839	18 yrs in 1846	Clark, Hiram	Ordered brought by sheriff 4March1839*
Reaves, Martha	1Apr1839	18 yrs in Jan1849	Hutchens, Thomas	Ordered brought by sheriff 4March1839*
Reaves, Rode	1Apr1839	18 yrs in 1852	Farmer, John D.	Ordered brought by sheriff 4March1839*

Name	Date	Age	Master	Notes
Reeves, Ann	1June1839		Hopkins, John	
Hooker, Willie	4Nov1839	21 yrs on 25Nov1846	Richa, David	Indenture confirmed 3Feb1840
Shortt, Bird	6Apr1840		Lane, James	Minor heir of Alfred Shortt. Entry X'd out. Whether guardianship or indenture unclear
Bethue, William H.	6July1840		Hayes, William A.	Until 20 yrs
Fields, Benjamin F.	Oct1842	b. 16Oct1836	Hopkins, Josiah	Heir of Lucy Ann Fields, Dcd. Farming
Fields, Absalon	Oct1842	b. 15Mar1838	Hopkins, Josiah	Heir of Lucy Ann Fields, Dcd. Farming
Gunter, Harry	7Aug1843		Rory, Lee	Orphan
Edward, Margaret	1Jan1844		Hubbard, William	Orphan
Edward, Mary Ann	1Jan1844		Martin, William B.	Orphan
Edward, Charles Harvey	1Jan1844		Gardner, Joshua	Orphan
Edward, Sarah	1Jan1844		Gardner, Joshua	Until 21 yrs. Orphan
Reaves, Rody	4Aug1845		Farmer, John D.	
Dean, Stephen	6July1846	15 yrs	Johnson, John	Orphan
, Rody	6July1846		Waggoner, Richard	Orphan
Williams, James	6July1846		Stuntson, Lewis	Orphan
Maynard, Mary Elizabeth	7Sept1846		Osborne, William C.	Servant
Reaves, Catharine			Collier, Henry	On 7Dec1846 indenture cancelled and child delivered to Bethel Reaves
Reaves, Roseanna			Wagner, Richard	On 7Dec1846 indenture cancelled and child delivered to Bethel Reaves
Records 1847 through 1852 missing				
Ford, John	7Feb1853	16 yrs	Manning, Kenneth	Orphan
Ford, Joseph H.	7Feb1853	Abt 15 yrs	Chappell, William	Orphan
Bynum, William T.	2May1853	7 yrs	Newton, James W.	Orphan. Farmer
Dabbs, Westley	4July1853	13 yrs	Robertson, David	Orphan. Farmer
Clark, Charles B.	4July1853	4 yrs	House, William H.	Orphan. Farmer. Cancelled 4Jan1854
Bigart, W[ilson] R.	5Dec1853	14 yrs	Riggsby, J. A.	Orphan. Farmer. On 5June1854 Rigsby acquitted of mistreatment of Biggert [sic]

Name	Date	Age	Master	Notes
Smith, Nancy			Perry, John E.	Orphan of John Smith, Dcd. On 6Dec1853 requirement to educate Nancy cancelled. Indenture cancelled 4Dec1854
Russell, Huston			Newton, William	Indenture cancelled 4Jan1854
Turner, James F.	5June1854	4 yrs	Myrack, A.	Orphan. Farmer
Turner, Nancy C. C.	5June1854	6 yrs	Myrack, A.	Orphan
Singalten, William H.	4Sept1854	8 yrs	Mitchel, James T.	Orphan
Murphey, John	4Sept1854	7 1/2 yrs	Cochran, J. W.	Orphan
Lewis, Paulina A.	2Oct1854	12 yrs	Goliman, W. G.	Orphan
Smith, Nancy	4Dec1854		Dent, T. E.	Orphan
Burden, William			Workman, W?. M.	Indenture cancelled 1Jan1855
Williamson, Mary	5Feb1855	7 yrs	Cooley, George	
Carter, John	7May1855	13 yrs	Carter, George	
Gunter, Randolph	6Aug1855	14 yrs	Shaw, D. B.	
Haroken, William	7Apr1856	4 1/2 yrs	Jones, M. G.	Taken from Gasten Jones 6Sept1858. To B. W. Ivie, Esq, until further action by the court
Richie, John W.	4Aug1856	14 yrs	Dudly, W. G.	On 11Apr1856 T. S. Perry appointed adm of Robertson Richie, Dcd. B. Ray a security for both Perry & Dudly. On 1Sept1856* John Elliott apptd adm of James M. Richie, Dcd
Sears, John Henry	6Jan1857	13 yrs	Higgs, Willis L.	Until 18 yrs. Orphan
Chapple, Elizabeth A.	2Mar1857	2 1/2 yrs	Chapple, William	Until 16 yrs
McDaniel, Peter Riley	7Dec1857	6 1/2 yrs	Shaw, D. B.	With written agreement of Rebecca Rudd, who had had possession of Peter
Dum?, George Washington	4Jan1858	15 yrs	Snow, James B.	Orphan
Pepkin, John Taylor	4Jan1858	11 yrs on 13Nov last	New, A. H.	Orphan
Cantwell, William		20 yrs in Feb1858	Scotis, Alexander H.	Bound 7 or 8 yrs ago as tanner. Scotis now dead. Cancelled 2Feb1858*
Sexton, V. I.	3May1858	Abt 15 yrs	Killgore, W. R.	Cancelled 6Aug1860
Sexton, James (or John) N.	2Aug1858	Abt 14 yrs	Nix, Jesse	Farming. Entry uses both forenames
Hooker, William	4Oct1858	Abt 11 yrs	Clary, Benjamin	Farming.

Name	Date	Age	Assigned to	Notes
Warren, Josiah	7Mar1859	Abt 12 yrs	Finch, Adam	Farming
Guy, Nathaniel B.	7Mar1859	Abt 8 yrs (from canc entry)	Cole, C. T.	Farming. Cancelled 6Aug1860, as Benjamin Guy
Pentecost, Samantha J.	5Apr1859	Abt 3 yrs	Reddeck, L. W.	
Partin, Nancy Ann			Sullivan, William	7Dec1857 her mother, Amy Parten, applied to have indenture cancelled. No action. 1Aug1869, Sullivan asked cancellation of indenture. No action recorded
Anderson, Walter	6Feb1860	Abt 12 mo	Anderson, G. W.	For 20 yrs. Farming. Left in county by persons unknown. Name assigned by court
Franklin, Percival K.	3Apr1860	Abt 15 mo	Cooley, George	For 19 yrs. Farming
Larry?, William	7May1860	Abt 8 yrs	Green, Thomas B.	Farmer
Thomason, Wesly	8Jan1861		Davis, Robert	For 7 yrs. Farmer
Spears, William H.	6Apr1863	15 yrs	Gailey, C. C.	Farming
Dickson, Joseph	7Nov1866		Gardner, Alfred	Orphan. Farmer
Hawkins, Green	4Dec1866	13 yrs	Hawkins, Thomas P.	Orphan. Farmer. Of color
Joseph	7Jan1867	10 yrs last Sept	Bell, Sarah L.	Orphan. Of color. Formerly a slave
Hannah	7Jan1867	8 yrs last August	Bell, Sarah L.	Orphan. Of color. Formerly a slave
George	8Jan1867		Cook, S. C.	Of color. Cook a female. Entry X'd out
Susan	8Jan1867		Cook, S. C.	Of color. Cook a female. Entry X'd out
Clara	9Jan1867	9 yrs	Gardner, Alfred	Seamstress. Orphan. Of color
Columbus	9Jan1867	9 yrs	Love, Solomon	Until 20 yrs. Freeman. Orphan. Farmer
George	9Jan1867	11 yrs	Love, Solomon	Orphan. Farmer. Of color
Glass, Charles	3Apr1867		Glass, Thomas	Of color. Entry X'd out
Glass, Hannah	3Apr1867	6 yrs	Glass, Thomas	Of color. Entry X'd out
Glass, Lucinda	3Apr1867		Glass, Thomas	Of color. Entry X'd out
Glass, Linda	6May1867	11 yrs	Glass, Malinda R. & Thomas	Orphan. Housekeeping. Of color
Glass, Hannah	6May1867	8 yrs	Glass, Malinda R. & Thomas	Orphan. Housekeeping. Of color. Rescinded 8Oct1868 at request of father, William Wiggins. Glass appealed
Glass, Charles	6May1867	9 yrs	Glass, Malinda R. & Thomas	Orphan. Farming. Of color. Rescinded 8Oct1868 at request of father, William Wiggins. Glass appealed

Name	Date	Age	Master	Notes
Paschall, Lucinda	3June1867	10 yrs	Paschall, Jerre. M	Orphan. House keeping. Of color
Paschall, Redmore	3June1867	11 yrs	Paschall, Jerre. M	Orphan. Farming. Of color
Higgs, Elbert	2Dec1867	9 yrs	Lynn, Mathew	Orphan. Farming. On 6Oct1868 Lynn apptd Higgs' guardian. Heir of Levie? Higgs. Canc 2Sept1872, "Ethelber" having left Lynn
Webb, William Edmund	8Jan1868	13 yrs	Palmer, Thomas H.	Orphan. Farmer
Martin, Peter	3Feb1868	5 yrs	Caldwell, Henry	Orphan. Farmer or spinning weel maker. Of color
Black William	3Feb1868	7 yrs	Taylor, Billington	Orphan. Farmer
Offal, Isham L	7Oct1868	3 yrs	Thomas, F. M.	Orphan. Farming
Offal, Mary	7Oct1868	5 yrs	Thomas, F. M.	Orphan. House keeping
Gardner, Stephen	6Jan1869	9 yrs	Wing, James	Orphan. Blacksmith. Of color
Tansell, Sam	6Jan1869	12 yrs	Blacknall, W. R.	Orphan. Farming. Of color
Kimbell, William H. C.	6Oct1869	4 yrs	Palmer, Thomas H.	Orphan. Farming. Cancelled 5July1870, request of Palmer and Martha E. Kimbrel. To possession of Kimbrel
Odile, Samuel	2May1870	8 yrs	Boucher, J. R.	Orphan. Farming
Odile, Jackson E.	2May1870	10 yrs	Dodson, W. H.	Orphan. Farming. On 30Apr1871 Mary Odle, mother, applied to cancel indenture. Action?
Mitchell, Alonzo	2May1870	5 yrs	Frazier, T. J.	Orphan. Farming
Haggard, Masey	1Aug1870	7 yrs	Caston, John H.	Until 21 yrs. Orphan. Female?. Farming
Haggard, Louisa	1Aug1870	5 yrs	Caston, John H.	Until 21 yrs. Orphan. Farming
Donall, Charles	6Sept1870	13 yrs	Jenkins, J. A.	Orphan. Farming
Tharp, Luticia	7Nov1870	14 yrs	Jones, John H.	Orphan. Housekeeping
Marten, Charley	5Dec1870	12 yrs	Duke, D. M.	Orphan. Farming
Jones, Dock	5Dec1870	9 yrs	Hughes, H. C.	Orphan. Farming
Smith, William	4Jan1871	8 yrs	Dunlap, J. E.	Orphan. Farming
Smith, Paralee V.	4Jan1871	11 yrs	Dunlap, J. E.	Female orphan. House keeping
Eskridge, John Bird	5Jan1871	13 yrs	Drake, P.	Farming. Orphan of J. R. Eskridge. Both parents dead 4Jan1871
Eskridge, George Thomas	5Jan1871	15 yrs	Parrish, Elizabeth	Farming. Orphan of J. R. Eskridge. Both parents dead 4Jan1871

Name	Date	Age	Notes
Fonvill, John	5Jan1871	3 yrs	Farmer. Son of Fasay & Sund (or Lind) Fonvill, both dead. Of color 4Jan1871*
Fonvill, Sanday	5Jan1871	9 yrs	Farmer. Son of Fasay & Sund (or Lind) Fonvill, both dead. Of color 4Jan1871*
Thompson, Emerson	5Jan1871	6 yrs	Orphan. Farming
Thompson, William	5Jan1871	11 yrs	Orphan. Farming. Of color
Fonvill, Joe	5Jan1871	14 yrs	Farmer. Son of Fasay & Sund (or Lind) Fonvill, both dead. Of color 4Jan1871*
Ward, Dock	6Feb1871	12 yrs	Orphan. Farming
Hatler, Daniel	6Feb1871	6 yrs	Orphan. Farming. On 5June1871 B. J. Roberts apptd administrator of estate of George Hattler
Hatler, Ada	6Feb1871	9 yrs	Orphan. Housekeeping. See above
Gardner, John Henry	6Feb1871	7 yrs	Orphan. Farming
White, Lucy	6Mar1871	11 yrs	Orphan. Housekeeping
White, Marcelas	6Mar1871	6 yrs	Orphan. Farming
White, Harmon	6Mar1871	9 yrs	Orphan. Farming
Gardner, Jeptha	5Apr1871		Orphan. Hostler
Cooper, Louesia	5June1871	9 yrs	Orphan. House keeping
Gardner, Bell	8Aug1871	11 yrs	Orphan. House keeping
Stow, Jack	8Aug1871	10 yrs	Without father or mother. Jack Thompson appealed. Jack Stow & Thompson of color
Elender, George	3Oct1871	7 yrs	Orphan. Farming
McClelland, George B.	4Dec1871	8 yrs	Orphan. Farming
Thomas, Eliza	4Dec1871	15 yrs	Orphan. House keeping
Thomas, Frank	4Dec1871	14 yrs	Orphan. Farming
Freeman, Julia	5Dec1871	10 yrs	Orphan. House keeping
Freeman, Alledonea	5Dec1871	12 yrs	Orphan. House keeping
Elner, James	5Dec1871	14 yrs	Orphan. Farming
Mitchell, Lou	2Jan1872	3 yrs	Orphan. House keeping
Elner, William F.	2Jan1872	10 yrs	Orphan. Farming
Elner, Sarah E.	2Jan1872	12 yrs	Orphan. House keeping. Cancelled 5Aug1872. Mcadams dead

Name column also includes apprenticeship masters:

Pointer, S. W. — Fonvill, John
Roberton, G. H. — Fonvill, Sanday
Hombeak, W. M. — Thompson, Emerson
Roberts, John J. — Thompson, William
Pointer, William L. — Fonvill, Joe
Vaden, L. R. — Ward, Dock
Hatler, Alean — Hatler, Daniel
Hatler, Alean — Hatler, Ada
Gardner, John A. — Gardner, John Henry
White, J. A. — White, Lucy
White, J. A. — White, Marcelas
White, J. A. — White, Harmon
Shaver, D. L. — Gardner, Jeptha
Parham, Thomas H. — Cooper, Louesia
Gardner, Joshua — Gardner, Bell
Stow, William A. — Stow, Jack
Taylor, Robert — Elender, George
Thomas, F. M. — McClelland, George B.
Thomas, F. M. — Thomas, Eliza
Thomas, F. M. — Thomas, Frank
Freeman, J. W. — Freeman, Julia
Freeman, J. W. — Freeman, Alledonea
Carlton, Obe — Elner, James
Caston, J. A. — Mitchell, Lou
Mcadams, J. B. — Elner, William F.
Mcadams, John — Elner, Sarah E.

Name	Date	Age	Master	Notes
Martin, Jim	5Feb1872	4 yrs	Martin, Thomas D.	Orphan. Farming
Martin, Dave	5Feb1872	7 yrs	Martin, Thomas D.	Orphan. Farming
Fonville, Mariah	5Feb1872	7 yrs	Martin, Thomas D.	Orphan. House keeping
Ennent, John	4Mar1872	14 yrs	Hawks, C. W.	Orphan. Farming
Simmons, Dick	3June1872	8 yrs	Thomas, C. G.	Orphan. Farming
Gardner, Tom	3June1872	10 yrs	Gardner, J. Almus	Orphan. Farming
Gardner, Walter	3June1872	7 yrs	Gardner, J. Almus	Orphan. Farming
Gardner, Sam	3June1872	4 yrs	Gardner, J. Almus	Orphan. Farming
Paschall, India	5Aug1872	7 yrs	Paschall, Martha	Until 21 yrs. Orphan. Housekeeping
Paschall, David	5Aug1872	9 yrs	Paschall, Martha	Orphan. Farming
Martin, Levy	2Sept1872	7 yrs	Gardner, John C.	Orphan. Farming
Nailing, Peter	7Oct1872	7 ys	Phillips, W. E.	Orphan. Farming
Powers, Walter	8Oct1872	10 yrs	Powers, Thomas	Orphan. Farming
Harrall, William	4Nov1872	12 yrs	White, A. B.	Orphan. Farming
Collier, John	3Dec1872	4 yrs	Collier, Martha J.	Orphan. Farming
Oldham, Puss	7Jan1873	14 yrs	Cole, C. T.	Orphan. House keeping
Akin, Charley	3Feb1873	5 yrs	Akin, A. C.	Orphan. Farming
Akin, Autrey	3Feb1873	2 yrs	Akin, A. C.	Orphan. Farming
Gilliam, Thomas L.	2June1873	4 yrs	Sanderfer, A. H.	Orphan. Farming. Cancelled 6Jan1875. To father, Lesly Gilliam
Gardner, Allice	5Aug1873	7 yrs	Gardner, Metta A.	Orphan. House keeping
Gardner, Ada	5Aug1873	3 yrs	Vincent, J. E.	Orphan. House keeping
Gardner, Lee	5Aug1873	1 yr	Vincent, J. E.	Orphan. Farming
Morris, George	1Sept1873	16 yrs	Stephens, D. H.	Orphan. Farming
Dunlop, Andrew J.	1Sept1873	10 yrs	Dunlop, R. W.	Orphan. Farming
Dunlop, Delia	1Sept1873	3 yrs	Dunlop, R. W.	Until 21 yrs. Orphan. House keeping
Edwards, Amanda	1Dec1873	9 yrs	Gardner, John A.	Orphan. Housekeeping
Brown, Deck	1Dec1873	4 yrs	Phelps, W. J.	Orphan. Farming
McDanel, John	1Dec1873	8 yrs	Denning, Thomas G.	Orphan. Farming
McDanel, Clinton	1Dec1873	14 yrs	Brumett, W. Y.	Orphan. Farming
Thompson, John H.	7Jan1874	3 1/2 yrs	Tansel, E. E.	Orphan. Farming

Name	Date	Age	Custodian	Notes
McDanel, Jacob	7Apr1874	6 yrs	Booth, Tapley	Orphan. Farming
Thomas, Scott	7Dec1874	13 yrs	Johnson, Tillman	Orphan. Farming
Thomas, Nevelly	7Dec1874	4 yrs	Johnson, Tillman	Orphan. Farming
Thomas, John	7Dec1874	9 yrs	Adams, Phillip	Orphan. Farming
Harris, Alx	6Jan1875	1 yr	Canady, James E.	Orphan. Farming
Owens, Anthony	1Mar1875	4 yrs	Edwards, J. J.	Orphan. Farming
Phepps, William S.	1Mar1875	14 yrs	Groom, J. M.	Orphan. Farming
Page, Byran	6Apr1875	4 yrs	Stephens, D. H.	Orphan. Farming
Page, Joseph	6Apr1875	2 yrs	Stephens, D. H.	Orphan. Farming
Mosley, Frank	3May1875	9 yrs	Capps, M. W.	Orphan. Farming
Todd, Nellie	2Aug1875	11 yrs	Glasgow, F. M.	Orphan. House keeping
Thomas, Harry J.	3Aug1875	11 yrs	Foster, Anthony	Orphan. Farming
Ray, Pink	6Dec1875	5 yrs	Tansel, E. D.	Orphan. Farming
Blakemore, Thomas	6Dec1875	11 yrs	Blakemore, B. D.	Orphan. Gardning
Semmons, George	4Apr1876	10 yrs	Janes, Ed D.	Orphan. Farming. Of color. Janes also to care for Semmons, a relative and the custodian of George. See adoption 5Mar1877 of Malecia Simmons, dau of Lemuel & Julia Simmons, Dcd, by W. R. & Martha Roberts
Martin, Harrison	4Apr1876	2 yrs	Wright, Frederick	Orphan. Farming
Kelsaw, James	1May1876	10 yrs	Boyd, Peter	Orphan. Farming
Kelsaw, Rip	1May1876	12 yrs	Boyd, Peter	Orphan. Farming
Patten, A. J.	4Dec1876	13 yrs	Stanley, J. F.	Orphan. Farming
Brasfield, Denis	8Jan1877	5 yrs	Caraway, B. R.	Orphan. Farming
Brasfield, Samul	8Jan1877	7 1/2 yrs	Hutcherson, Asa	Orphan. Farming. Cancelled 8May1877
Taylor, Harvey	5Feb1877	4 yrs	Malvan, R. W.	Orphan. Farming
Trantham, Thomas R.	5Feb1877	11 yrs	Smyth, A. M.	Orphan. Farming. Will of R. F. Trantham probated 2Jan1877. On 5Mar1877 J. R. Deeson appointed guardian for Rebeca Trantham, lunatic. 4Apr1877*
Knight, Robert E.	7May1877	8 yrs	Newton, Robert	Orphan. Farming
Brasfield, Samel	8May1877	8 yrs	White, J. J.	Orphan. Farming. Of color. 7May1877*
Thomas, Thomas J. A.	6Aug1877	3 yrs	Rucker, G. W.	Orphan. Farming

Name	Date	Age	Master	Notes
Shannon, Charles	6Aug1877	7 yrs	Prestwood, J. B.	Orphan..Farming
Brasfield, Notice	6Aug1877	10 yrs	Loony, E. J.	Parents dead. Housekeeping. Of color. Cancelled 5Oct1881, Notice having deserted
Bondurant, Bell	7Aug1877	8 yrs	Pointer, B. M.	Orphan. Housekeeping. Of color. Bound at request of mother, Mariah Bondurant
Simmons, A. L.	5Nov1877	9 yrs	Campbell, J. J.	Orphan. Farming. See George Semmons
Pratt, Isaac	4Feb1878	6 yrs	Lowery, S. W.	Orphan. Farming
Lee, Ernest	4Aug1879	5 yrs	Dent, E. R.	Orphan. Farming. Of color
Lee, Thomas	4Aug1879	7 yrs	Edwards, W. A.	Orphan. Farming. Of color
Parker, William	7Jan1880	10 yrs	Burton, H. B.	Orphan. Farming. Perhaps one of 3 sons of Eliza Parker 5Feb & 3Mar1879
Holiday, Albert Ross	3May1880	15 yrs	Foster, A.	Orphan. Farmer. Cancelled 4Jan1882, Albert having left Foster
Rowlett, Eddie	7Oct1880	9 yrs	House, E. A.	Orphan. Farming. Son of Peter Rowlett, Dcd 3Aug & 7Sept1880*
Simmons, Ben	7Oct1880	2 yrs	Simmons, G. W.	Orphan. Farming
Reese, Thomas	10Jan1881	13 yrs	Bobo, W. R.	Orphan. Farming
Prewett, Henry	2May1881	4 yrs	Rice, D. F.	Orphan. Farming
Arn, Walter	5Oct1881	7 yrs	Climer, W. H.	
Welch, Almus	10Oct1881	11 yrs	Rogers, P. M. & M. A.	Recorded in Guardian Bond Book p 353
Jones, Tom	10Oct1881	11 yrs	Rogers, P. M. & M. A.	Recorded in Guardian Bond Book p 354. Son of Alonzo & Emma Jones 5Oct1881
Simons, James	6Dec1881	6 yrs	Banter, J. M.	Orphan. Farming
Bell, Simon			Phillips, W. E.	Canc 6Feb1882, Simon having left Phillips
Gleason, Earnest	5Apr1882	4 yrs	Little, J. D.	Orphan. Farming
Cooper, Lee	10Apr1882	7 yrs on 1Jan1882	Johnson, David N.	Orphan of Joe Cooper, Dcd. Mother, Mary Cooper, unable to provide. Sibs Amanda D. & William Grant Cooper. Farmer.
Cooper, Mandy	1May1882	12 yrs	Farmer, R. P.	Orphan of Joe Cooper, Dcd. Mother, Mary Cooper, unable to provide. House keeping. Dau of Joe Cooper, Dcd 10Apr1882*
Winston, Aleson	5June1882	6 yrs	Malon, R. W.	Orphan. Farming
Parham, Paraline	4Dec1882	9 yrs	Farmer, R. P.	Orphan. House keeping

Ryan, Andy	3Sept1883	13 yrs	Stunston, Lewis	Orphan. Farming
Simmons, Lee	3Dec1883	15 yrs	Simmons, B. L.	Orphan. Farming
Houston, Green B.	5Aug1884	5 yrs	Boone, G. D.	Orphan. Farming
Simmons, James	1Sept1884	9 yrs	Pentecost, William	Orphan. Farming
Hoggard, Finus U.	7Apr1885	5 yrs	Meek, F. M.	Orphan. Farming. Prob one of 5 children of M. C. Meek's sister (d. 22Feb1885). See his adoption of Berdie & Penolar Haggard 7Apr1885. Deserted by father"
Hoggard, James Allen	7Apr1885	8 yrs	Meek, F. M.	Orphan. Farming. See above
Hoggard, J. W.	7Apr1885	10 yrs	Mahon, J. W.	Orphan. Farming. See above
Morgan, John W. H.	7Oct1885	7 yrs on 10Oct1885	White, T. P.	Orphan. Farming
Gillean, George Edgar	7Apr1886	9 yrs on 18Dec1885	Brock, S. M.	Orphan. Farming
McMahan, Alice	10June1886	11 yrs	Scott, R. B.	Orphan. House keeping
Hughston, Green B.	2Aug1886		Perch, J. W.	Orphan. Farming
Irvine, Willie	13Sept1886	5 yrs	Somers, A. J.	Orphan. Farming
Brannon, John Henry	6Dec1886	13 yrs	Taylor, M. L.	Orphan. Farming
Webb, Jennie A.	5Oct1887	6 yrs in March1887	Roney, Margaret (Mrs)	Orphan. House keeping
Taylor, Lea	1Feb1888	9 yrs	Caston, J. H.	Orphan. Farming
Mansfield, Ida E.	7May1888	9 mo	Perry, R. G.	Orphan. Housekeeping

NOTE: Name may appear more than once on a page.

J. J. C., 108
Loan, 108
Miles, 52
Peter, 108
William, 29,
   108
William J.,
   112
Bivins
   Lewis C., 137
Black
   Alfred, 153
   Amos, 59
   Charles, 60
   H., 60
   Jeremiah, 12
   Nancy J., 9
   Nancy Jane,
      9, 10
   Narcisses,
      120
   S. A., 59
   Samuel, 9
   Walker, 59
   William, 9,
      160
Blackburn
   Joseph L., 20
   R. H., 20
Blackcome
   Jacob, 9
Blackman
   James W.,
      117
Blacknall
   W. R., 160
Blackwell
   Bayles C., 28
   Bayliss, 28
   Bettie, 47
   Betty, 48
   Dilsy, 51
   Hiram H., 28
   Jasper W., 28
   John, 27, 28
   Lewis, 51
   Nathan B., 28
   Newton G.,
      28
   Polly, 28
   Polly A., 28
   Solomon G.,
      28
Blair

A. B., 129
Andrew, 11
Felix, 11
George D., 39
Lizzie, 36
Blake
   James G., 71
Blakeley
   J. P., 119
Blakely
   Thomas, 69
Blakemore
   B. D., 163
   Thomas, 163
Bland
   Morris, 54
Blane
   Celia Ann, 99
Blank
   Joseph, 1
Blankenship
   D. W., 72
   J. W., 96
Blanks, 1
   John, 1
   William L., 1
Blanton
   Albert C., 39
   William F.,
      69
Blaylock
   Jesse, 63, 64
Bleckley
   Calvin, 145
   James, 145
   Malvina, 145
   Milley, 145
   T. C., 145
Bledsoe
   A. B., 22
   Duncan C.,
      105
   W. E., 45
Blevins
   Wilson, 74
Blickly
   T. C., 134
Block
   Alfred
   Jeremiah,
      12
Blount
   John B., 9
Blythe

A. J., 91
James, 106
Board
   G. F., 130
   John, 130
Boarding, Sr
   John, 149
Boatman
   John G., 119
Bob, 110, 111,
   112
Bobbett
   Samuel M.,
      105
Bobo
   W. R., 164
Bogguss
   R. D., 21
Bohannan
   Lizzie, 148
Bolen
   G. M., 3
Boler
   Ren, 37
Boles
   John T., 103
Bomar
   Betty, 107
   Calvin C.,
      107, 108
   Phillip, 107
   Rins, 108
   Willis, 87
Bomer
   R. J., 3
Bond
   Abram, 79
   Angeline, 82
   Cicily, 79
   Clancy, 117
   Eliza, 101
   Eva, 117
   Frank, 117
   Freeman, 117
   Granville, 4
   Henry, 82, 85
   Jackson, 80
   James, 88,
      101
   James Polk, 2
   James W.,
      113
   Jesse, 118

John, 82, 85,
   101, 113
Lovey, 117
Thomas, 77
W. T., 80
W. W., 79
William W.,
   81
Willie, 117
Bonds
   Elizabeth, 2
   Newton, 4
Bondurant
   Bell, 164
   Mariah, 164
Bone
   James P., 35
Bonner
   C. H., 131
   Thomas, 103
   Walter N. R.,
      94
   Willis, 87
Booker
   Frances M., 8
Boon
   Benjamin, 38
   Billy, 24
   D. M., 119
   Henry, 23
   Willard, 23,
      24
Boone
   G. D., 165
Booth
   David C., 29
   Tapley, 163
Borren
   Willis, 38
Bostic
   J. S., 94
Bostick
   Samuel
      Alexander,
      125
Bostin
   Jacob, 11
Boston
   Hannah, 125
   Jacob, 10
   Jessee, 10
   Samuel, 10
   Sandy, 125

Browder
  D. A., 17
  J. J., 119
  W. T., 119
Brown
  A. J., 94
  Ben, 144
  Benjamin C.,
  142
  C. P., 50
  Deck, 162
  Elijah, 151
  Gracy, 117
  H. B., 66
  Hiram R., 130
  Hollis, 151
  Isaac, 15
  James
    William,
    50
  Jesse A., 87,
  88, 90
  John, 76, 86
  Jordan, 151
  M. H., 50
  Malindy J.,
  93
  Martha, 135
  Mary, 140
  Mary Jane,
  145
  Milton, 108
  Oliver, 117
  R. C., 102
  Samuel, 78
  Silas, 130
  Simon, 48
  Solomon, 35
  Thomas B.,
  75
  W. A., 148
  Whit, 151
  Wilbourne,
  144
  William, 76,
  139
  William A.,
  18
  Wilson, 7, 8
Brumett
  W. Y., 162
Brumley
  Jefferson C.,
  70

Willis, 69
Brumly
  William A.,
  71
Bryant
  Andrew, 33
  Benjamin, 77
  Charley, 114
  DAvy, 33
  Eli, 77
  John Thomas,
  77
  Joseph, 77
  Martha, 77
  Nancy, 77
  R. A., 15
  William A.,
  132, 133
Bryum
  James, 3
Bucey
  John M., 90
Buchanan
  Ama, 109
  Daniel, 87
  Henry F., 87
  Thomas N.,
  109
Buck
  Albert, 16
  Henry, 80
  Laura, 80
Buckingham
  H. G., 140
Buckley
  John T., 126
  Joseph, 126
  Solomon O.,
  126
Buckner
  Virgil, 155
Bucks
  Henry, 101
Buford
  Alex, 66
Bugance
  John H., 7
Buggs
  Baker, 121
  Charles B.,
  121
  Ella, 121
  Franklin, 121
Bull

H. F., 129
Bullington
  D. A., 15
Bunch
  Albert, 75
  Elijah, 132
Bunnell
  Isaac, 23
  W. A., 23
Burden
  William, 158
Burford
  Mary, 84
  Pat, 80
  S. C., 80
Burges
  Madison, 56
Burke
  Amanda, 147
  R. A., 100
Burkhead
  Alfred, 122
  Andy, 122
  Peter, 122
  Thomas O.,
  122
Burks
  Henry, 101
  Patsey, 68
Burnet
  Daniel H., 77
  John, 77
Burnett
  Eliza, 77
  Frances, 77
  George, 77
  James, 77
  James
    Thomas, 77
  John, 77
  Martha Ann,
  77
  Thomas, 77
  Thomas M.,
  52, 149
Burns
  Anthony, 46
  Maggie, 116
  Robert H., 46
Burras
  Julius, 92
  Mary Ann, 92
Burrel
  Taylor, 154

Burris
  J. B., 127
  John, 94
  Thomas
    Wyley, 94
Burrough
  Alice, 79
Burroughs
  Henry W., 21
Burrow, 8
  Ephriam, 7
  Freeman, 32
  Green, 8
  Hezekiah, 7
  Jincy, 7
  John J., 13
  John S., 8
  John W., 32
  Martin, 8
  Matilda, 12
  Peter, 13
  Phillip, 8
  Rebeca, 7
  Robert, 32
  William, 7
Burt
  William S.,
  28
Burton
  H. B., 164
Bush
  Rheuben, 92
Bushart
  John, 86
Busich
  John, 9
Butcher
  Alice, 148
Butler
  A. J., 13
  Ben G., 101
  Billy, 124
  Cath, 124
  E. T., 46
  James J., 20
  Johma, 10
  John, 143
  Rese, 13
  S. Mozello,
  26
  W. F., 20
  William, 101
  William
    Leroy, 122

John, 14
Nancy, 13
Sarah, 13
Clement
  Lewis T., 8
  R. H., 131
Click
  Jordan, 1
Clifton
  Eldridge, 71
  Nancy, 74
Climer
  Carroll, 104
  Harvey, 105
  Milton, 104
  W. H., 164
Clingan
  David, 70
Clinten
  Robert, 29
Clinton
  Ellen, 61
  Henry, 4
  M. L., 61
Cloar
  John E., 128
  T. C., 130
Coates
  Amanda L.
    M., 63
  Catherine, 63
  George, 63
Coats
  W. G., 19
Cobb
  Alfred, 97
  Henry, 98
  Jesse, 97, 98
  Martha, 98
  Mary, 98
  Nancy, 98
  Paul, 98
Coburn
  Ginny, 62
  James L., 62
Cochran
  J. W., 158
Cock
  Dilla, 110
  John C., 110
  Thomas, 110
  Thomas A.,
    111
Cocke

Ann E., 33
Leana, 33
Roberta, 33
Thomas R.,
  34
Codswell
  John, 143
Cody
  A. H., 75
  George, 147
Cogshall
  Boyd, 79
  Charlie, 79
  J. C., 79
Cogswell
  A. M., 143
Coldwell
  David, 84
  Elias, 84
  Henry, 84
  Joe, 84
  John P., 126
  Marshall, 84
  VanBuran, 84
Cole
  Allen, 116
  C. T., 159,
    162
  Ivie, 116
  J. M., 130
  James M.,
    127
  M. A., 115
  Mittie, 142
  Rachel, 116
  Roxie, 117
  S. H., 39
  Sue, 142
Coleman
  A. A., 59
  Charley, 115
  E. G., 61
  E. N., 102
  Ellen, 115
  George, 115
  J. F., 46
  James M.,
    137
  John A., 98
  Joshua, 128
  Loyed, 93
  Silas, 115
  W. A., 154
Colier

James, 1
Collier
  Henry, 157
  John, 162
  Louisa, 60
  Martha J.,
    162
  Violet, 153
  William, 65
  Z. T., 15
Collins
  R. A., 134
  W. N., 13
Collinsworth
  Jesse, 103
Collister
  James, 136
Columbus, 159
Colvin
  B. F., 102
  Joseph L.,
    102
  Rebecca, 102
  V. L., 102
Colwell
  Elvira, 77
Coly
  George, 147
Compton
  Jackson, 83
Conan
  Isaac F., 40
Connally
  Thomas M.,
    105
Connell
  James, 42
  William, 134
Connelly
  Guss, 131
Conner, 62
  Malinda, 99
  William, 76,
    99
Converse
  Elam, 146
Conway
  Jane, 81
Conyers
  John, 9
Cook
  Archibald,
    105
  D. C., 93

John, 40
John W., 80
Jordan, 80
Mary, 148
S. C., 159
W. C., 93
Cooksey
  Mary Ann, 86
Cooley
  George, 158,
    159
  James, 5
  William, 4
Cooney
  John, 89
Coop
  G. B. H., 48
Cooper
  Amanda D.,
    164
  George M.,
    121
  Grace, 50
  Henry J., 36
  Homer B.,
    115
  Isaac, 13
  Joe, 164
  John C., 27,
    29
  John H., 1
  Lee, 164
  Louesia, 161
  Mandy, 164
  Mary, 164
  S. M., 129
  Tilda, 13
  Whiton C., 40
  Whitson, 42
  William, 15,
    92
  William D.,
    149
  William
    Grant, 164
Cooxey
  Jemimah, 5
  Joseph, 5
  Samuel, 5, 86
Copeland
  Solomon, 70
Coples
  William T.,
    42

Alice, 5
Delapp
 Anderson,
  106
Demington
 James A., 129
Demmington
 Jesse, 129
Demsey
 A. W., 151
Denning
 Thomas G.,
  162
Dennis
 Stephen, 86
Dennum
 Wilson, 69
Denny
 Alfred, 96
 Thomas, 96
Densford
 James, 151
Dent
 E. R., 164
 T. E., 158
Derington
 J. W., 89
Derrington
 Laura T., 91
Dewberry
 Amarintha,
  51
 John, 51
Dick, 109, 112
Dickens
 John, 132
Dickenson
 Isaac, 67
 Mollie, 67
 William, 67
Dickerson
 Cora, 62
 Elvin
  Amariah,
   107
 Jack, 62
 Jesse, 62
 John L., 1
 Lucinda, 1
 Nancy
  Caroline, 1
 William, 1
 William E.,
  99

Dickey
 David, 40
Dickins
 Richard, 38
Dickson
 Adeline, 143
 Ella, 143
 Emma, 49
 Jackson, 37
 Joseph, 159
 Thomas, 31 '
 William
  Jefferson
  Davis, 49
Diggs
 Jacob, 93
Dilday
 J. H., 14
Dildy
 J. F., 14
Dill
 Jemmiah H.,
  39
Dillian
 Joseph, 4
Dillingham
 William H.,
  104
Dillon
 Jackson, 155
 Joseph, 75
Dinah, 105
Dinkins
 Edward G.,
  70
Dix
 Fayette, 141
Dixon
 Adeline, 147
 Betsey, 142
 Ella, 147
 George, 142
 Millie, 142
Dodd
 Nancy, 50
 Sammie, 50
 W. T., 81
 Willie, 50, 76
Dodds
 John A., 75
Dodson
 Archer, 59
 Belle, 44
 Buck, 44

George, 61
W. H., 44,
 160
William H.,
 40
Dolan
 Catherine,
  145
Dollins
 Jesse E., 129
Dolsen
 Benjamin S.,
  23
Donahoo
 John D., 72
Donaldson
 Benjamin, 51
 Calvin, 51
 Charles, 44
 Ebenezer, 44
 Harriet, 44
 Leonidas, 51
 Lucinda, 44
 Mattie, 51
 Milly, 51
 William, 44
Donall
 Charles, 160
Donnel
 George, 25
Donnell
 R. A., 131
Dora, 33
Doran
 W. P., 75
Dorch
 Columbus, 88
Dord, 112
Dorns
 Felix P., 92
Dorris
 Anna, 94
 Henry P., 104
 Laura, 94
Doud
 William, 40
Dougherty
 Eliza, 128
 Emma B.,
  128
 George Ann,
  128
 James F., 128
 Polly, 128

Douglas
 Ellen, 26
 Franklin, 120
 George T.,
  146
 Jane, 26
 John T., 151
 Nick, 26
Douglass
 Amanda, 14
 Guy, 23
 Henry L., 147
 Matilda, 23
 Shela, 27
 Soran, 27
 Thomas, 29
 W. A., 93
Dourtheage
 Sarah, 104
 William, 104
Dowdey
 William, 70
Dowell
 Wiley, 23
Dowley
 Annie, 148
Downey
 Mary, 19
Doyle
 Sarah, 4
Dozier
 Billie, 14
Drake
 Haywood, 80
 Jeremiah, 103
 Jeremiah M.,
  106
 John, 80, 81
 P., 160
 Thoms, 80
Drane
 Jo, 23
 John M., 23
 Sallie, 23
Driggers
 James, 9
 William, 9
Droffin
 Elizabeth,
  155
 Jesse John
  Calhoun,
   155
Dudly

181

Fraser
  William L.,
    34
Frazier
  Constantine,
    92
  George, 92
  John W., 131
  T. J., 160
Fred, 144
Freelan
  William W.,
    104
Freeling
  J. H., 117
Freeman
  Adeline
    Catherine,
    69
  Alledonea,
    161
  Benjamin
    Rush, 69
  Elizabeth
    Ann, 70
  George W.,
    16
  J. W., 161
  James Jasper,
    69
  John L., 70
  John Lewis,
    69
  Julia, 161
  Sarah, 70
  Sarah Jane,
    69
  William
    Andrews,
    69
  William P.,
    69
Frely
  Andrew J., 70
  Martin, 70
  Sarah, 70
French
  Berry, 87
  Brown, 20
  Leslie, 20
  Noah, 86
  Reuben, 20
Frizell
  Asa, 156

Frost
  Wilson, 25
Fry
  G. W., 12
  George W.,
    13
  Henry, 150
Fryer
  R. N., 24
Fryor
  Thomas C.,
    91
Fulerton
  Elijah, 30
Fuller
  Amanda, 23
  Ann, 23
  George, 23
  Jane, 118
  Jefferson, 68
  Jeremiah,
    106, 113
  John, 23
  W. G., 11
  William, 23
Fullerton
  David, 1
Fulleton
  Elijah, 30
Fulshen
  William, 149
Fulton
  John, 156
  Joseph, 156
  Susan, 156
  William, 156
Fumbanks
  A. L., 24
Funk
  Peter, 138
Fuqua
  John, 47
Furgerson
  Harris J., 39
  Samuel H., 13
  William A.,
    41
Furlong
  Viola, 119
Fussell
  Wyatt, 107
Fussell &
  Norwood,
    106

Futell
  Richard, 103
Futington
  George
    Washingto
    n, 29
Gailey
  C. C., 159
Gainer
  William, 86
Gaines
  A. M., 99
Gainess
  Oscar, 123
  Robert, 123
Gaither
  J. G., 34
Gammill
  Arch, 75
  Ebenezer, 68
Gannaway
  James
    Walker,
    104
  Mary D., 104
  May B., 103
  Samuel
    Lancaster,
    103
Gant
  J. H., 134
  John H., 133
Gardner
  Ada, 162
  Alfred, 159
  Allice, 162
  Andrew, 129
  Bell, 161
  Cornelius, 32
  D. S., 129
  Eli, 111
  Elizabeth, 32
  J. Almus, 162
  Jeptha, 161
  john, 26
  John, 74
  John A., 161,
    162
  John C., 162
  John Henry,
    161
  Joshua, 157,
    161
  Lary, 6

Lee, 162
Marcus
  Lafayette,
    150
Mark, 129
Mary, 129
Mary
  Elizabeth,
    32
Melindy, 6
Metta A., 162
Miles, 129
Sally, 129
Sam, 162
Sidney, 129
Stephen, 160
Thomas, 150
Thomas J.,
    54, 55
Tom, 32, 162
W. H., 130
Walter, 162
William, 48
William F.,
    115
Garner
  Jashua, 71
Garnett
  John H., 36
Garratt
  Ted, 64
Garret
  Mary Ann,
    119
  McD., 119
Garrett
  Henry, 30
  Martin Lee,
    146
Gary
  Martin O., 49
Gaskins
  T. R., 12
Gates
  Mare A., 90
  William A.,
    29
Gaulden
  Fletcher, 26
Gay
  William, 144
Gaynor
  Isaac, 147
Gee

John, 38
John P., 38
General, 136
Gentry
William, 26
George, 81,
110, 113, 127,
159
Isaac, 28
George, Sr
Benjamin, 76
Gerr?
Edmond W.,
6
Gibbon
Clara, 62
Henry, 62
Gibbs
Coonrod, 68
Gibson
E. P., 56
Elizabeth, 88
Felix, 127
James Henry,
56
Jeremiah, 9
John, 10
Sphen, 4
Wiley P., 9
Gidcombe
John, 101
Samuel, 101
Gilbert
Joe, 16
Vina, 16
Giles
James C., 38
T. L., 138
Thomas N.,
29
Gill
Alexander,
117
Julius, 85
Philus, 85
Tom, 85
Gillam
Lesly, 162
P. A. (Miss),
141
Phebe, 141
Gillean
George
Edgar, 165

Gillespie
James, 96
Gilley, 97
Gilliam
Thomas L.,
162
Gillis
Murdock, 5
Gillstrap
Barnett, 96
Gilmore
Robert, 156
Gilstrap
Amanda, 96
Barnett, 96
Rebecca, 96
Susan, 96
William, 96
Gingery
Israel, 99
Jacob, 99
Given
John, 133
Stephen, 27
Tenilla, 27
Givens
Lucy, 48
Moses, 133
R. S., 50
Rebecca, 133
Robert H.,
111
Samuel W.,
103
Givins
S. D., 50
Glasgow
F. M., 163
Glass
Charles, 159
Faranklin, 88
Hannah, 159
Linda, 159
Lucinda, 159
Malinda R.,
159
Thomas, 159
Glasscock
Scarlett M.,
40
Glease
German, 147
Gleason
Earnest, 164

Timothy, 45,
50
Glenn
Betsy, 76
Cassa, 76
Cassiah, 76
John, 76
Kizzia, 76
Malinda, 98
N. C., 98
Nancy, 98
Glidewell
James, 56
Glisson
George W.,
39
William N.,
39
Glover
George, 6
Jesse T., 129
John M., 126
Joshua, 129
Glowson
Jones, 9
Godwin
D. Y., 146
Goff
John C., 113
Gold
John, 89
Goldsmith
Charles, 122
Francis, 122
Jessee, 122
Goliman
W. G., 158
Gonzales
Manuel
Farina, 135
Gooch
J. G., 121
Good
Alex M., 41
Daniel, 6
Jefferson, 6
Nelson, 41
Patrick, 41
Goodell
Austin, 115
Goodloe
M. H., 41
P. R., 49
Goodlow

George, 104
Goodman
Isaac, 153
James
Vincent,
102
Jane, 153
Goodrum
G. W., 13
Gordon
Calista, 40
Fredonia, 114
John, 40
John W., 40,
41
Tennessee,
114
Wilson, 40
Gorforth
Alfred, 71
Gorman
Daniel, 118
Gorsell
F. W., 120
Gough
Jesse, 53
Gouse
T. G., 102
Goyne
Aaron, 132
Grace
John L., 86
Gragg
J. W., 148
Graham
Daniel, 87
Dock, 64
G. W., 64
James, 68
John D., 132
John Henry,
64
Robert, 64
Grainger
William
Henry
Harrison,
88
Gram
William F.,
90
Gran
Jesse G., 38
Granberry

Charles, 35
Grant
 J. E., 142
Grantham
 James Henry,
  56
 Lewis, 56
 Sion, 56
Granville, 108
Graves
 E. A., 79
 Tom, 79
Gray
 John, 139
 Thomas, 69,
  70, 86
 W. C., 64
Grayton
 William, 36
Greaves
 E. A., 98
 Henrietta, 98
Green
 A. A., 100
 Claiborne, 99
 David, 99
 Delia, 99
 Erasmus, 44
 Fannie, 140
 Frances, 141
 Harriet, 140
 Henry, 99
 Jacob, 140,
  141
 James L., 99
 John, 86, 154,
  155
 Joseph, 7
 Lee, 154, 155
 Louiza, 100
 Margaret,
  140, 141
 Martha, 7
 Mary, 45
 Mary A., 128
 Minnie, 154
 Mozela, 100
 Nice, 154
 Rebecca, 100
 Sally, 127
 Samuel, 93
 Sarah A., 85
 Thomas, 100

Thomas B.,
 159
Victoria, 154
William, 92
William N.,
 128
Greer
 John, 3
 Joseph, 14,
  149
 Lucinda, 149
 Thomas A.
  Guillom,
  46
 Tilda, 112
Greggs
 John, 151
Gregory
 Albert, 84
 America, 84
 Charles T.,
  148
 Henry, 84
 John H., 115
 M., 84
Gridley
 Chance, 76
Griffin
 Henry, 90
 Richard
  Calvin, 90
 Thomas, 88
 Thomas J., 26
 Timothy, 24
Griffine
 Calvin, 89
 Richard C.,
  90
 William H.,
  90
Griggs
 Henry C., 36
Grimes
 Flora L., 123
Grinage
 James M., 70
Grissom
 C. W., 16
Grissum
 Willis, 4
Groom
 J. M., 163
 W. C., 16
Grooms

Elizabeth, 12
Harriett, 12
Henry, 12
Grove
 Agga, 58
 Allen Osker,
  58
 Annie, 84
 Ellen, 60
 Isabella, 84
 J. H., 60
 Julia, 84
 Laura A., 58
 Margaret C.,
  58
 Osker, 58
Groves
 Thomas H.,
  101
Gudyer
 M. W., 97
Guin
 Jacob, 88
Gum
 Boyd, 128
 Feby, 128
 Fillis, 128
 W. N., 128
Gunter
 Charles, 156
 Harry, 157
 Randolph,
  158
Guthrie
 Felix, 55
 Robert, 88
 W. W., 66
 Warner, 146
Guy
 Benjamin,
  159
 Nathaniel B.,
  159
Guyman
 James, 87
 John, 87
 Noah, 87
 Thomas, 87
Gwin
 Edward, 6
Gwyn
 Pattie, 62
 Sallie D., 62
Gwynne

A. J., 129
Hadley
 Isaac, 67
 Lemuel, 135
Hagar
 Steely, 96
Haggard
 Berdie, 165
 Louisa, 160
 Masey, 160
 Penolar, 165
Haily
 Robert, 37
Hair
 William Bell,
  123
Haire
 Cason, 68
 Martha, 68
 William, 68
Hale
 J. P., 47
 Jesse, 4
 Meshac, 133
 Rebecca, 134
 Robert, 25
Haley
 Betty, 129
 Michael, 49
Hall
 Alfred D., 38
 Calvin, 38
 Elam, 153
 Esther, 135
 Esther
  Narcissa
  Manerva
  Jane, 134
 Hansford N.,
  40
 Harriet, 34
 Henry, 63
 Herrod, 41
 Isham, 153
 John B., 130
 Johnathan, 38
 Jonathan, 113
 Julius, 38
 Kitty, 34
 Lucy, 153
 M. W., 63
 Martha, 153
 Robert S., 96
 Sallie, 153

187

188

Archelous, 42
Elisha S., 41,
42
J. G., 41
Jessee, 41
Keathly
Archelous, 41
Kee
John, 14
Nelson, 14
Keeton
Reason, 71
Keithly
John, 78
Keller
A. J., 66
Uriah, 135
Kelley
John, 133
Kelly
Hillman, 18
James, 55
John, 2
Samuel, 18
W. O., 48
Kelough
John N., 9
Kelsaw
James, 163
Rip, 163
Kelsoe
J. F., 80
Keltner
Jacob B., 96
Keltner. M.,
102
Kemp
George W.,
123
Kemper
Jackson, 20
Kendall
Andy, 91
Peter, 88
R. A. (Mrs),
91
Richmond D.,
87
Richmond G.,
87
Samuel, 91
William G.,
88
Kennedy

Oscar, 141
Peter, 141
Trenton, 141
Kennen
Robert, 99
Rosetta, 99
Kennon
William B., 9
Kent
George, 109
Richard, 23
Kerr
Andrew, 70
German, 147
Thomas A.,
69
Kery
James P., 89
Kesen
David, 28
Saah Ann, 28
Ketchum
John W. N.,
26
Richard T.,
26
W. L., 26
Key
L. C., 128
Kilbreath
A. M., 3
Lovey F., 3
Moulton A., 3
Sarah, 3
William, 3
William H., 3
Kile
E. S., 8
Kilgore
James D., 87
Killen
Elizabeth, 15
Killgore
W. R., 158
Killin
Sarah Ninie,
15
Killough
Charles H., 8
John N., 8
Samuel D., 8
Kimbell
William H.
C., 160

Kimble
J. T., 75
Kimbrel
Martha E.,
160
Kincaid
William, 132
Kincannon
James F., 73
Nancy E., 73
Rebecca J.,
73
Thomas W.
P., 73
King, 98
Anna
Lennetta,
46
Charles, 129
Chesley, 8
Elias, 144
Eliza, 56
Enoch, 55
Henry A., 50
J. C., 11
James H., 127
Jennett, 130
Jennie, 82
Joseph Martin
A., 56
Mathew, 29
Nelson
Franklin,
38
Thomas, 130
William, 55
William D.,
128
William
Henry, 29
William J., 2
Kinnard
James, 55, 56,
57
Thomas, 55
Kinsey
John, 76
Kirby
Allen, 80
Benjamin, 97
Betsy Jane,
129
Charles, 129
Eliza, 80

John, 93, 122
Rebecca, 93
William R.,
93
Kirk
Catherine,
132
John, 132
Polly, 132
Thomas, 132
Kirkland
Henry, 52
Kirkpatrick
Alexander, 52
Jackson, 97
Robert, 97
Kirkpattrick
Plumer, 29
Kirlen
Bernard, 123
Kite
E. J., 12
Kizer
Sophia Ann,
118
Klink
James Henry,
107
Martha, 107
Tennessee A.,
107
William F.,
107
Knight, 130
Robert E.,
163
Knott
Green, 39
Henry, 39
John, 39
William, 39
Knowland
Lucinda, 147
Koker
Ben F., 30
Mary, 30
Nevil S., 30
Kyle
E. J., 15
Laberque
Vincent, 137
Lackey
B. F., 101
James A., 95

John W., 49
Thomas, 49
Neal
Eliza Jane, 75
James W., 126
Richard M., 126
Sidney G., 126
Thomas, 150
Tom W., 23
Neale
Crawford, 149
Thomas, 149
Neblett
Emily, 33
J. D., 33
Neeley
Daniel, 24
James B., 111
Neely
Ada, 113
Amanda, 24
Andrew, 5
Ellen, 113
Henry, 116
J. J., 65
J. S., 63
James C., 66
Jo, 25
Joseph, 116
Robert H., 25
Samuel, 10
Neill
John M., 118
Pinkney H., 118
Nelms
Calvin, 141
Clinda, 141
Joanna, 141
Kate, 141
Richard, 124
Sandy, 141
Nelson
A. W., 147
G. F., 49
George H., 11
Henry, 100, 116
Jane, 153
William J., 11

William R., 146
Nesbit
Robert N., 30
Nesbitt
Ed, 16
Henry, 28
Peter, 47
Robert, 47
Sampson, 16
Wilson, 7
Nevel
R. J., 42
Nevill
Alexander, 69
New
A. H., 158
Adeline, 63
Early, 63
John, 63
Jordan, 63
Martha, 63
W. H., 146
Newbern
Anna, 60
David J., 59
Henry, 59
Jason, 117
Thomas, 59
Newbone
Tom, 84
Newby
Catcy, 113
Catherine, 113
Eliza, 113
James, 113
Laura, 113
Martha, 113
Missy, 113
Sallie, 113
Wales, 32
Wiley, 113
Newell
Florence, 142
Jane, 142
John W., 89
Newhouse
Allen, 43
Emma, 43
F. M., 43
Newman
Henry, 73
L. C., 85

Nelly C., 150
Wesley, 73
Newsom
Hannah, 65
Henry, 114
Jack, 82
John F., 115
Thomas, 132
William, 82
Newson
Sarah, 132
Newton
James W., 157
Robert, 163
Sarah, 154
William, 154, 158
Niblett
Alfred, 80
J. T., 80
July, 80
Niceler
Allert, 10
Nicely
Moses, 10
Nichol
David, 5
Nichold
Lazarus, 44
Nichols
George, 54, 74
James H,, 125
James W., 17
John, 17
Noah, 54
Sarah, 125
William, 125
Nina, 98
Nix
Franklin, 71
Jesse, 158
Nixon
Edward, 101
Loiza, 101
Noah
F. L., 131
Nobles
William A., 106
Nolen
H. C., 82
John, 104

Nolin
Allen C., 39
Nora, 25
Norman, 11
Dilly, 149
Jackson, 149
Rhoda, 149
Sarah, 149
William, 87
Northern
Henry, 118
Jack, 118
Norton
Jacob A., 57
Nowell
Andrew, 105
Barnibas, 105
Caladonia, 4
Dempsy, 105
Elizabeth, 105
Jeptha G., 4
Thomas, 105
W. B., 5
Nuckells
Richard, 66
Nuckolly
John, 54
Null
Louis J., 10
Richward G., 7
Nunn, Jr
D. A., 17
Nusum
John, 132
Oakes
John, 54
Oar
Gilbert, 126
John Hawkins, 126
Oates
Eliza Jane, 60
Fannie G., 60
O'Daniel
Alexander, 39
J., 48
Stephen, 39
O'Dell
James A., 26
Odile

Prewett
Henry, 164
Prewitt
Robert E.,
116
Price, 144
Agnes, 26
James, 50,
121
John, 50, 132
Joseph, 4
Reuben T., 87
Sally, 28
Terrell, 87
William, 28,
86
Priest
Franklin, 8
Prince, 105
Ephaine, 15
James, 20
Miles
Morgan, 94
William, 13
Printz
William, 134
Pritchard
Allen, 13
Charles, 13
David L., 132
Willis, 13
Pritchett
Benjamin, 39
Hannah, 52
Judy, 52
Lucy, 52
Privett
Miles, 18
Pruden
John, 147
Thomas, 147
Prudett
W. F., 3
Pryor
Henry, 127
W. S., 92
William, 90
Pucket
Columbus, 61
Susan, 61
Winnefred,
61
Puckett
Peter P., 38

Pugh
Ann, 61
Eliza, 61
Rose, 61
Pulley
Henry, 102
Pulliam
J. L., 35
Pullin
Fayette J., 32
Judie, 32
Purvis
Starkey, 125
William T.,
77
Puryear
W. W., 147
Pybas
James S., 42
Pybass
James, 62, 65
Pybor
Nathanial, 38
Pyles
Bedford, 108
Carter, 108
James M.,
108
Robert, 27
Queen
David C., 134
Quin
Judy, 115
Scylla, 115
Quinn
G. W., 15
John K., 96
Thomas, 15
Rachel
Barney, 50
Henry, 50
Judge, 50
Lawyer, 50
Newton, 50
Sue, 50
Ragland
Milton E., 34
Ragsdale
James, 119
Peter, 38
Raines
A. W., 51
Amanda M.,
53

Clara, 53
James F. M.,
121
James W., 53
Stephen, 53
Ralston
John, 132
Ramsey
A. M., 131
Alex, 66
Henry C., 71
Julia, 66
Maronda C.,
9
William, 53
Randle
Bert, 93
George, 92
W. G., 92
Randolph
Callie, 113
Henry, 82, 83
Rix A., 70
Tom, 113
Randoph, 111
John G., 123
Rank
S. G., 47
Rankin
David, 118
Ransom
John, 139
Rasberry
John J., 14
Rash
Jackson L.,
29
Ratcliff
Jean, 53
Rate
Emanuel, 33
Rateree
James E., 90
Raulhoe
George G.,
155
Rawlings
Kitty, 135
Rawls
Madison, 86
Ray
B., 158
Benjamin, 14
Betsy, 53

Elizabeth, 71
Emanuel F.,
72
John, 51
Mary, 51
Pink, 163
Richmond, 51
Samuel G., 53
Thomas, 24
William F.,
125
Raybern
Henry, 2
Rayburn, 133
Raynor
Eliza Jane,
142
May A., 142
Rose, 142
Read
Isaac H., 81
James B., 41
Laura E., 101
Mary J., 40
Peter, 40
Samuel A., 52
Seamon, 83
W. B., 83
Reamey
Sarah J., 25
Rease
Charly, 19
Reaves
Bethel, 157
Catharine,
156, 157
Henderson,
156
John, 134
Martha, 156
Rode, 156
Rody, 157
Roseanna,
157
Thomas C.,
107
Rebecca, 104,
114, 120
Reddeck
L. W., 159
Redden
Fannie, 78
Margaret, 78
Sarah, 77

David, 157
Elizabeth,
124
J. F., 17, 18
James Erwin,
131
Jane, 107
Jeff D., 24
Johnothan, 17
Mary, 67, 144
Narcissa
Elizabeth,
56
P. A., 144
P. F., 66
Patrick F., 56
William R., 2
Willis, 66
Robins
George W.,
38
John L., 38
Mary E., 136
Sarah
Alexander,
70
Thomas D.,
137
William J.,
135
William N.,
38
Robinson
Alexander
M., 135
D. A., 62
David, 70
Dawson H.,
69
Elizabeth,
124
Gabriel, 78
Harry R., 150
J. C., 107
J. W., 72
James, 69
James H., 60
James L., 66
James W., 44
P. A., 144
Robert, 136
Spencer, 107
Wiley G., 72
William, 147

Robison
Amandy Jane,
95
Anna, 95
Elijah W., 95
Thomas, 95
William T.,
95
Rodgers
Alexander,
124
Chance, 58
H. E. (Mrs),
140
Jake, 61
Jeff, 58
John Wesley,
124
Louisa, 33
Lucinda, 140
Mariah, 124
Mary, 124
Nathaniel,
124
William, 124
Rody, 157
Roe
Green, 43
Jessee, 43
John A., 43
Rogers
Bob, 94
Charlie, 94
David, 53
John, 53
John W., 155
M. A., 164
Mary H., 145
Nancy, 8
O[re] U., 38
P. M., 164
Richard, 61
S. C., 146
S. J., 129
W. O., 56
William, 88
William A., 9
William E.,
145
Rogers, Jr
C. B., 121
Rolling
Alain, 8
Romine

J. H., 123
Roney
Margaret, 165
Rook
A. T., 64
Amon Y., 55
Roper
David T., 13
J. R., 16
Rory
Lee, 157
Rose
Catherine,
154
Roseberry
J. S., 10
Roseman
George, 17
J. W., 17
Samantha, 17
Ross
Charles H.,
39
Daniel T., 6
David, 126
E. P., 92
George W.,
38, 39
James C., 122
James C/, 104
James T., 74
John G., 87
Samuel, 7
William A.,
74
Roswell
Lewis, 3
Mary L. B., 3
Roten
E. H., 120
Rousey
James H., 123
Rowe
John M., 13
Rowland
Aaron, 9
Rowlett
Eddie, 164
Peter, 164
Rucker
G. W., 163
Rudd
Rebecca, 158
Rudder

James W., 23
Ruff
John L., 7
Ruffin
James D., 144
John B., 107
T., 60
Rumley
Henry, 7
Joseph, 7
Madison, 7
Sarah J., 7
Runnells
Jefferson, 45
Rush
Carroll B., 96
William, 63
Rushing
Mark, 72
Richard, 24
Richard B., 3
W. F., 20
William F.,
19
Russel
Hannah, 156
James Petty,
156
Jonah, 156
Majah
William,
156
Priestley, 14
Rachel, 156
Russell
Alexander, 71
Buckner, 156
George Mc.,
116
Henry A., 15
Huston, 158
James, 94
John W., 12
Thomas P.,
14
William, 6,
70, 71
Rust
Jeremiah T.,
6, 8
Ruth
James V., 101
Rutherford
Charles, 123

Andrew, 24
Bidwell, 140
Erasmus, 24
Horace, 140
Jim, 48
Luitene, 24
Malinda, 46
Scott, 24
William, 47
William P.,
13
Shaver
D. L., 161
Shaw
D. B., 158
J. W., 100
James A., 106
Martha S., 60
Miller, 66
Minnie, 14
Prince, 100
Samuel, 40
Sarah, 146
Solomon, 37
Susan, 60
Willis, 37
Zachariah, 37
Shearin
G. W., 66
Sheffield
Rachel, 75
Shelby
Charles A.,
42
Shelley
James T., 8
Shelton
Catherine,
107
Eliza, 140,
145
Franklin C.,
17
Henry W.,
107
Joanna, 153
John F., 136
Jonah, 153
R. W., 145
R. W. (Mrs),
140
Sallie, 17
Shepherd
I. N., 147

Mark, 148
Thomas M.,
39
Sherman
John L., 84
Sherrell
H. N., 116
W. A., 123
Sherrill
C. E., 154
Frances I.,
154
M. A. (Mrs),
153
Sarah E., 155
Sherry
P., 137
Sheton
Joanna, 153
Jonah, 153
Shields
Archabald,
123
Shim
J. M., 81
Nelson, 81
Richard, 81
Shinault
Alfred, 67
Shipman
Exeline, 131
Shirley
J. T., 140
Richard, 90
Virginia Ann,
140
Shivers
Elin, 60
Louis, 36
Mattie, 36
Shobell
John F., 132
Shofer
Frederick, 56
Rufus, 56
Shofner
Sarah F., 14
Willis, 14
Short
J. L., 4
Pheby S., 7
Shortt
Alfred, 157
Bird, 157

Shoultce
Anoline, 47
Rutha, 47
Shoultse
Rutha, 47
Shrimpf
Charles, 137
Shrum
Mary, 156
Shull
Joseph, 71, 72
Joseph B., 72
Shunkle
William, 89
Sidney, 111
Silas, 109
Sills
J. M. M., 63
John, 63
Reuben I., 63
Silsby
L. H., 21
Simmins
John, 10
Simmonds
Bartley P., 1
Simmons
A. L., 164
B. L., 165
Ben, 164
Dick, 162
F. T., 22
G. W., 164
Henry, 18
James, 165
John, 103
Julia, 163
Lee, 165
Lemuel, 163
Malecia, 163
S. F., 46
Viola Jane, 20
William L.,
116
Simon, 111
Simons
James, 164
John, 5
Simpson
Clinton, 93
James P. S.,
91
John, 90, 127

Lawrence,
132
William, 5
William B.,
120
Willis H., 121
Sims
Alexander,
155
Amanda, 47
Clifford
Stanley,
143
Elmos, 47
G. W., 47
George, 139
James
Washingto
n, 47
John J., 155
John Mills,
47
Malissa, 108
Martha, 47
Mary
Elizabeth,
47
Nancy, 139
R. W., 108
Sarah, 47
Susan
Leonora,
47
Sinclair
Daniel, 56
Dick, 44
J. F., 17
Singalten
William H.,
158
Singleton
W. H., 101
Sisba
Lorenzo, 135
Sisco
Z., 30
Skeggs
Charles B., 32
Skinner
Minerva S.,
49
Robert A.,
103
Skipwith

214